RONDOUT

ALSO BY BOB STEUDING

Ashokan: Poems

Gary Snyder: A Critical Biography

Winter Sun: Poems

The Last of the Handmade Dams: The Story of the Ashokan Reservoir

A Catskill Mountain Journal

The Heart of the Catskills

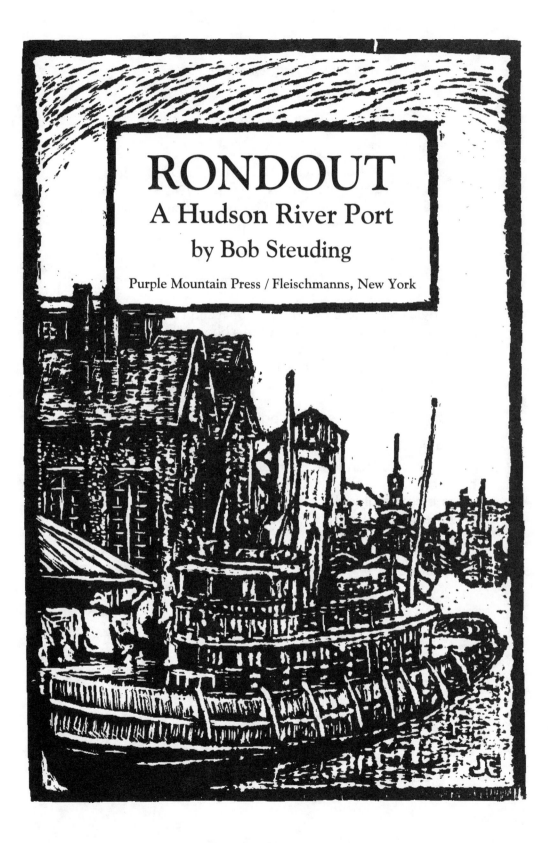

RONDOUT
A Hudson River Port
by Bob Steuding

Purple Mountain Press / Fleischmanns, New York

Rondout: A Hudson River Port

Published by
PURPLE MOUNTAIN PRESS, LTD.
P.O. Box 309, Fleischmanns, New York 12430-0309
845-254-4062, 845-254-4476 (fax), purple@catskill.net
www.catskill.net/purple

First edition 1995, second printing 2009

Library of Congress Cataloging-in-Publication Data

Steuding, Bob.
    Rondout : a Hudson River port / by Bob Steuding. -- 1st ed.
        p.   cm.
    Includes bibliographical references (p.   ) and index.
    ISBN 0-935796-70-3 (alk. paper)
    1. Rondout (N.Y.)--History.   I. Title.
F129.R844S73   1995
974.7'34--dc20   95-42766
                                                       CIP

Manufactured in the United States of America.
Printed on acid-free paper.

For my Mother
Dorothy Groene Steuding
Who loves both history
and books

Contents

PREFACE

Most readers of this book will never have seen old Rondout. Others who lived and worked in this interesting locale will know it in a way I never can. For, although I was born in Kingston a few short miles from Rondout, I must admit that I grew up in Hurley, New York, and was raised a country boy. Nonetheless, Rondout has always fascinated me, and my life, and that of my family, has been touched by Rondout from time to time.

My father and uncle knew Rondout well. They worshiped in Rondout, visited the relatives there, and performed as professional musicians on the Hudson River Day Line. They have told me stories about the *Skillypot,* which ferried their Model-T Ford across the Rondout Creek to Sleightsburgh on a chain. And they have recounted to me how the bridge was built on Wurts Street, which made this beloved craft obsolete. I have been told what it was like to ride on the *Mary Powell,* and I have shared, through their remembrance, the giddy pleasures of a day spent at Kingston Point Park.

As a young boy, my parents often took me to Rondout. We went there to purchase school clothing at Yallum's, to buy building materials at John D. Schoon-maker's Island Dock, where the D & H Canal coalyards had been, to see the tall Freeman Building on the Strand, and best of all, to enjoy the Orpheum Theatre, where I saw my first western. In summer, we rode the ferry across the Hudson. It was a great, windy adventure I shall never forget. To me, in those days, Rhinecliff seemed as exotic and remote as the moon. I can still see in my mind's eye the long line of cars waiting on Ferry Street, their engines shut off, the thick, green color of the creek, the boats docked, the oily smell. Then, on the ferry, as it moved down the stream, me standing at the bow—the pounding engines below, the lighthouse coming up on the port side, the pull of the current on the big boat as we cleared the creek. I recall that my elementary school held its annual picnics in Hasbrouck Park, which had been mined and owned by the Newark Lime & Cement Company in earlier times. This soon became one of my favorite places, for here I could view Rondout, the river, and the creek from its historic ramparts. In 1777, rebel cannons fired from this point on the British squadron which later burned Rondout and Kingston.

Today, I know a great deal more about Rondout than I did as a youth, or even a decade ago, when I first began the research for this book. Yet, surprisingly, this increased familiarity with Rondout and its colorful past has not diminished my initial childhood delight and interest in this place. In fact, the long and gradual process of discovery which I have undertaken has only whetted my appetite for more knowledge of old Rondout. Clearly, this Hudson River port has seeped into my blood.

The story I have written traces Rondout's history from its early sighting by the explorer Henry Hudson in 1609 to the present day. During these four centuries, the reader will meet many interesting women and men and watch a myriad of surprising things occur. By reading this book, like a ride on a magic carpet or a trip in a time machine, the reader may experience, in some measure, what it was like to live in a particular spot on earth over a long period of time. It is my hope that the reader's journey be found an enjoyable and a memorable one.

Bob Steuding
Olive Bridge, New York
Summer 1995

1 : The Beautiful Land

 It flows through "as beautiful a land as one can tread upon," exclaimed Captain Henry Hudson, as he viewed the great estuary which now bears his name. On that late summer day in 1609, Hudson hoped that this great expanse of navigable water would eventually lead him to the riches of India. An intrepid English explorer hired by the Dutch East India Company, Hudson had sailed his ship the *Halve Maen* (*Half Moon*) to North America during the first decade of a century seething with violence, greed, and turmoil.

At that historic moment, Hudson's employers held high hopes for his quest. The recently independent Dutch Netherlands was becoming an economic power of profound significance. In fact, the possessions of the older, declining powers, such as Spain and Portugal, were soon to fall to Holland. And even England and France, Holland's immediate rivals in the New World, would in the coming years gain great respect for the commercial ambitions of these Dutch entrepreneurs whom Henry Hudson would ably represent.

Hudson and his crew of eighteen sailors would search for the Northwest Passage to the Orient for some time, sailing the coast from Newfoundland south to Virginia. Unsuccessful, they would return north. Finally, disappointed but hopeful, they would anchor off Sandy Hook near what was to become the City of New York. Remaining a week below Staten Island, they noted that the shores were covered with tall oaks. Indians clad in feathers, skins, and furs, and carrying bows and arrows, paddled out to the ship in canoes made from hollowed trees. While in this area, a fight broke out between the crew and the Indians, and a sailor was killed, shot with an arrow. At last, entering the bay and proceeding up the river, which Hudson named the Mauritius, the crew smelled the delicious fragrance of wild grapes wafting from the shore. On the right bank, unbroken forest stretched as far as they could see, and on the left, the rocks of the Palisades pushed toward the sky. Along the way, they traded with friendly Indians, obtaining beans and oysters, tobacco, pumpkins, and corn.

On the morning of September 15, 1609, the crew awoke to find the river covered in mist. Soon, however, the sun rose, quickly burning off the mist, and the day became hot and clear. Weighing anchor, Hudson and his men continued up the river about twenty leagues, a distance of roughly sixty miles. Nearing the Catskill Mountains, about midway between the present cities of New York and Albany, "The Land grew very high and Mountainous," writes Robert Juet, the chronicler of the expedition (Van Zandt, 111-12). Describing the river that warm, bright day, Juet states that its depth was from six to thirteen fathoms (nearly eighty feet). At this spot, situated on the west shore of the river somewhere between the mouths of the present Rondout and Esopus Creeks in what is today Ulster County, New York, the crew fished and obtained "a great store of very good fish," especially "salmons." Here, they met "a very loving people, and very old men" who treated them hospitably, wrote Juet. And thus, in strikingly prosaic terms, the momentous first encounter between Europeans and the inhabitants of the setting of our story is described.

As fair weather persisted, the explorations of the *Half Moon* were resumed. Leaving the area and sailing to a point north of present-day Albany below the falls at Cohoes, the explorers realized that the great river did not lead to the Orient. During this very summer, the Frenchman Champlain had reached the same conclusion about the St. Lawrence River. And so, the *Half Moon* turned and headed south, passing the mouth of Rondout Creek at the present-day city of Kingston on September 27 or 28.

Farther downriver, meeting Indians once again, the crew was offered food, including boiled cornmeal, pigeon, and most notably, a fat dog, which was killed and skinned with clam shells. At this point, Juet describes the Indian habitations as "well constructed of oak bark and circular in shape, with an arched roof." Inside, mats of interwoven bulrushes were spread on the floor, where the Indians sat and ate from red wooden bowls (Johnson, 11). Soon however, trouble erupted once again between the Whites and the Indians, and off Manhattan Island nine attacking Indians were killed by cannon fire. Finally, one month after entering New York Bay, Hudson reached the Atlantic and set sail for Holland.

After making landfall at Dartmouth, England, however, Hudson, by order of the king, was detained and prevented from returning to Amsterdam with the *Half Moon* and the rest of his crew. Thus, the following year, still possessed with the desire to find a quick route to the Orient, Hudson sailed westward again on his fourth great voyage, this time in command of an English ship. In June, he reached Greenland and eventually entered the bay in present-day Canada that would be given his name. Unfortunately, from November until the following summer, his ship was imprisoned in the ice at the southern end of this bay. Nonetheless, with radically diminished food supply, Hudson determined to continue his quest once the ice melted and the ship was released. The crew, however, many of them recently liberated convicts, disagreed, and three days after leaving their winter prison, in the summer of 1611, the crew, among them Robert Juet, mutinied. They placed Henry Hudson, his son, and others who remained faithful to Hudson in a shallop, or small boat, gave them a gun, powder, shot, an iron pot and some grain, towed the shallop free of the ice, set it adrift, and then sailed the ship back to England themselves.

Once the fate of Hudson and the others was revealed, a rescue expedition to Hudson's Bay was mounted. No trace of Hudson and the others, however, was ever found. No more than forty-five years of age, Hudson had died in the frozen North, unsuccessful in his ambition to reach the East, and leaving a wife, children, and a house near the Tower of London.

The story of Henry Hudson, however, does not end here. Surprisingly, in the trial that followed, the mutineers were found not guilty. And the faithful old *Half Moon*, which Hudson had sailed to the New World on his first voyage, later reached the Indies by sailing the long route around the Horn. In 1616, at the island of Sumatra, it was last heard of, when, like Hudson and his faithful comrades, all hands were lost at sea.

Hudson, of course, did not discover the Hudson River, nor was he the first European to see it. As early as 1524, Verrazano, the Italian navigator, had ascended the Hudson, at least as far as the Palisades, calling the river, "The River of the Steep Hills." The following year, an unnamed Spanish captain noted the existence of the great North River, as it was later called. It is also thought that Frenchmen sailed to the location of the present-day city of Albany and traded with the Mohawks some years prior to Hudson's voyage. Be that as it may, what Hudson accomplished, if unintentionally and unknowingly, was to open the territory to more extensive and systematic trading, and thus, ultimately, to settlement. Hudson represented the vanguard of Dutch imperialism, which, driven by international competition, sought the vast possibilities of wealth to be obtained in the New World. After Hudson's trip, Dutch expansion was to continue for over fifty years, ceasing only when all Dutch holdings in the New World were lost in 1664 to the English.

Of added interest may be the fact that only two years before Hudson's voyage Jamestown had been founded in Virginia by the English, and a year before that Quebec had been settled by the French. In the same decade, Cervantes published the first installment of *Don Quixote*; Shakespeare wrote his masterwork *Hamlet*; England crowned James I upon the death of Queen Elizabeth, who had reigned for nearly fifty years; and the translation of the King James edition of the Bible and the invention of the telescope by Kepler were soon to occur. Within ten years of Hudson's exploration of the Hudson River, Europe would become embroiled in the Thirty Years' War, a period of bloody religious conflict which would devastate sections of Europe, exhaust its populations, and generate a significant wave of migration of people to North America. Although Hudson had not succeeded in finding a passage to the Orient as he had intended, like Christopher Columbus and other explorers before him, he had accomplished something of greater importance.

Following Hudson's explorations for the Dutch East India Company, the Dutch moved quickly to capitalize on his discoveries. In the year that Hudson disappeared, fur trading with the Indians began in earnest along the Hudson River, and in 1612 Dutch merchants sent Adriaen Block on the first of a number of trips to the New World. He named Block Island after himself, as well as Hells Gate, Rhode Island and the Connecticut River. His explorations also revealed that Manhattan and Long Island were not connected.

In 1614, Dutch burghers organized the next of the great Dutch commercial companies. It was called the New, or United Netherland Company, and it was awarded a patent which gave it a three-year monopoly on trade between the fortieth and fiftieth parallels in North America. Although the company's patent was not renewed, for a number of years its traders continued the exploration of the river, traded with the Indians, and constructed forts at New Amsterdam on Manhattan Island and near the present city of Albany. It is possible, even probable, that by the early 1620s United Netherland Company traders occasionally stopped at the mouth of the Rondout Creek, then called Esopus (or *Groote Esopus*, Great Esopus), to trade with the Indians, whose name was assigned to this place. According to one historian, it is said that it was "a good place to rendezvous and trade. . ." (Fried, 13). Prior to this time, the name Esopus had been used to represent both sides of the Hudson, but by the early 1620s, Esopus had come to refer to the territory only on the west side.

In 1621, a successor to the United Netherland Company was found, and the most powerful of all the Dutch commercial companies was established. Given a twenty-four-year monopoly on trade in America—eight times longer than that assigned the United Netherland Company—the Dutch West India Company gained the power not only to trade, but also, in effect, to conduct what today would be called foreign policy. In fact, the company was so powerful that it was almost a state within a state. Its vast authority was exercised through a resident director general, or governor, who was given near despotic power. Restricted by no charters or representative assemblies, as his English counterparts were, the Dutch governor, for the most part, could do as he wished.

In the year of its establishment, the company began the settlement of the Hudson Valley, sending five families to the New World. Delaying to issue a plan of government for these settlers until 1624—possibly for political reasons, because England complained strongly about this settlement—the company exercised absolute, centralized control and gave the colonists no voice in their governance (Currey, 17). Dutch colonies on Manhattan Island and at Albany, first called Fort Nassau and in 1624 Fort Orange, were ruled rigidly by a private body, or joint stock company, more interested in profits than supporting settlers. "Caprice, pettiness, and tyranny" on the part of the company and its governor were not uncommon, writes one scholar (Currey, 18). Such cavalier conduct was to produce profound consequences and to result, in effect, in the founding of the settlement of Esopus.

What might be considered the actual beginning of planned settlement of New Netherland occurred in 1625. In that year, Willem Verhulst, the first governor, plotted several farms on Manhattan Island. When Pieter Minuit arrived in spring of the following year, replacing Verhulst, who was considered incompetent, Minuit established *bouweries*, or small farms, to be allotted to the company's indentured servants, or *bouwlieden*, who were beginning to arrive. By the end of 1625, New Amsterdam, the Dutch village on Manhattan Island, was becoming a lively, bustling center of agriculture and trade. Living there were not only the Dutch, but also Scandinavians, Scots, Irish, English, Germans, Jews, and Blacks. By 1643, after the monopoly of the Dutch West India Company had ended, new development resulted, and New Amsterdam became a cosmopolitan city of some 400 souls, its inhabitants speaking eighteen different languages.

During the first years of Pieter Minuit's tenure, however, growth was slow. The company therefore attempted to stimulate settlement by establishing a system of baronial land holdings. In 1629, it issued what was called the "Charter of Privileges and Exemptions," which allowed any member of the company certain privileges if he established a community of persons anywhere in the New Netherlands. This entrepreneur, taking the title of *patroon*, would be allotted sixteen miles of land along one side, or eight miles on both sides of a navigable river. The holding could extend inland as far as he wished, or as far as he could control. His settlers were bound to cultivate the patroon's land for up to ten years and not to leave it without his permission. They were to give the patroon the option to purchase their surplus produce, to have their grain ground at the patroon's mill at his price, and to allow the patroon to settle small disputes in his own court. Settlers also were prevented from making cloth or from hunting or fishing on the patroon's property. It is not surprising, therefore, that tenants quickly became dissatisfied with this arrangement.

Such was the case of Thomas Chambers, an English carpenter and early immigrant to the New World. Redheaded, tall and thin, Chambers was a man of unusual courage and enterprise. Impulsive, inventive and able, Chambers first appears in the records of New Amsterdam in 1642. In this year, he contracted to build a house for Jan Jansen Schopmoes. It was to be "enclosed all around and overhead with clapboards, tight against the rain." This method of construction was new to New Netherland, and the ability to construct such a house resulted in notoriety for Chambers and his earning the name of *clapport*, or in variant spelling *clabbort*.' Certainly, there was no lack of work for a carpenter with Chambers' innovative abilities. In fact, this situation may have motivated Chambers to emigrate to New Netherland in the first place. Chambers does not seem to have been a particularly pious man, driven to seek freedom from religious persecution, as were his countrymen who settled further north in New England. New Netherland, although Dutch, was actually more relaxed and open in terms of personal conduct than New England. Thus it was a place of greater opportunity and promise, more appropriate to a person of Chambers' character and lifestyle. This may have been why he moved there.

Nonetheless, four years after his appearance in New Amsterdam, Chambers was working 150 miles up the Hudson River in Rensselaerswyck, near the present city of Troy, in the colony established by the patroon Kiliaen Van Rensselaer. A member of an old and wealthy Dutch family, Van Rensselaer had invested heavily in Dutch commercial ventures in the New World, and he was an impassioned advocate of patroonship. He had married well, and thus possessed a considerable fortune, which he devoted wholeheartedly to his ambitious project at Rensselaerswyck. By 1640, Van Rensselaer was not only hoping to make his colony profitable as a grain exporting center and a supplier of furs, but also as a provisioner of immigrants coming to the upper Hudson Valley region. Indeed, he aspired to become a major merchant trader. Van Rensselaer, however, was not to enjoy the success he savored. He died in 1643, and his son Johannes, who felt no commitment to the enterprise, succeeded him. Johannes, giving the colony no further thought, promptly relinquished his patroonship to his alcoholic uncle, the former and unsuccessful governor of New Amsterdam, Wouter Van Twiller.

It was into this context of greed, neglect, mismanagement and financial chaos that Thomas Chambers stepped. In 1646 he contracted to build a kitchen and chimney in the house of Dominic Magapolensis, and on September 7 of that year he leased a farm opposite the flat on the east side of the Hudson between two *kills*, or creeks, for a term of five years. And so, Chambers became a leaseholder, and thus found himself subject to the whimsical control of the Dutch Van Rensselaers. By 1648, Chambers had married Margrita Hendricks Jansen, a widow with four children, three unmarried. Whether unhappy as a farmer, unfulfilled as a married man, or dissatisfied with his life in general, the carpenter appears to have developed a problem with alcohol. In the court records of Rensselaerswyck, the name of Thomas Chambers appears frequently, he being fined for drunken and riotous conduct. Such behavior, however, does not seem to have limited Chambers' involvement in the affairs of the colony, for in October 1650 Chambers joined other settlers in a peace mission to the Mohawk Indians who threatened their settlement. Nonetheless, involvement with alcohol would, in fact, later get him into deep trouble, and it would have a profound and negative impact, indeed, on the new settlement in Esopus.

In 1651, Jan Baptiste Van Rensselaer, the second son who had been too young upon the death of Kiliaen to become patroon, assumed control of the colony. He was shocked at what he found. Wouter Van Twiller had mismanaged the enterprise totally. Crops were unplanted. Tenants were failing to work; some were even leaving. It was at this time, when Jan Baptiste and his younger brother Jeremias came to America to attempt to restore order, that Thomas Chambers' lease ran out. Undoubtedly, Chambers had made up his mind to leave Rensselaerswyck before this time. The rules of the charter, to say nothing of the inept and heavy-handed feudalism of the patroon and his director of affairs, Barent Van Schlictenhorst (Brandt Van Schlectenhorst), must have irked Chambers and made it clear to him that further investment of time and effort in this colony was foolish.

So Chambers set out to find suitable land in an unsettled place, one which no patroon controlled. Thus it was inevitable that Chambers would search downriver, for he would wish to continue to live along the main route of transportation. By 1624, the mouth of the Rondout Creek at Esopus was "already a familiar geographical location" (Fried, 13). Catelyn Trico, who had sailed on board the Dutch West India Company ship *New Netherland* with the first families of settlers going up river, remembered sixty-four years later how the ship had stopped at Esopus on its journey in May 1624. She cites seeing boats that had been left there by the Dutch, who had traded with the Indians the previous year.

On April 27, 1640, during his own journey up the river to Fort Orange, the patroon David de Vries also passed the mouth of the Rondout Creek. He remarks in his journal, published in 1655, "We came to Esoopes, where a creek runs in; and there the savages had much maize-land, but all somewhat stony" (Fried, 14). Although no European settlement existed at Rondout at this time, the place had been clearly marked on the map and was familiar to and anticipated by river travelers, being perceived as a distinct location to be found half way between New Amsterdam and Fort Orange. So, considering that Catskill, a few miles upriver from Esopus, had been settled a year or two earlier, and Esopus was well known, Chambers made the most obvious and best possible choice for settlement.

It was to this place of maize (corn), where a creek runs into the river, that Chambers came a bit more than a decade after de Vries' visit. Chambers had visited Esopus, or *Atharhacton* as the Indians called it, at least once previously in order to arrange for the purchase of land. Then, on June 5, 1652, he met with Kawachhikan, or Ankerop as he was also called, and Sowappekat, two Indians living in Esopus, and there he paid for, "from the first penny to the last," and received a parcel of land "extending Southwest and Northeast. . .with a path from the said land to the river. . ." (Brink, 1: 80-83).

By the next year, most likely after the ice on the river had melted, Chambers and other settlers began to arrive. It is not known whether general disaffection with life in Rensselaerswyck prompted an agreement between the colonists to move to Esopus, or what seems more likely, that once Chambers purchased his piece of land and settled on it, others decided to follow. Certainly it would seem that Chambers' initiative and courage acted as a catalyst and a focus for the settlement of Esopus, for it was not long before Chambers was acknowledged as a community leader. Whatever the case, by the summer of 1653, several people had purchased land at Esopus, and many were to follow.

One was Johannis Dyckman, commissary and vice director at Fort Orange, who purchased and sold land at Esopus, though he may never have lived there. Others were Juriaen Wesphaelen (possibly also called Westvael) and Jacob Jansen Stoll, called "Hap," and later referred to as Jacob Jansen Slicoten. Hap Stoll was a violent person, a wife-beater and an Indian-hater. He once threw burning pieces of wood at his wife. Another settler, Evert Pels, had come to New Netherland from Pomerania. He was farming at Esopus by late 1659, but also maintained a farm in Rensselaerswyck until 1661. Pels owned a yacht, which he used commercially. Johan de Hulter purchased land at Esopus from the Indians in 1654, but died before he could patent it (a form of official registration). It was not until nearly three years later that his widow Johanna de Laet, the daughter of an historian, was granted the patent. One of the first women to settle in Esopus, Mrs. de Hulter was a person of great ability and presence of mind. In 1658, when the stockade was built on the plains above Rondout, she engaged carpenters to dismantle, remove, and reassemble her house, barn, and sheds in the stockade. During an Indian raid, her horses were killed and she sued for, and received, compensation in the form of land. In 1659, she married Jeronimus Ebbingh and joined her considerable lands with his. Cornelius Barensten Slecht (Sleght) also settled in Esopus. For a time, Slecht cooked for Chambers, then rented and farmed part of the Ebbingh-de Hulter tract. By 1662, the enterprising Slecht had established himself as a successful brewer. Not to be outdone in industriousness and energy, Slecht's wife was herself a successful practicing midwife. Mattys Hendricks (Hendrix) in one source is also mentioned as an original settler, but this is doubtful; according to local historian Marc Fried, his name appears nowhere in provincial records (Fried, 21).

One of the most colorful of the first settlers was Christofell Davits (Davis). "Kit" Davits, as he was called, was a free-wheeling pioneer. Like Chambers, he was also an Englishman, who had first come to Rensselaerswyck from Chaucer's Canterbury in 1638. He had accompanied Chambers to Esopus and had purchased land at the Strand at the mouth of the Rondout Creek on the Hudson River. Davits was the first white man to live on the banks of the Rondout. It was here that settlers landed, unloaded their possessions, and took the footpath through the cliffs up to the plains and the fertile farmlands of Esopus. This location seems to have been ideally suited to Davits' interest in trading. Here he sold brandy illegally to the Indians, an act which angered his fellow settlers and won him a reprimand from none other than Peter Stuyvesant, the governor of New Netherland. In a letter from the governor, Davits was told to stop inciting the Indians and to "regulate" himself. A "bold and independent soul," Davits seems to have been "more interested in trading and frolicking with the Indians than in farming. . ." (Fried, 25). Unmoved by disapproval, this Chaucerian figure promptly named the creek after himself, calling it *Kit Davits Creek.*

Born in 1615 or 1616, Davits was certainly not a man to avoid a fight. It is recorded that in a fight in Rensselaerswyck he not only beat his opponents black and blue, he struck them with post and tankard. Davits was married more than once and had at least three sons and a daughter. One of his sons, like Davits, could speak the language of the Indians. Davits himself acted as interpreter for the settlers and was hired as a scout during the Indian Wars because of his knowledge of the wilderness and its inhabitants. During these wars, Davits paddled a canoe from Manhattan to Esopus, sleeping with friendly Indians en route. Davits, however, was never trusted by the settlers, possibly due to his commercial interests and because his house had been commandeered by the Indians and used as a lookout in Rondout harbor during the troubles of 1663. He was accused of "spreading dangerous rumors" and of "arousing the Indians." Nonetheless, Davits' house was subsequently burned to the ground by the Indians, and, as a result, he was forced to sell his land to Evert Pels in March 1667. Pels, in turn, leased the land to Samuel Oliver (Fried, 148-9). Davits, however, owned land elsewhere, and is thought to have maintained for a time a number of residences of sorts, one at Beverwyck (Albany), and another at Claverack (near Hudson, in Columbia County).

After 1682, the name of Kit Davits disappears from the public record. It is probable that by this time he was dead. Yet the legend of Kit Davits remains. Although eccentric, difficult and uncooperative in his relations with his neighbors, often perceived by them as a problem to be dealt with, Davits, in his independence of mind and his intrepidity of spirit, clearly represents one type of individual who in the coming centuries would epitomize the spirit of the American frontier.

The place to which these settlers first came in 1652 or 1653, called in turn *Atharhacton* by the Indians and *Esopus* by the Dutch, was wild and forbidding. As they approached the gateway to this area at the port of Rondout, they saw darkly wooded hills faced with steep precipices, which loomed 200 feet above them like the palisades of a castle. Imagine each settler grasping the rail and staring intently in fear and expectation at the shore. Imagine the lush vegetation crowding the creek and the cliffs. Imagine the incredible silence.

Entering the creek, they passed mud flats on their port side. Possibly this is where David de Vries had seen the Indian maize-land. To starboard, a brief stretch of level land could be seen, where one day the village of Rondout would stand. About eighty-five miles up the Hudson River from Manhattan, Rondout (part of present Kingston) can be found on the map at 41° 51' 30" north latitude, 73° 59' 00" west longitude. Within a radius of a few miles of this point, the Esopus Creek, the Wallkill River, the Rondout Creek, and the Hudson River meet, making Rondout the ideal location for the development of a rich commercial center. However, at its greatest point of expansion in the late nineteenth century, the boundaries of Rondout itself would enclose only about 228 acres, of which approximately only three-quarters were usable. Clearly, space was limited in Rondout, and all activities would have to be confined to the lowlands along the creek. As one visitor observed over 200 years later, Rondout was "all hills and valleys, with many ups and downs" (De Lisser, 60).

And so, in that the settlers' first sight of the area must have been a bit daunting, and space for farming severely limited—only Kit Davits initially settled there—it is not surprising that not long after disembarking at the Strand, or beach at the base of the hills, the settlers began moving up the Indian footpath that breached the wall of rock above the landing. Here they passed through the notch in these hills, crossed the plains above Rondout, and headed toward the alluvial flatlands spread out along the Esopus Creek to the northwest. For it was, in the words of Dominie Megaploensis, "an exceedingly good country" there. In this fertile and open land some two to three miles from the port of Rondout—still farmed today after centuries, possibly millennia, of cultivation—the first extensive settlement occurred.

The derivation of the name Rondout itself is difficult to trace with any exactness. The name may first have been given to the area of Esopus where today's Rondout Creek flows into the Hudson River because, although no true fort or redoubt existed there before 1660, a few huts from which to trade with the Indians may have been built at Kingston Point or at Ponckhockie (referred to by the local Indians, variously, as the burial ground, or a high place of land) as early as the second decade of the seventeenth century. The first reference to the construction of a "redoubt at Esopus," however, occurs in 1657, when the settlers, in fear of the Indians, petitioned the new governor of New Netherland, Peter Stuyvesant, to finance its construction. Although funds were not forthcoming for three years, a fort was built at the mouth of the Rondout Creek in 1660 for the avowed purpose of tax collection or trade, but also for convenient employment during Indian conflicts.

Complicating the process of determining the word's derivation is the view of one historian that in Dutch *rondhout* means standing timber, and *rounduit* means out-of-round (Van Buren, 132-133). In French, *rond* and *ronde* also mean round, but *redout*, as it does in English, denotes a fort. Added to this is the fact that the Dutch equivalent of the English word *redoubt* is *reduyt*, and yet in Dutch records the creek is written *Ronduyt*. Be that as it may, it might be suggested that *ronduyt* is close enough. Certainly, as eighteen different languages were spoken in New Netherland, and many of the settlers at Esopus were English, it is not surprising that there is some confusion. By 1663, the captain of the militia sent to protect Esopus, Martin Cregier, refers in a letter to the location as "the creek which runs past the Redoubt." And by the 1670s, the name appears in land surveys as *Round Doubt*, *Roundoubt*, and *Rondout*. Suffice to say that from its earliest inhabitation Rondout was associated with defense and commerce, and that whatever structure or structures were erected there for these purposes gave their name to the area and to the creek.

2 : Heartless Provocations

INLAND from the port of Rondout, which remained for the most part sparsely inhabited, and also up and down the river, settlement was well underway by 1658. About five years after the first settlers stepped ashore at the Strand in Rondout, more than sixty people, mostly farmers and their families, had carved homesteads for themselves out of this new and fertile land. Living mostly apart from each other in individual land holdings, they soon found themselves exposed and in danger of Indian attack. In response to the destruction of their crops by settlers' hogs and cows, Indians killed settlers' livestock, threatened women and children, and in general humiliated the settlers by forcing them to plow the Indians' maize land. In September 1655, drunken Indians had killed Harmon Jacobsen on board his sloop anchored at Rondout, and had burned to the ground in nearby Ponckhockie the houses of Andires Van der Huys and Jacob Andriaensen (Adriance). Shockingly, Adriaensen was blinded and his little child killed. Some settlers returned to Fort Orange for a time, afraid for their lives. Thus, as hostilities between Whites and Indians continued, fueled by alcohol, competition for land, and the problems created by the proximity of two very different peoples, the settlers petitioned Governor Stuyvesant for protection.

When Stuyvesant landed at Rondout and reached Esopus in the spring of 1658 with a force of seventy militia, trouble was brewing, and things were nearly out of control. Unhesitatingly, as was his manner, the governor informed the settlers that unless they moved to Fort Orange or to Fort Amsterdam, or constructed and inhabited a fortified village, they should cease their petitioning and trouble him no further. No one wished to leave his farm of course, but finally, most of the settlers, among them Thomas Chambers, agreed to Stuyvesant's proposal, and so a stockade was built on a hill overlooking the Esopus Creek and the lowlands a few miles from Rondout at what is now Kingston. Only Kit Davits refused to participate in the project, continuing to live in Rondout on the banks of the creek near the river.

The man who gave this ultimatum to the settlers, and who three years later granted them a charter conferring municipal powers on Esopus, which was to be called Wiltwyck (wild place), had been governor of New Netherland for more than a decade when he strode into Esopus on his one good leg. He had succeeded Willim Kiefft, who had assumed the governorship from Wouter Van Twiller, known as "Wouter the Doubter" and later immortalized in Washington Irving's *Knickerbocker History*. Van Twiller himself had followed Pieter Minuit, who, in 1629, had been recalled. When Kiefft arrived in New Netherland in 1637, he found matters very much in disarray. Van Twiller had been incompetent beyond belief; employees were trading furs illegally, and smuggling, gunrunning, drunkenness, theft, and murder were commonplace. Kiefft, unusually authoritarian and unyielding even for Dutch governors of the time, quickly responded and promptly alienated the colonists by issuing numerous, heavy-handed proclamations which were impractical and impossible to enforce. He also initiated a "murderous" policy toward the Indians, which greatly incited them against the Dutch. As a result, in 1641 a protracted war with the Indians began. From 1641 to 1645, nearly 2,000 settlers were killed by Indians in retaliation for Kiefft's brutal tactics. Finally, after ten long and dispiriting years, Kiefft was censured and recalled to Holland. On the voyage, his ship was wrecked and Kiefft drowned. Some might consider this just retribution.

Nonetheless, it had been a discouraged and fearful people that Stuyvesant had met when he assumed his duties in 1647. Certainly, it had been a difficult task for him to overcome the effects of Kiefft's misgovernment and his mistreatment of the Indians, and the new governor had not been completely successful. However, by 1658, Stuyvesant had made significant progress in restoring order to New Netherland, though relations with the Indians remained volatile and somewhat unstable.

A tall, dark man in his sixties, Stuyvesant was the son of a clergyman. He had worked for the Dutch West India Company for many years, serving in numerous capacities. As a soldier, he had lost his right leg in a fight with a Portuguese on the island of Curacao. The wooden leg, which thereafter was decorated with silver nails and bands, gave rise to his nickname, "Old Silver Nails." Stuyvesant carried a sword at his side, wore a velvet jacket, a full, puffed shirt, knee breeches with slashed hose fastened at the knee by a knotted scarf, and rosettes on his shoes. Attired in this fashion, he addressed the settlers at Esopus.

An able governor, Stuyvesant demanded and received respect. His uncontrollable temper and his lack of tact, however, often angered his subjects. In his later years, Stuyvesant would, with regret, sign the Articles of Capitulation, which would surrender New Amsterdam to the English in 1664. The colonists, alienated by years of his behavior, refused to respond to the governor's call for defense. Stuyvesant, after accounting for his action in Holland, returned to the New World and spent the rest of his life in the newly-named city of New York. Mellowing in retirement, he became more companionable in his last years, even becoming warm friends with the English. Living peacefully on his farm in what is now lower Manhattan, he inhabited a wooden, two-story house approached through a garden of bright flowers arranged in geometrical beds. These were the happiest years of his life, it is said. In 1672, remembered by his enemies and friends, he died at the ripe old age of eighty.

At first, the Indian response to Stuyvesant's visit to Esopus and to the construction of the stockade there was obsequious. The Indians referred to the governor as

"The Grand Sachem," and they willingly relinquished the site of the stockade to the Dutch and to Stuyvesant, wishing, as they said, to "grease his feet," since he had traveled so far to meet with them. They even agreed to consider the possibility of selling all their land near the stockade and moving to the interior, as Stuyvesant had requested. After Stuyvesant returned to New Amsterdam, however, the tentative peace which he had negotiated did not last for long. Due to mistrust on both sides, and because of lingering bad feelings, disagreements and other incidents occurred and tensions remained high. Once again, in this time of danger and fear, the red-headed *clabbort*, Thomas Chambers, reappeared.

It was nearly autumn in 1659, and Chambers had hired some Indians to help him with his harvest. It was late in the day, and the Indians had husked a great deal of corn. Thirsty, they asked Chambers for a drink of *boisson*, as the Dutch called liquor. Generously, but unwisely, Chambers gave the Indians a large jug of brandy. Possibly this was done in lieu of wages, or as a tactic which Chambers employed in order to avoid making proper payment. Possibly it was simply a gift. No one knows. Nonetheless, drinking the troublesome beverage near the stockade that night, then purchasing another bottle from a soldier, the Indians soon became riotously drunk and made such a loud disturbance that they terrified the settlers and kept them awake. In response, and against the advice of Ensign Smit, who had been sent to Esopus to command the militia, Jacob Stoll and a number of other settlers surrounded the drunken Indians at their campfire. Stoll had lost a house to the Indians a year previously, and he intended to teach them a lesson. In the fracas that followed one Indian was killed, another wounded, and a third taken prisoner. Later, Stoll told Smit, "We wanted to slap their mouths, for the dogs have vexed us long enough."

Realizing that a fatal mistake had been made, Stoll and Chambers, who had both been in part responsible for this sad state of affairs, raced to Rondout accompanied by a party of soldiers. There they hired a yacht and sent it south, carrying a letter informing Stuyvesant of the dire situation. On their return journey to the stockade, at the corner of Hone and Pierpont Streets in Rondout at a place where a *Kaatsbaan*, or ball court was situated, they were ambushed by the Indians; one settler was killed and thirteen captured. Many of the captives were eventually tortured to death; among them was Jacob Stoll, who was tied to a stake and finally burned alive. Chambers' fate was happier, however; he was exchanged soon thereafter for an Indian prisoner.

Now, the First Esopus War, as it was later called, began in earnest. For two and one-half weeks, literally hundreds of Indians kept constant siege on the stockade. The Indians fired burning arrows into houses and barns and slaughtered livestock. A number of settlers were wounded and Jan Barensten Slecht was killed. Finally, Stuyvesant reached Esopus with a company of nearly 200 men. By that time, however, the Indians had retreated to the interior and could not be pursued due to heavy rains, so Stuyvesant and his troops prepared to return to New Amsterdam. While waiting at the port of Rondout to set sail, the Dutch forces heard a rustling sound in the bushes. Fearing it was Indians, they panicked and many of the troops jumped into the water, though no Indians were seen. It was later learned that the noise that had terrified them had been made by a dog. In shame and disgust, Stuyvesant and his untrained and inexperienced soldiers returned to Manhattan.

An unstable truce was maintained into the next year. Then, in late winter of 1660, Ensign Smit and his men, while on patrol, broke the peace, surprising a large group of Indians a few miles from the Esopus settlement. They killed and captured some of these unsuspecting Indians and burned their food supplies. Subsequently, these captives were sent to Curacao by Stuyvesant to work as slaves for the Dutch West India Company. More than anything else, this heartless act on Stuyvesant's part served to anger the Indians.

Further skirmishes followed, in which the Indians were pursued and harassed, their villages and forts destroyed. In one such instance, Smit marched with nearly 100 men to the confluence of the Rondout Creek and the Wallkill River. There he found another Indian village and the old chief named Premaeken, or Preymaker. The sachem, who had spoken to Smit arrogantly and was considered too aged to travel, was not taken as a prisoner; without remorse, Smit confiscated Preymaker's weapons and killed him with a blow to the head from his own hatchet. And so, the atrocities of war continued along the Rondout. Preymaker's name, it is interesting to note, was given to a small brook known as Preymaker's Creek near Hurley on the west side of the Esopus Creek.

Meanwhile, other river Indian tribes interceded with Stuyvesant on behalf of the beleaguered Esopus Indians, who were now isolated and without support. Finally, in July 1660, an armistice was granted by the Dutch, a peace treaty signed "under the blue sky" at Esopus, and the First Esopus War came to an end. As the Kingston historian Marius Schoonmaker wrote more than 100 years ago, "Much of what we. . .know is not complimentary to the humanity. . .of the Whites." And, as Schoonmaker concluded, "Would that an impenetrable veil could have been drawn over. . . the heartless provocations by which [these] Indian Wars were. . . provoked. . ."(Schoonmaker, 20).

Three years of peace followed. During this time, a wagon road was built to replace the old footpath from Rondout to Esopus (generally following what is now Broadway); Esopus was renamed Wildwyck (now written Wiltwyck), and the settlement assumed municipal powers, an indication of the area's growing economic and political importance as the grain basket of New Netherland. By this time, the major emphasis of the settlement and the Dutch West India Company had shifted from trade with the Indians to agriculture. Thus the settlers, no longer needing the Indians to procure furs for them, felt even less inclination to maintain amicable relations than they had earlier. Arable land was important now, and the Indians still owned some of it. In addition, more and more settlers were arriving at Wildwyck, generating a corresponding demand for more and more land. By the time the fort was constructed at the mouth of the Rondout Creek, development had reached three miles south of Wildwyck to Nieuwe Dorp (Hurley), where a "new village" was begun by colonists from Rensselaerswyck with names such as Crispell and Roosa. Without a doubt, the Indians were being crowded and dispossessed. A peace founded on such inequity could not last.

On June 7, 1663, at noon, while most of the male settlers were out working in the fields, the Indians entered the village, as was their custom, seeming to sell produce such as maize and beans. No one at Wildwyck at the time knew that the Indians had already destroyed Nieuwe Dorp to the south. But when word reached the stockade and the alarm was raised, the Indians, already inside, attacked, murdering settlers, burning and plundering houses, and carrying off women and children. During the massacre, Baret Gerritsen, a distiller, was killed in front of his own house. So too were sixteen other adults and two children, among them Harry Olferts, a Black belonging to Thomas Chambers, who himself was wounded. One child was burned alive. As Dominie Blom, the first cleric in Esopus, lamented, there were "burnt and slaughtered bodies" everywhere. It was "frightful to behold" (Schoonmaker, 32). At Hurley, three men had been killed, and eight women and twenty-six children taken prisoner.

The attack, once repulsed by the settlers who had returned from the fields, was not renewed, however. Possibly, as one historian suggests, the raid was undertaken to bolster the Indians' sagging self image, with no thought given to the consequences (Fried, 60). Whatever the case, Chambers, the captain of the local militia, issued orders to secure the gates and to use the cannon, and these acts may have turned the tide in the settlers' favor and forced the Indians to flee.

A week later, Governor Stuyvesant visited Wildwyck and gave orders to the wartime government of the settlement, placing military matters in the hands of the commander of the garrison, Sergeant Niessen, until the arrival of Martin Cregier, the new captain-lieutenant of all military forces in New Netherland. Cregier's new job was to wage war on the Esopus Indians. Once at Esopus, he pursued his task for the next six months with a vengeance. He dispatched scouting parties in all directions in an attempt to gain information about the Indians.

At first, little was learned. Then, on July 10, while returning to Wildwyck from Rondout, a troop of soldiers was ambushed. Two days later, another detachment discovered a group of Indians across the Hudson River (near the village of Tivoli). The soldiers killed some Indians and took others prisoners. On the journey, one soldier was bitten by a rattlesnake and died. Throughout the summer and into the autumn, Cregier and his forces, called "Cregier's Army," accompanied by Kit Davits as interpreter, relentlessly harried and harassed the Indians. Skirmishes were frequent, with the increasingly demoralized and over-matched Indians usually getting the worst of it. On the march, Cregier's forces took cannon and wagons, and thus found the travel strenuous due to the difficult terrain and the frequently wet weather. In these expeditions, Indian forts were sometimes found; they would be destroyed, their barkhouses plundered and burned, and all the inhabitants killed or taken prisoner. On one such expedition, an Indian child who was unable to keep up with her captors was thrown into the Rondout Creek, where she drowned. Once, Cregier was guided by an escaped prisoner named Madam Gysbert Van Imborgh. On another occasion, his garrison at the redoubt on the Rondout was surprised to see a young woman appear out of the woods on the opposite side of the creek and stand silently looking at them. Taken across the water, she informed them that she, too, had escaped from her Indian captor, who lived a few miles up the Rondout Creek. Quickly, a detachment was assembled and sent upstream to attempt to capture the Indian. When they reached his camp, however, he had fled, and was nowhere to be found.

The year 1663 had been an exceptionally trying time for everyone. In addition to the massacre of Whites and Indians, a severe earthquake, unusual in the region, had struck the Hudson Valley. Its effects were felt from Fort Orange to New Amsterdam, and its reverberations noticed as far north as Canada. As a result of the quake, the Hudson River overflowed its banks, and devastating floods had destroyed much of the precious corn crop. Both settlers and Indians had also suffered from a strange disease, with many sick at Esopus. No cause could be found. By January of the following year, the disease had not abated. As Sergeant Niessen reported, "the disease here does not diminish, but increases daily. . ." (Fried, 106). Wolves also continued to be a problem, and each household was directed to provide money for bounties.

And, of course, the Indian war dragged on in desultory fashion. As Niessen said, "woeful times" continued. Finally, a truce was called. And although the truce soon expired, fighting did not resume, for everyone had endured so much. In addition to the losses of war, they had suffered earthquake, flood, famine, and disease. And, as if this were not enough, their suffering was increased by the lack of shoes and socks during an exceptionally severe winter. The Indians, on their part, were exhausted, "sick and very lean because of the want of food. . .all provisions destroyed" (Fried, 108). And so, the war simply stopped. A few months later, when most of the prisoners had been exchanged, a treaty was officially signed by the Dutch and by Seuwacken-amo and other Esopus Indian sachems, but it was only a formality. Everyone was glad the war was over, and no one wanted to fight anymore.

The terms of the treaty, however, were severe. Reparations were to be paid by the Indians, and all lands taken from the Indians were to be retained by the settlers. The Indians, if armed, were not allowed to approach the settlers. And no more than three canoes, preceded by a flag of truce, could come to the redoubt in Rondout to trade. Although in the coming years rumors would surface of potential Indian uprisings, and the Indians would remain a threat to peace and security, raiding outlying farms 100 years later during the French and Indian Wars, open warfare never again occurred. The power the Indians had once held was lost forever.

The Indians who inhabited the valleys of the Rondout and the Esopus creeks and who had been defeated and dispossessed by the white settlers were an Algonkian-speaking people, members of small clans of the third tribe, the *Minsi*, or the Wolf tribe, of the Delaware Confederacy. The Dutch first called them *Wilden* (wild people) and, more specifically, Esopus Indians (from the Algonkian *sepus*, meaning river), but the Indians called themselves the *Lenni-Lenape*, or the Original People. Slender and small-boned, with thin faces and delicate features, the Esopus Indians looked little like the Indians of the cinema and the wild west. As Adriaen Van der Douck described them in his famous account of New Netherland published in 1655, they were "well proportioned, and equal in height" to the Dutch. Their hair, he wrote, was "jet black, sleek and uncombed, and nearly as coarse as a horse's tail." The color of most Indians' eyes was brown; their skin was commonly "yellowish . . . like the Tartans," although many Indians had skin as fair as that of the Dutch. The men were generally beardless. "It is true," Van der Donck stated, "that they appear singular and strange" at first glance, "but this, on acquaintance, is disregarded." To the Dutch, they were pleasant in appearance, for the most part. In fact, as Van der Donck points out, "Their women are well favored and fascinating" (Van der Donck, 72-73). It is estimated that their numbers may have ranged from 1,000 to as high as 2,000 persons before the arrival of the Europeans. The language of these people, spoken by Kit Davits, was noted for its great beauty, as well as its qualities of emphasis, flexibility, and conciseness. It is said that the thought of an entire sentence could be expressed in one word, by taking the most important syllable of each word in that sentence and creating a new word. The words *Mohonk*, or "on the great sky top," and *Shatamuck*, "on the Hudson River," offer good examples of this fact (Brink, 1: 73, 75).

For the most part, the Indians and their highly coherent and successful culture have been forgotten in Esopus. During the American Revolution, the Esopus Indians were driven from the area, and by the early nineteenth century most of the Delaware tribes had been transported to Indian reservations in the West. There is a legend, however, that one old Indian remained until 1830, living in a shanty on the bank of the Rondout Creek. But this person, the last of the indigenous peoples, if he existed at all, was probably not a pure-blood Indian. Sad to say, however, no monuments or even simple gravestones memorialize the Indian presence in Esopus. We only find evidence of Indians in the residue of their language and in the bones and tools left beneath the soil. One record, however, does (or did) exist early into the present century, and was noted by many people. It was found in the Town of Esopus, on the west bank of the Hudson River, and was incised into a large rock on the shore. It was a figure of an Indian, possibly a sachem or chief, who wears plumes on his head and holds a gun in one hand and a wand of some sort in the other. The Indian gazes out at the great river upon whose waters his people first watched Henry Hudson's *Half Moon* sail. With the benefit of many centuries of experience since the first Indian-European encounters, one can only wonder what this silent sentinel might say now, if he could only speak.

With the peace established at Esopus, the garrison was quickly removed to New Amsterdam because England, at this time, was actively seeking control of the Hudson. Nevertheless, dissatisfaction and disaffection were widespread with many settlers discontented with Dutch rule. Consequently, Stuyvesant was unable to muster enthusiasm for the defense of New Amsterdam against the English; thus the fall of Dutch suzerainty was inevitable. And so, ironically, within three months of the declaration of peace with the Indians at Esopus, the territory which Dutch commercial interests had developed for more than half a century was lost, without the firing of a single shot.

On August 27, 1664, the Duke of York took formal possession of New Netherland, and in 1669 Wildwyck was renamed Kingston, the name deriving from Berkshire, England, and having personal significance to the English Governor Lovelace. The Dutch reclaimed and won New Netherland briefly nine years later, when Kingston temporarily became Swaenenburgh. However, the Dutch could not retain their position of political and economic power in the region, and in 1674 New Netherland was ceded permanently to the English.

Significantly, when English rule, which was frequently heavy handed and undiplomatic in its administration, was first established in Esopus, there was little local resistance. In the early years of this rule, the population of Kingston (including Rondout) numbered about 900, with adult males somewhat outnumbering females. And, although the English ruled New Netherland, now called New York, very little changed. Even the temporary corruption of the English Governor, Lord Cornbury, had little impact on the day-to-day conduct of things. The Dutch kept their lands, and Dutch customs and their particular way of life endured and prevailed. Some even say that pockets of Dutch-speaking people could be found in far corners of the Hudson Valley until the late nineteenth century.

What we know of the Dutch endears them to us. Without a doubt, they were more liberal in matters of faith and lifestyle than their New England neighbors, respecting individual and personal privacy. And yet they were fundamentally conservative, loving the land, resisting change, and keeping to themselves. In general, these "individualistic Yorkers," according to one historian, were anticommunitarian, recognizing no common bond beyond that of neighbor (Blumin, 48-49). They seem to have lived life simply and forthrightly, asking nothing more than to do their work and to be left alone.

Living in comfortable houses constructed of brick and stone, with steep, sloping roofs and deep-set windows, split "Dutch doors," and large chimneys fitted with "Dutch ovens," the Dutch made a number of significant contributions to American cultural life. Among these are the culinary delights of hamburgers, coleslaw, cookies, crullers, and doughnuts; the activities of ice-skating, sleighing, sledding, and bowling, of quilting bees and apple cuts. They have given us Santa Claus (St. Nicholas was the patron saint of New Amsterdam) and the Easter egg. They taught us to hang our socks over the fireplace at Christmas. And it was the Dutch who distributed pipes, tobacco, and gin at funerals. Although the Dutch enjoyed ballroom dancing to the music of the violin, large evening parties were not common, the Dutch preferring to gather in the afternoon. Remembered not only in their architecture and customs but also in their language, the Dutch have left behind many colorful and descriptive words. A myriad of place names, such as the Bronx, Yonkers, Harlem, Tappen Zee, and more local varieties, are obvious examples of their tenure in the Hudson Valley. Words such as *spook*, *scow*, *yacht*, *stoop* (front porch), *brief* (letter), *kill* (creek) and many others are still used today. Certainly, the emphasis which the Dutch placed on hard work, self-sufficiency, and the simple life, offers an example that we might well reexamine with profit today.

By the 1670s, people had already begun to build dwellings and to live outside the stockade once again. Among these intrepid souls was Thomas Chambers, who, as an Englishman, welcomed his new masters, and was rewarded by having his extensive landholdings and house (near current Manor Avenue and Kiersted Avenue) designated an autonomous manor. Chambers was also given the power by the English king to dispense justice and to write his own laws, interestingly, not unlike the patroons he had hated so much. Fox Hall, as Chambers' estate was called, became the focus of his vast energies. In 1681, he also bought land in Rondout on the Strand from Evert Pels, and there he constructed a house and a mill, important later in our story.

However, at this spot in Rondout, in the previous spring, a person of acute perception and sensitivity had landed. Searching for a site suitable for the founding of a religious colony, the Labadist Minister Joseph Dankers had found little development and not much that impressed him at Rondout. In his journal he wrote, "At the mouth of the creek. . .there are some houses and a redoubt, together with a general storehouse. . . ." He added, "The woodland around the Hysopus is not of much value, and is nothing but sand and rock." An interesting incident occurred, nonetheless, during Dankers' brief sojourn in Rondout. He mentions how a man had approached Dankers and his companion, and with great animation had begged them for help, since the man was "sorely afflicted with an internal disease." The sick man had heard that the ministers understood medicine and could prescribe for him. The pair informed the suffering man that they were not doctors and had little medicine with them. However, Dankers' companion diagnosed the man's ailment as best he could and informed him that, although he could do nothing for him at that time, he would send him "a brackish powder" which had done some good in similar cases. Finally, Dankers reports, "this poor wretched man" returned "sorrowfully" to his house, and the ministers, soon boarding their boat, reached the entrance to the Highlands by evening (Van Zandt, 31, 308).

Traveling under assumed names and pursuing a secret mission, Dankers and his companion were members of a sect following the mystical teachings of Jean de Labadie, which had been persecuted in both France and Germany. In the more than two weeks they spent searching along the Hudson River and during the nine months in which they toured the Atlantic seaboard, their lives, at times, were clearly in danger. Although, unlike the settlers from Renssalaerswyck, they found Esopus unsatisfactory to their particular needs, their reflections on the area and the adventures they reported are of undoubted interest, for they record the first non-commercial, unselfish acts of Europeans exhibited toward fellow human beings at Rondout.

But back to Thomas Chambers. Although married twice, Chambers left no children of his own. Attempting to keep his manor intact and to perpetuate his name after his death, Chambers added an unusual provision to his will. According to the will, only if his stepson, Abraham Van Gasbeek, and his heirs took Chambers' name would they inherit his estate. Although Abraham agreed reluctantly, Chambers' carefully laid plans were doomed from the start. For even before his own death, Abraham broke the will, and the property was divided, thus showing that there are some things which even money cannot buy.

In another matter, the choice of Chambers' burial site, the man who had possessed such power and prominence in life was once again foiled. Chambers had directed, also in his will, that he be buried in Rondout near the house which he had recently built, rather than, as might be expected, at Fox Hall on the plains. It was as if Chambers had wished to return to the place where he had begun forty years earlier. Even in this desire Chambers was also thwarted, for his remains were not allowed to rest where he had intended. More than a century after his burial, Chambers' remains were disinterred and taken by hearse up the hill from Rondout to the Montrepose Cemetery, where they were unceremoniously interred, the plot marked only by a plain bluestone slab. Chambers' original tombstone, bearing his initials and the date of his death, was embedded into the foundation of Jansen Hasbrouck's new brick house, built in 1850 on the site of Chambers' first grave. When the Hasbrouck house was demolished, the original tombstone was removed and placed on display in the Senate House in uptown Kingston. It would not be until the first decade of the twentieth century, more than 250 years after Thomas Chambers, Kit Davits and others stepped ashore at the Strand in Rondout, that a granite monument in Montrepose Cemetery would be erected to the memory of this red-headed carpenter turned lord of the manor. However, a pear tree, thought to have been planted by Chambers himself at his gravesite in Rondout, continued to grow until 1926. Certainly, this is the best and most appropriate of all monuments for the man who helped to plant the fruit of European civilization in Ulster.

From the creation in 1683 of Ulster County (named for James Stuart, Duke of York, Earl of Ulster, and later King James II), and throughout the time of renewed Indian troubles, when raids were made on outlying homesteads in the county, Thomas Chambers had continued to hold public office and to consolidate his position in Ulster. Amassing considerable wealth and power during the last quarter of the seventeenth century, Chambers was the first of many commanding personages, "white sachems," or captains of commerce to inhabit and to exploit Esopus and the Rondout. When Chambers died on April 8, 1694, not only the century, but also an era, had nearly come to an end. Kingston and Rondout were no longer the frontier. Settlement had been firmly established; the roots of a new culture had been deeply planted in the rocky, alluvial soil; and agricultural and limited commercial interests had been developed and were secure. Esopus, or Ulster as it was beginning to be called, was now important. It had become the recognized food basket, or granary, of the English colonies.

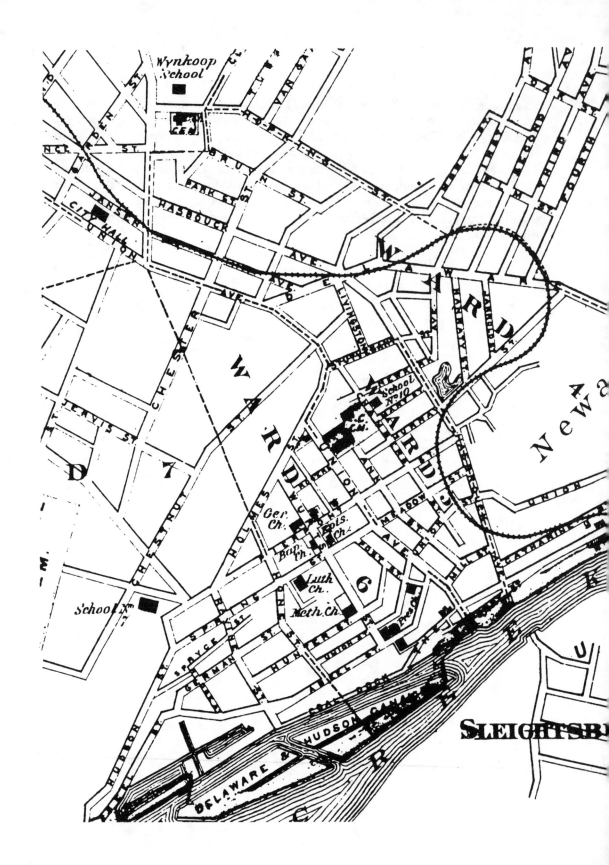

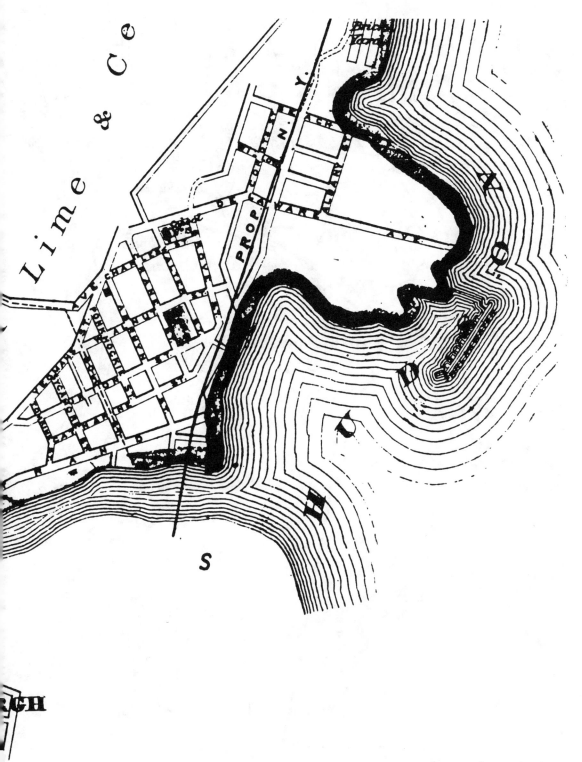

Rondout in 1875.

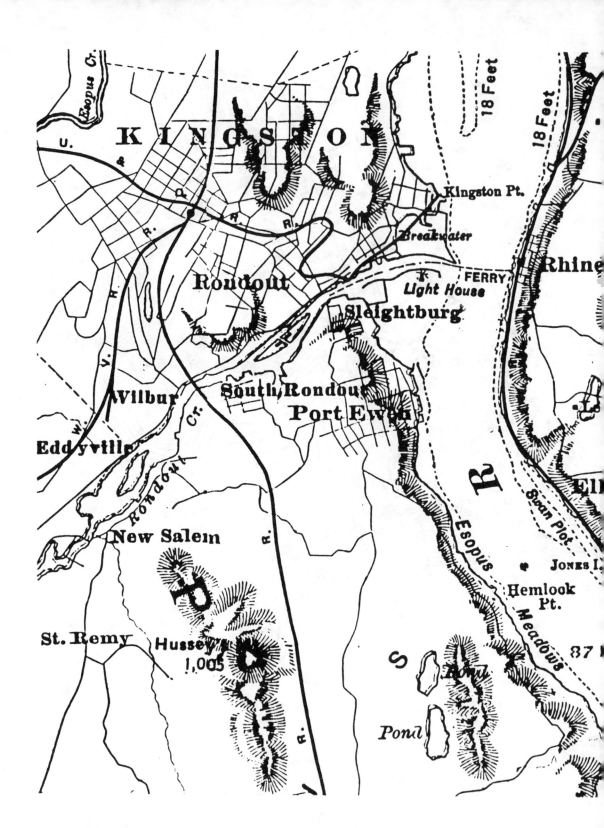

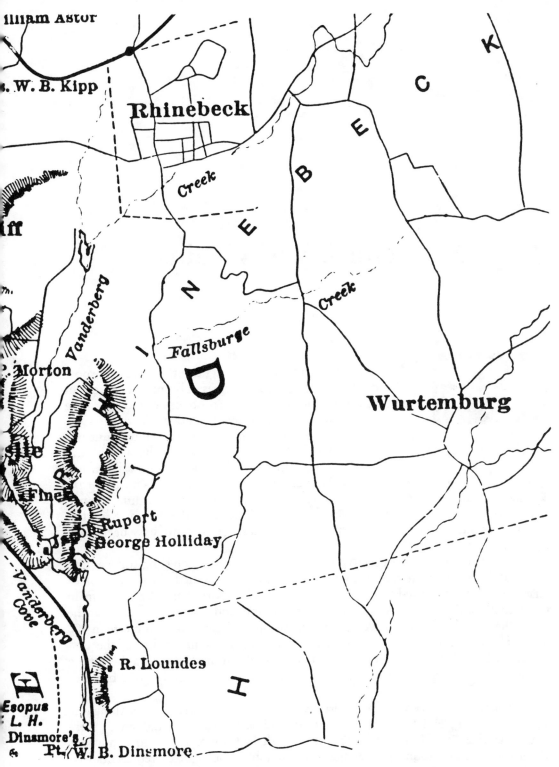

Rondout in 1897.
Rand, McNally & Co.

3 : A Nursery of Villains

DURING THE FIRST HALF of the eighteenth century, the port of Rondout began to play an increasingly important role in the life of the area. More and more produce poured out of the rich and beautiful lands of Ulster and moved down the river to the great city. In ample, wide-bottomed sloops, built not unlike the big, squat Dutch barns which dotted the landscape, the agricultural products of Ulster were sent to a growing market. Two sloop lines sailed from Rondout. One line was operated by Abraham Hasbrouck, who owned the *Martin Wynkoop*, possibly the most famous sloop on the river, and the other line was run by a Major Swarts. Soon, a dock would be built at Columbus Point (now Kingston Point), and a public ferry established to take an increasing number of passengers back and forth across the river.

In this regard, it is interesting to note that between 1653, when Kingston was first settled, and the end of the century, when Thomas Chambers died, the population of what would later be called the United States increased more than four times, from 52,000 to 214,000. By 1750, it had reached one million, and within a decade, near the end of the French and Indian Wars, it was to become 1.5 million, an increase in 100 years of nearly thirty times the original population. As William Smith, the first historian of the Province of New York, stated at mid-century, Ulster was becoming a populous and prosperous land, an area noted for flour, beer, and a good breed of draft horses.

Of course, things were far from perfect. There *were* problems. For one thing, the colonists and England had their differences, and as English rule tightened, these differences increased. For one thing, the English had imposed certain conditions which the colonists found intolerable. Most notably, the right of representation, which had been enjoyed for some time in Ulster, was withdrawn. For another, strictures were placed on education and the press. And the colonists were taxed more and more heavily for the maintenance of English troops in New York, who were

34

fighting the French and Indians to the north. In addition, as these fruitless and costly campaigns continued, Ulster men were conscripted and local food supplies were requisitioned. Perversely, however, Ulster was abandoned by the English and left to defend itself against Indian molestation. As a result of such mismanagement of the war and the rigid and cavalier manner in which the English treated the colonists, by the second half of the century the physical and moral resources of this once prosperous region had become severely strained.

Even after the end of the French and Indian Wars in 1763, English oppression of Ulster and the colonies did not cease. In fact, appropriations actually increased, as England continued to press the colonists, and although a native of Ulster County was made governor in 1760, no improvement of the situation for Ulster, then in dire straits, occurred. In fact, the British Parliament, represented by the new Governor Cadwallader Colden, imposed even heavier duties on navigation and trade. The notorious sugar, stamp, and quartering acts were enacted. Such insensitivity to the problems of the colonists increased hostilities already bred by years of neglect, tyranny, and injustice. Often, these bad feelings erupted into violent altercations between colonists and English soldiers, as provisioning and quartering of British troops continued. It was not long, therefore, before matters came to a head. And as all students of the American Revolution have learned, the Boston Massacre resulted in 1770, the famous tea party in 1773, and the meetings of the first and second Continental Congress in the next two years. By 1775, the colonies and England were at war.

Of course, there had been portents of impending conflict and disaster earlier in the century. Swarms of locust had covered the county periodically, and severe wind and hailstorms, with hail as large as eggs, had broken windows and destroyed gardens and orchards. There had been a number of devastating floods, which had drowned livestock, washed away mills, and spoiled the grain crop. Seething masses of worms had appeared, and great amounts of caterpillars (possibly the gypsy moth) had ravaged the oak and apple trees. In 1737, the rain had frozen, and many trees had shattered from the weight.

Military action began in New York in May 1775, when Ethan Allan and his Green Mountain Boys took the British fort at Ticonderoga. In rapid succession, other forts were captured on Lake Champlain by the patriots. Some three thousand men had been recruited and organized into regiments, and upper Manhattan and both sides of the Hudson River as far as Lake George were fortified. Soon, the records of the colony were moved to Kingston, and the new provincial congress began to meet at White Plains. There, on July 9, 1776, the Declaration of Independence, which officially separated the colonies from England, was approved. Not long afterward, Lord Howe invaded and took New York City with superior forces, and George Washington successfully evacuated his troops, encamping at Harlem Heights. After a series of battles, Washington retreated to White Plains and then to New Jersey.

About this time, a man named John Holt, fleeing Lord Howe and his troops, moved his New York *Journal* to Kingston. Proudly proclaiming the motto, "unite or die," it was the first newspaper to be published in Ulster County. Holt and his paper would remain in Kingston, along with the records of the colony, until events of the fall in 1777 would send him running once again.

To understand how these events unfolded, we must first consider the nature of the British plan for the taking of the Province of New York. In 1777, it was decided, Lord Howe would sail north up the Hudson. General Burgoyne, who had created the plan, at the same time would march south from Montreal. The third English general, St. Leger, would cross the Mohawk Valley from the west. These three men and their forces, it was expected, would meet in Albany, dividing, and therefore conquering the state—in effect splitting the colonies in half. The plan seemed simple and faultless; it could not fail, it was thought. And yet, greatly surprising the arrogant British, it did fail, miserably. St. Leger was defeated in the bloody battle of Oriskany; Burgoyne was surrounded at Schuylerville near Saratoga, and surrendered to General Gates soon thereafter; and Lord Howe had headed in the opposite direction, and thus failed to play his assigned part.

An impatient and obstinate man, Sir William Howe had not been enthusiastic about Burgoyne's plan in the first place. Leaving his command at New York in the charge of Sir Henry Clinton, Howe had sailed off along the Atlantic coast in search of the rebel enemy, while Burgoyne and St. Leger marched on Albany. When he learned that Burgoyne was encountering difficulty near Saratoga, Sir Henry had dispatched Admiral James Wallace up the Hudson to create a diversion. Wallace, in the *Friendship*, a full-rigged, three-masted frigate, was accompanied by Sir John Vaughan, the military commander of the British fighting men. On October 3, with great loss of life, they took the forts at the Highlands and rammed and broke the chain that had been stretched across the river at Stony Point. It seemed like nothing could stop them.

When word of the inexorable advance of the British forces reached Kingston, there was great consternation. Once again, as during the troubles with the French and Indians, Kingston was left to defend itself alone; General George Washington's forces were engaged by that time with Howe at Germantown, Pennsylvania, and General George Clinton, hampered in his attempts to muster the necessary men, was unable to reinforce satisfactorily the rebel ranks at Kingston. Nonetheless, what could be done was done. Records, which had been moved earlier from New York City to Kingston, were sent to other locations. Every male sixteen years old and over was called to arms. Women, children and livestock were moved to Hurley and Marbletown. A Dutch poem of the time stated in part, "Run, boys, run, the red-coats are coming. Harness the horses before the wagon, and to Hurley ride" (Schoonmaker, 309). And so, prepared for the worst, but inadequately, Kingston awaited its fate.

The third largest settlement in the state, Kingston had been chosen as the site of New York's first Constitutional Convention earlier in 1777. In fact, the New York State Constitution had been written there and first read publicly on the steps of the uptown courthouse, all the churchbells ringing. The assembly had met in a local tavern, the senate in the gracious stone house of Abraham Van Gaasbeck, now called the Senate House, and Chief Justice John Jay had called the first Supreme Court into session. Just three months earlier, in this first capitol of the state, an Ulster County native, George Clinton, had been elected the first non-colonial governor and had taken his oath of office. The local Tappan House had become the executive mansion (Clinton's wife was a Dutch-descended Tappan).

Late on the morning of October 15, the Committee of Safety, which was meeting at Kingston, learned that to the north Burgoyne had been defeated. This was good news, indeed, and all were pleased. However, such information was not to be savored, for it was followed soon thereafter by further news from the south, which was bad. The British fleet under Wallace had been sighted anchored off Esopus Island, a short distance from Rondout. Accounts differ, but there seem to have been approximately thirty naval vessels in Wallace's squadron—an awesome sight, to be sure. All of them were armed to the teeth. The *Friendship*, with its distinctly inappropriate name, carried twenty-two guns alone. And aboard these ships were 1,600 select infantry regulars, eager for revenge. Facing these battle-hardened men, on the morning of Thursday, October 16, stood a pitifully inadequate rebel force. Nonetheless, the militia on Breast-works Hill above Ponckhockie (later known as the Vlightberg) and the crew of the two-masted rebel ship, *Lady Washington*, commanded by a Captain Cook and anchored at the mouth of the Rondout opposite Columbus Point, waited, as the British approached. It was not long before the British "opened a vigorous cannonade" upon the *Lady Washington* and upon the two batteries on the cliffs above Ponckhockie. In response, the rebel militia, commandered by colonels Pawling and Snyder, discharged five light cannons, which had been moved hastily into position. In her turn, the *Lady Washington* fired her own thirty-two-pound gun, but to little effect.

By the early afternoon, the British troops, encountering little resistance, prepared to come ashore. Observing this, the rebel militia on the heights spiked their guns, and with their wounded, fled. The *Lady Washington* turned and sailed up the Rondout Creek, chased by a party of British seamen, who later landed at South Rondout (now Connelly) and destroyed the house of William Houghtaling. Scuttled and abandoned by the rebels at the falls in Eddyville, the *Lady Washington* disappeared beneath the murky waters. Other ships anchored in the port were burned and sunk by the British. During this engagement, the *Dependence*, a British ship, was damaged and its crew and commander, a Lieutenant Clarke, injured in an explosion.

Since the early days of the war, Kingston had been burdened with the maintenance of a large number of political prisoners, most of them Tories, who had remained faithful to the English king. From all over the east coast, these people had been sent to Kingston, among other locations. When the jail in Kingston became filled to overflowing, prisoners were sent to Rondout, where they were incarcerated in vessels anchored in the creek. On July 10, eighty additional prisoners had been sent from Albany in two sloops, compounding the problem. Ironically, approximately a week before the British invasion, these luckless prisoners, who might have been liberated during the British attack, had been sent to Connecticut. Nonetheless, the craft which had housed them were boarded by the British and put to the torch.

By the time the British infantry came ashore, split into two divisions, one landing above Columbus Point (near the abandoned brickyards of today), and the other making a beachhead at the Strand in Rondout, the day had become unusually warm, for Ulster had been experiencing a period of good weather, called locally, "Indian Sumner." Facing little opposition, the British division in Rondout promptly burned the few buildings which stood there, and then climbed the hill to meet the Columbus Point contingent, which had probably followed the road from the point which today is called Delaware Avenue. Once the forces rejoined, they headed toward Kingston, guided by a Black whom they had captured. On the way, they met a Tory named Jacob Lefferts. This brief meeting was significant, for Lefferts, it is said, informed

Vaughan that Burgoyne, who had been defeated by Gates at Saratoga, would surrender (as it turned out the next day) at Schuylerville (Pratt, 136). Certainly, it was
apparent to all who heard this information that it was now unnecessary for Vaughan
to create a diversion for Burgoyne, as he had been commanded. Vaughan, however,
who considered Ulster County "a Nursery for almost every Villain in the Country."
(Pratt, 139), had also been "instructed to scatter desolation in his track"(Wilstach,
116). Thus, following these instructions to the letter, Vaughan decided to perform
his mission completely, and would not be deterred.

Angered by the defeat of Burgoyne, and realizing that his men were bent on
plunder, Vaughan was in no mood to turn back. It might be suggested, in this regard,
that his orders simply provided him with a rationalization for what he and his men
apparently wished to do anyway. Knowing that winter was near, Vaughan decided
to show no mercy. As Vaughan was to write with pride in a dispatch which he
composed the next day aboard the *Friendship* off Esopus, his men and officers had
"behaved with the greatest spirit" during the sacking of Kingston. And so, on this
hilltop high above Rondout, Vaughan made what might be considered one of the
most disastrous decisions in the history of settlement.

Realizing they could not retain control of the area, and fearing that the forces
commanded by George Clinton, which were en route from New Windsor to the
south, might reach Kingston at any moment, Vaughan and his men moved quickly,
systematically firing and plundering all the structures in the village. Only one house,
the Van Steenburgh house (at the corner of Wall and Franklin Streets), a barn owned
by Benjamin Low, and the brewery of Johannis Sleght were left untouched. Truly,
the British troops were dedicated to their task. When the jail and the courthouse on
Wall Street, which had been the site of the constitutional convention seven months
earlier, burst into flames, these troops cheered. Even the church and schools were not
spared. As described in the New York *Gazette* on November 3, 1777, 326 houses,
with an almost equal number of barns, "almost every one of them filled with flour,
besides grain of all kinds" and much valuable furniture, were lost. Although this
figure, cited by a British-held newspaper, seems quite exaggerated—a number of about
115 dwellings seems more realistic (Schoonmaker, 305)—the suffering, nonetheless,
was no less great, whatever the exact amount. An eyewitness, Abraham Hasbrouck,
who watched as his own possessions burned, wrote in his diary, "When the enemy. . .
came to Kingston. . . and burnt my dwelling-houses, barn, cider-house or stone-house,
and another barn, wagon-house. . .and also a small out-kitchen. . . the enemy. . . laid
everything in a rubbish of ashes, fences and everything they came to. . . . My loss. . .
I compute no less than £5000 at least" (Sylvester, 80).

In only three hours, the British, who retreated immediately afterwards to their
ships in Rondout, had reduced Kingston and Rondout to smoking ruins. Vainly,
George Clinton had attempted by forced march to reach Kingston in time. But the
militia he commanded were more concerned for the safety of their own families, and
were willing to fight only during the day and to return home at night. And so, the
rebel forces had hesitated. Earlier, Clinton had requested that Ulster County men
who were serving in the five regiments from New York in the Continental Army be
returned. He had implored the other generals to send him reinforcements, but none
had come. All he could do during his prior inspection of the area was to direct that
defense be established at Rondout and that every male over sixteen be made ready to

fight. All these requests and preparations, however, proved inadequate; on the very day that Vaughan burned Kingston, Clinton's own troops—little more than 1,000 men—had been able to reach only Marbletown, tantalizingly close, but nonetheless a few miles to the south. It is said that at this location Clinton commanded his tired soldiers to bivouac. Once this was accomplished, he rode ahead to Kingston with a small detachment of scouts. On a hill called the *Keykhout* (meaning "lookout" in Dutch, the present-day Golden Hill) above the village, Clinton watched in sadness and horror. Before him he beheld the ruins of Kingston engulfed in flames.

With limited resources and under difficult circumstances, this untrained, grass-roots commander had done his best, and it had not been enough. In a letter dated October 19, General Gates, in response to the burning of Kingston, wrote to Vaughan, "With unexampled cruelty, you have reduced the fine village of Kingston to ashes, and most of the wretched inhabitants to ruin." One day, stated Gates, Vaughan would suffer "the just vengeance of an injured People" (Schoonmaker, 301-2). Many years afterwards, the American writer James Fenimore Cooper was to describe the burning of Kingston in his novel *The Pioneers*. Natty Bumppo, or old Leatherstocking, as he was called, remembers seeing the event from high on the Catskill escarpment: "I was on that hill when Vaughan burnt 'Sopus, in the last war, and I seen the vessels come out of the Highlands. . . . The day the royal troops burned the town the smoke seemed so nigh that I thought I could hear the screeches of the women."

Although troubled by his inability to save Kingston, George Clinton went on to serve his state and country with distinction, not only as a general, but as a citizen elected to some of the highest offices in the land. As seven-term governor of New York, from 1777 to 1795 and from 1801 to 1804, Clinton held this position of public trust longer than any of his successors. Clinton also twice became vice-president of the United States, from 1805 to 1812, once under Thomas Jefferson and again under James Madison. In 1807, Clinton had even been a serious, if unsuccessful contender, during the Democratic-Republican caucus, for the office of president.

After the Revolutionary War, Clinton became a leading exponent of states' rights, publishing his anti-Federalist "Letters of Cato," in which he opposed ratification of the Constitution because it did not include a bill of rights and amendments which would, in his view, adequately protect the people and the rights of states. The state of New York had fought hard and had lost much during the Revolution, stated Clinton—Kingston provided clear example of this fact—and it was not inclined to return to the tyranny of centralized government, giving up freedoms which it had won. Consequently, Clinton and his followers withheld their support for ratification of the Constitution for some time, even threatening separation from the Union. It was only after ten states had ratified the document that Clinton and the New York delegation reluctantly agreed to fall into line, realizing, as the practical politician he was, that further discussion was impossible and their position untenable.

Clinton was born in 1739, in what was then southern Ulster County. In 1768, as a young lawyer, he was elected to New York's provincial assembly, where he became a leader in the anti-British faction. In 1775, before being appointed as a Brigadier General in the Continental Army in charge of the protection of the Hudson Highlands, Clinton served in the Second Continental Congress. A fleshy man of commanding presence, with prominent nose, full eyebrows, and long white hair in later years, Clinton, who counted himself a personal friend of George Washington, significantly died in the momentous year of 1812, as his country, once again, prepared to fight its second war of independence against England. Appropriately, Clinton is buried in the cemetery at the Old Dutch Church in Kingston, the village he attempted valiantly, if unseccessfully, to save. A granite obelisk marks his grave.

When those who had been evacuated to Hurley returned along the flats, across the Esopus Creek, and up the hill to Kingston a few days after Vaughan's retreat, they must have looked at the smoke-blackened walls of their old homes and then sat down in the ashes and wept. It had been a good harvest, the green, fertile fields along the creek having yielded a bountiful grain crop. But now that was mostly gone. Some people must have wanted to quit. In fact, some did leave to live with relatives elsewhere. Constructing as best they could makeshift shelters and lean-tos in the foundations of the burned houses, the remaining villagers awaited winter and its first snows with anger and fear in their hearts. Building materials and labor became so scarce and expensive that many could not afford to rebuild, and some despaired. As Andries De Witt of Kingston wrote to Governor Clinton, " Their spirit to rebuild is good, but their abilities weak. Assistance for that purpose would be exceedingly agreeable, and greatly revive the drooping spirits of many of the poor sufferers" (Schoonmaker, 321).

Although Clinton was to send some help, the most encouraging assistance came from unlikely quarters. From across the Hudson river, the wealthy and powerful Robert Livingston, who also had lost his house and barns to Vaughan, granted the citizens of Kingston five thousand acres deep in the Catskills (a community that would be called New Kingston), and patriots as far distant as South Carolina sent food and money.

Even in these darkest times, however, those in Kingston did not loose their own sense of generosity and patriotism. That same cold winter of 1777–78, when George Washington and his troops were encamped at Valley Forge, Kingston contributed its share to the foodstuff collected in Ulster County to aid the starving soldiers. Four months after the city had been burned, sleighs loaded with whatever food could be collected set out for Valley Forge. Tradition says that even the lead which had survived the burning of Kingston in Ben Low's barn was made into bullets and was also contributed to the Continental Army cause.

Nonetheless, few places in the colonies suffered such devastation, or gave so much to the fight for liberty. As a result of this sacrifice, and because of the extreme situation in which Kingston now found itself, its militia of two companies was exempted from further military service until the village could be rebuilt. Thus, there is no record of service of Kingston men in New York State regiments of the Continental Army after this time.

On Friday, the day after the holocaust, the British troops, who had beaten a hasty retreat to the port of Rondout, sailed up the Hudson River, landing a few miles above Rondout. There they torched the isolated and abandoned farmhouse of Petrus Ten Broeck, along with his storehouse and barn, and also burned the house owned by the Whitaker family. A detachment of soldiers was sent across the river, where several houses were burned on the Rhinebeck Flats, in addition to the house of Robert Livingston at his manor to the north.

It was feared that the marauding British might return to Rondout, or even attempt to occupy Kingston, for although Burgoyne had surrendered at Saratoga, Wallace and Vaughan strangely hesitated, their British forces remaining in the area. As Clinton had written to General Gates on October 21 from Hurley, "If they land in Force I must either retreat, or sacrifice my few men and lose seven valuable pieces of field artillery." Clinton added with emphasis, asserting his view of Kingston's predicament, "If I retreat this whole County will be ravag'd and destroy'd. . ." (Pratt, 150).

On October 23, Clinton's worst fears, it seemed, were realized, for the British ships, like figures in a bad dream, returned and anchored off Columbus Point. That night, panic must have run through the desolated streets once word reached Kingston from Rondout. As anyone who was superstitious could have pointed out, it was the same day of the week as when Kingston had been burned. Villagers who had begun the resurrection of the town only a few days earlier must have wondered what would happen next. Must the village be evacuated once again?

Deterred by the presence of Clinton's forces and low on ammunition, the British did not attack, however. With the coming of dawn, as if the prayers of the townspeople had been miraculously answered, the *Friendship* and its flotilla weighed anchor and headed downriver to join the British fleet at the Highlands, its tall sails disappearing at last around a bend. At this moment, Rondout and Kingston must have breathed a collective sigh of relief, for with the exit of Wallace and Vaughan the British presence in the area ended, and Clinton's troops could return to New Windsor.

Before sailing into the port of Rondout in the fall of 1777, Admiral James Wallace had served as a naval commander for fifteen years. Noted for his severity and brutality, he was rewarded in later life for his services to the crown by being made the governor of Newfoundland. He died in London on March 6, 1803.

General John Vaughan had been a career army officer. He entered the British forces at the age of eight, never married, and served there for nearly fifty years. He was a brave soldier who had reason to fear and hate rebels and their guns, for in 1775, after landing on Long Island, he had been wounded in the thigh and had been disabled for some time. In 1777, during the British attacks on Forts Clinton and Montgomery, his horse had been shot out from under him. After the American Revolution, Vaughan was assigned to the Leeward Islands as commander-in-chief. Later, he was made the governor of Fort William in Scotland. Other appointments followed, as well as his acceptance of the Order of the Bath. At the age of fifty-seven, on the island of Martinique, Vaughan died suddenly and mysteriously. Some historians believe he was poisoned. If this is true, one could suggest that General Gates' angry prophesy, made eighteen years earlier, had finally come to pass. The man who unnecessarily and mercilessly had razed Rondout and Kingston had himself, through violent treachery, been killed.

With hostilities between the colonies and England ending in 1782 after the surrender of Cornwallis at Yorktown, Virginia, the previous year, Rondout and Kingston awaited with anticipation the arrival of the conquering hero, George Washington. General Washington had visited the area in 1777, during the dark days of the war, when the lower Hudson River had been occupied by the British. He had taken a circuitous route from New Jersey to West Point, and on this journey he had passed through Marbletown and Hurley en route to the river at Rondout. At Hurley, he had been addressed by a very old man named Wynkoop, who spoke with such a thick Dutch accent that Washington could not understand a word. A tall, erect, and dignified man, Washington nonetheless had listened to the old man, politely sitting upon his horse in the middle of the road, hat in hand, in a driving rain.

Five years later, on November 16, 1782, after attending a public reception with Governor Clinton and his wife in Hurley, Washington once again rode into Kingston, where he was met with great public rejoicing. Speeches were delivered, offering the famous and beloved general congratulations and "the most unfeigned love and esteem." (Schoonmaker, 337). His wisdom and fortitude, which had led the colonies to victory, were extolled. "May your well-earned fame run parallel with time and your felicity last though eternity," Henry Sleght, the speaker of the town trustees, told Washington.

Aware of the great losses Kingston had suffered during the Revolution, Washington warmly and diplomatically responded:

> While I view with indignation the marks of a wonton and cruel enemy, I perceive with the highest satisfaction that the heavy calamity which befell this flourishing settlement, seems but to have added to the patriotic spirit of its inhabitants; and that a new town is fast rising out of the ashes of the old. That you and your worthy constituents may long enjoy that freedom for which you have so nobly contended is [my] sincere wish. . . (Schoonmaker, 337-338).

That evening, after attending a large reception given in his honor where he was introduced to the town dignitaries and their ladies, he spent the night with his staff at the public house of Evert Bogardus. The next morning, bright and early, he boarded a ship at Rondout and continued his journey to West Point. This occasion and the memory of George Washington were to endure in Ulster County for many years. Although not a man of imagination or initiative, Washington, according to a noted historian, "typified the idea of union as nobody else could" and commanded "a sort of awe." He was dignified, as people thought a leader should be. "At receptions he would enter dressed in black velvet and satin, with diamond knee buckles. . .his military hat under his arm, and a dress sword in a green scabbard at his side" (Nevins, 117-18). As late as the mid-nineteenth century, according to a prominent Rondout citizen, formal parties were given on the date of Washington's birthday, and his revered name was toasted, everyone "standing in silence" (Booth, I: 322).

Not until nearly a year after Washington's visit, on September 3, 1783, was the final Treaty of Paris signed, recognizing the United States as a nation. Then, finally, on November 25, to the great relief and joy of all, British troops, who had troubled the colonists since 1664, were evacuated from New York at last.

This chapter of our story, however, is not yet complete. For earlier that same year, as improbable as it may seem today, Kingston petitioned the Congress of the Confederation to consider making Kingston the site of the capital of the new United States. Governor George Clinton had approved the petition, and one square mile within the limits of the village had been set aside for this purpose. If this proposal had been taken seriously by the delegates who were meeting at Philadelphia—which it was not—the history of Kingston might have been altered and Rondout might have become a Hudson River port of a very different nature. But this was not to be. The efforts of the trustees and prominent businessmen of Kingston ultimately proved futile. In a tersely worded response to their proposal, Alexander Hamilton, a

Federalist delegate from New York unsympathetic to upstate interests and an antagonist of Governor Clinton, had answered the hopeful citizens. You should have offered two acres, he informed them contemptuously. In disappointment and shame, the trustees realized that it was useless to revise and resubmit their proposal. Thus, no further steps were taken, and Kingston never heard from Hamilton or the Congress of the Confederation on this matter again. Quickly, Kingston and Rondout returned, almost gratefully, to their earlier state of peaceful obscurity. This condition, however, would continue only until early into the next century, when individuals from outside the area would create dramatic changes once again.

4 : The Great Emporium

BORN IN KINGSTON on October 15, 1775, near what is today the corner of Wall and John Streets, John Vanderlyn grew up in the ashes of revolutionary Kingston. One can imagine this gifted child, who would become a world-renowned artist, sketching the ruins of the burned village. The third son of Nicholas Vanderlyn, a blacksmith and artisan, and Sarah Tappen, Johannis, as he was christened, was recognized early in life for his artistic talent. Subsequently studying at Kingston Academy (situated at the present Academy Green), at age seventeen, with the support of his generous patron Aaron Burr, John Vanderlyn worked in Philadelphia in the studio of one of the most famous of all American portrait painters, Gilbert Stuart.

An intelligent, good-looking young man, with fair skin, curly hair and proud, sensitive eyes, Vanderlyn, whose Dutch grandfather also had painted, became the rage of Paris when he was introduced to its best salons by Burr at the age of twenty-one. Something of a dandy in his youth, Vanderlyn liked to dress well and in the fashion of his day. Although many men still wore the knee breeches and stockings of colonial and revolutionary times, Vanderlyn's wardrobe reflected the Americanization of the latest, contemporary English Regency and French Empire styles. In his self-portrait, he is fashionably attired in stylish velvet cutaway coat, striped satin vest, and over-the-chin white cravat. Although not apparent in this picture, he undoubtedly wore wool or denim trousers stuffed into "Hessian" boots, and when walking out of doors, sported a long, caped overcoat and a flared top hat made of beaver.

In 1801, at the beginning of Thomas Jefferson's first term as president, Vanderlyn returned to America from Europe at the suggestion of Burr. During his ensuing travels in America, Vanderlyn visited places of geographic interest, making sketches, most notably of Niagara Falls. Returning to Europe soon thereafter, Vanderlyn continued to cultivate his interest in landscape painting and decided to become a nature painter in the tradition of the English painters Constable and Gainsborough. In Paris,

Vanderlyn viewed with great interest the panoramic exhibitions that were receiving such enthusiastic response from the general public. First painted by Robert Barker in the year of Washington's inauguration, the panorama was a picture or series of pictures of a landscape presented on a continuous surface, encircling the spectator so as to give the impression of an unlimited view in all directions.

Typifying the entrepreneurial spirit of his newly liberated nation, Vanderlyn decided to try the panorama in his own country, where energetic and dedicated investors were meeting with unprecedented commercial success, since the heavy restrictions that had been imposed by the British had been lifted. With high hopes, not only for his own financial advantage but also for the future of the fine arts in the new nation, Vanderlyn returned to New York and leased, at great personal expense, a building which he called the New York Rotunda. Here, he exhibited large panoramas, some representing awe-inspiring scenes of grandeur from the American landscape which, years later, would become the stock-in-trade of highly successful painters such as Albert Bierstadt, Frederic Church, and other members of the Hudson River School.

Unfortunately for Vanderlyn, Americans at this time were not ready to appreciate such a new type of art, and his experiment failed miserably. In his later years, he even petitioned Congress to establish a national art museum to house these and other works of American art, but without success. Largely unrecognized for his efforts to promote native American art and frustrated in his attempts to educate the American people to the value of non- utilitarian art, as embodied in his 12-by-160-foot *Panorama of the Palace and Garden of Versailles* and his monumental *View of Niagara Falls*, Vanderlyn was forced to paint portraits and historical scenes in order to survive. In 1839 he painted the landing of Columbus in America on a panel of the rotunda in the nation's Capitol. Best known for his portraits of both ordinary and famous personages, among them Presidents Washington, Madison, Monroe, Jackson, Van Buren, and Taylor, Vanderlyn despised these "face paintings," as he called them, disdaining the aesthethic taste of an earlier era. Yet, ironically, it is these beautiful, haunting portraits, as well as the work inspired by classical and historical themes, for which Vanderlyn is most remembered. His *Ariadne* caused an uproar when it was exhibited as the first nude painting displayed in America. And his *Marius on the Ruins of Carthage*, entered in competition in Paris, was awarded the Emperor's Gold Medal by Napoleon himself. When Napoleon expressed his wish to purchase the historical painting with the intention of installing it in the Louvre, characteristically, Vanderlyn refused to sell, preferring to return it to the United States as evidence of America's cultural nativity. Appropriately, this cultural patriot has written of himself, "the main object of my life has been to acquire some eminence in my art, less in the hope to acquire fortune thereby than to reflect some credit on my country" (Dumond, 27).

With extensive training and experience in the dominant neo-classical style of the time, with its restraint, balance, and preoccupation with Greek and Roman mythology and antiquity, and yet with strong romantic tendencies embodied in his personality and art, Vanderlyn pointed the way toward a new American art and culture. Although he died impoverished, unhappy, and alone—in a cheap Kingston hotel room in 1852—when the type of art he had pioneered had long been applauded in the works of others, Vanderlyn might take satisfaction in the fact that today art historians are beginning to recognize his importance in the development of American art and the contribution he made to American landscape painting.

In a life which spanned more than seven decades and two cultural eras, Vanderlyn, the painter of big, expansive canvases, reflective of the spirit, size, and hopefulness of the new nation, was both nationalist and cosmopolite. In the early years of the Republic, Vanderlyn, as did America, looked back with mixed feelings toward the older, more mature culture of Europe which was fast receding. His life and work, and the influences which shaped it, epitomize the distinctive qualities of the new nation.

After his death, in the early fall of the year in which Harriet Beecher Stowe published *Uncle Tom's Cabin* and Franklin Pierce became the fourteenth president of the United States, Vanderlyn's remains were buried at the Wiltwyck Rural Cemetery at public expense. His friend and biographer, the noted lawyer, state senator and congressman Marius Schoonmaker, relates that a crowd attended the service held in Kingston's largest church, but that no monument was erected to mark the grave. In the following years, Vanderlyn's unsold paintings and his effects were handed down through his family; eventually many of them were lost. The gold medal which Vanderlyn had received from Napoleon had long before been pawned.

On October 1, 1852, in the month following Vanderlyn's burial, a strange and perplexing eulogy appeared in a Rondout newspaper called the *Courier*. Mentioning that, prior to his death, Vanderlyn had chosen and paid for a burial site in Montrepose Cemetery "on the heights above Rondout," and that Vanderlyn had visited the location frequently in his last years, saying that he had experienced a sort of peace of mind while standing there, the eulogist pointed out that even in death, as in life, Vanderlyn had been disappointed. Whether Vanderlyn, in need of funds, as was often his situation, had sold the deed to his beloved plot or had misplaced or lost it, is not known. Nonetheless, sadly, the artist, who had loved the wide, sweeping view of the Hudson River from above Ponckhockie and Rondout, and who had painted this landscape so beautifully and lovingly, was not laid to rest in the site he had carefully chosen. For unknown reasons, Vanderlyn was buried in the Wiltwyck Rural Cemetery, now at the end of Pine Grove Avenue, set back more than a mile from Rondout and the river. Also of interest is the fact that, when Vanderlyn's corpse had been found, it was noticed that his hand had been raised as if in the act of transferring paint to canvas. How troubling it must be, then, for the spirit of this great artist, who may have been painting some great landscape in his imagination even as he died—possibly of Rondout and the Hudson River—to find himself situated for eternity in such an unfavorable location.

During the lifetime of John Vanderlyn, the United States experienced many changes—from colony to independent country, from monarchy to democracy, and from rural agrarian to urban commercial society. America saw the beginnings of large-scale manufacturing, prohibited before the Revolution, as well as an explosion of creativity and entrepreneurial energy and effort, released when English control was removed. It saw the construction of roads, turnpikes and canals, and the invention of new and more rapid means of transportation, such as the steamboat and steam locomotive. Anthracite coal replaced charcoal in smelting and the production of iron, a commodity which, in turn, made the development of industry possible. At this time, America saw the creation of a nationalistic foreign policy, reflected in our advocation of the Monroe Doctrine and the concept of manifest destiny. Covered wagons trundled westward, following the trails of the fur trappers, who had first explored the great western wilderness of Jefferson's Louisiana Purchase, and settlers from the eastern states and from all over Europe, in a great wave of immigration, washed across the country, displacing once again the indigenous people. By the fifth decade of the century, the pressing, unanswered questions of slavery and race could no longer be suppressed, and Congress made the compromises that obfuscated these issues and led the new nation inevitably toward civil war. About this time, a precious, yellow-colored metal was discovered on the far western coast of the continent, driving many Americans "gold crazy." And clipper ships sailed around the globe in search of other forms of wealth, such as silk and tea, traveling even to fabled Cathay.

The political, economic, and social consequences of independence were profound. When Vanderlyn died in 1852, the population of the United States exceeded twenty-three million; at his birth in 1775, at the dawn of the Revolution, it had been less than three million. Between 1789 and 1850, the percentage of Americans engaged in nonagricultural occupations increased by over 30 percent. With abundant labor eager to work, with new capital available to be invested, with the invention of efficient, specialized machines, and with the development of steam as a source of power, the configuration of American industry changed. During the first half of the nineteenth century, the production income of manufacturing alone rose nearly 100 percent each succeeding decade. And agricultural expansion, generated by increased population, new markets, and improved transportation, for a time kept pace. With the growth of free institutions and the end of privilege (for many, but not all), Americans of this time lived in a heady environment, one which, as Harvard historian Oscar Handlin has put it, "stimulated enterprise, rewarded investors, and encouraged dynamic innovation" (Handlin, I: 478). According to Hector St. John de Crevecocur, who in 1782 had published *Letters From an American Farmer*, the American was truly "a new man," one who "acts upon new principles." Fifty years later, the French observer Alexis de Tocqueville, in his American travel diary, *Democracy in America*, would note the "strange unrest" of America. And the great poet and essayist Ralph Waldo Emerson would call America "a country of beginnings, projects, of designs, of expectations." Truly, at the time, the open spaces seemed vast, the resources inexhaustible, and the economic possibilities unlimited. Most everyone wanted to take advantage of the situation.

In this parade of optimism, economic development and growth, Kingston and Rondout were not left behind. Of course, at first, things went a bit slowly. After the burning of Kingston, the farmers returned to their fields, and the gradual process of rebuilding began. With peace declared and the business of creating a government now being enacted elsewhere, the inhabitants of Ulster County resumed their earlier, settled pattern of existence. Washington Irving's Dutch character Rip Van Winkle would have felt at home here as before.

Four sloops, carrying local commodities, once again sailed down the Hudson River from Rondout to New York City, but only on Fridays, and the round trip took two weeks. For the most part, Rondout was poor farmland owned by the Van Gaasbeek family—possibly descendants of the stepson of Thomas Chambers, who had broken the entail and lost Chambers Manor—and by Abraham Hasbrouck, an owner of one of the two Rondout sloop lines.

In 1820, a small settlement stood at the Rondout Landing, or the Strand, near the mouth of the Rondout Creek. According to Schoonmaker, it consisted of a few houses—about one-half dozen—some buildings used for storage, and a small grist mill. Most of the structures were made of stone. There was no church, no school, and no public buildings. Van Gaasbeecks, Hasbroucks, William Swart, who owned one of the two sloop lines, a man named Wood, who lived in a house on Swart's dock, and probably a few other hardy souls lived in Rondout at this time (Schoonmaker, 469). In a landscape painting of Rondout by John Vanderlyn, who painted the sleepy scene from the hill above the Strand, one sees depicted a single stone house, with two other dwellings situated nearby, a solitary sloop moored at the wharf, a mill, millpond and miller's house, an old Dutch barn and another outbuilding, and across the creek in what is now Sleightsburgh the house of John Sleight. In this painting, the mouth of the creek is rendered accurately, with a low green point running out into the river on the south side and a high rock outcropping protruding to the north. In the early nineteenth century, this promontory became known as the Vlightberg. Later, it was mined for cement, and in the twentieth century it became a part of today's Hasbrouck Park.

Upstream from Rondout about a mile, at Twaalfskill (meaning "striped bass" in Dutch), at present-day Wilbur, there were two grist mills, a distillery, and a few houses. A mile and one-half farther, at the head of tidewater at the falls at Eddyville, there were also a few buildings and a small cotton factory. No direct road had been constructed along the creek this far. Down the creek from Rondout in Ponckhockie sat the homestead of William Tremper, and further along the road to the point the house of Wilhelmus Hasbrouck. At Columbus Point, to the north of the mouth of the creek, stood a dock, a one-story stone building which housed the ferry, and a number of other unoccupied stone houses which had fallen into ruins.

By 1820, although New York had passed Virginia to become the most populated state in the Union, the population of Kingston and Rondout only approached three thousand, with better than 300 being Blacks, of which more than sixty were free persons. And although Dutch had ceased to be spoken in church services after 1808 and Dutch ethnic consciousness had declined markedly since 1688, 153 of the 262 trustees of Kingston continued to be accounted for by only twenty-seven surnames, among them the still-familiar names of De Witt, Elmendorph, Sleght, Dumond, Dubois, Delemater, and Wynkoop (Blumin, 40). Clearly, although some things were different, the old families still dominated the area, and significant change had yet to come.

Money, combined with breeding and race, divided the locals into four classes. On the bottom were the slaves, freedmen, and poor whites. Next were white hired hands and village workers. Farmers, storekeepers, craftsmen, and professionals comprised the third class. These individuals were considered respectable. Finally, on top rested comfortably the elite, or gentlemen—those set apart from the respectable class by property, polish, or public office (Blumin, 39). Of the eighteen town officers elected in 1820, ten bore the names of the leading thirty-two families, and seven of these names can be traced back to the trustees during the seventeenth century (Blumin, 41).

But dramatic change did come to the area in the third decade of the nineteenth century. For although Kingston and Rondout were long-settled rural communities, seven generations removed from their frontier experience, they were not isolated from the changes in transportation and commerce which were imminent. In 1820, as historian Stuart Blumin has pointed out, Kingston and Rondout were poised on the "urban threshold," and they would soon cross that point of no return, becoming a "small but robust commercial city" (Blumin, xii). To understand how this happened and to learn how this peaceful agricultural area awoke from its eighteenth century slumber to join the rest of the northeastern United States in its scramble for money, power, and position, we must go back to the beginning of the century.

Alarmed at the rapid growth of American commerce and shipping after the Revolution, and especially during its war with Napoleon and France, England took advantage of its superior seapower and the general military unpreparedness of the United States. It blockaded European ports with which the neutral United States traded; it confiscated cargoes; and it impressed American seamen into the British navy. In response, President Jefferson persuaded Congress to pass the Embargo Act of 1807, which prohibited all American ships from trading with Europe. Although this was an unpopular piece of foreign policy that was repealed by the end of his administration, relations between the United States and England became even more strained during the presidency of James Madison (1809-17). The disruption of commerce, bitter sectional rivalries and partisan struggles over domestic and foreign policy, as well as crumbling confidence in the republican system of government, made it necessary that the new republic demonstrate that it could survive and succeed. The idea of war with England, however, was unpopular. Soon, though, Madison, provoked by continued British contempt and insolence, entered the conflict with reluctance. Only a few months after Madison's second inaugural address, the British, on August 24, 1814, sacked and burned the White House and the Capitol, which had been situated in Washington since 1800. During her hair-raising, last-minute escape from the British troops, the First Lady, Dolley Madison, it is said, had rescued the Declaration of Independence and a valuable portrait of George Washington.

The war with England did not leave Ulster County unaffected. In response to the capture of Washington, soldiers of the local militia were ordered south to Staten Island and to New York City. On September 7, 500 to 600 men from the brigade of General Frederick Westbrook of Ulster County were sent to defend New York Harbor. Embarking aboard sloops at the port of Rondout, the men sailed for New York. Newspapers of the time report that "their apparent cheerful obedience and devotion to their country's claim repressed all sorrow and struck dumb all grief" (Schoonmaker, 401). But one doubts the truth of such patriotic assertions, for some of these men must have remembered the Revolution, ended only about thirty years earlier, and the great price Ulster County had paid. When they had learned of the White House and the Capitol's fate, they must have thought of the burning of Kingston and Rondout in 1777.

Those not called up were asked to contribute potatoes and other vegetables to the war effort—even money, if possible. There was much talk of a "union of sentiment" and "union of exertion." Committees of relief, defense, and correspondence were formed. The response was quite spirited.

After three months' service, the Ulster Militia was discharged in December and relieved of guard duty in New York. Luckily, the men had seen no action. Less than a week after the sloops carrying the militia embarked from Rondout, Lieutenant Thomas Macdonough, with only four ships and ten gunboats, had destroyed a British flotilla on Lake Champlain near Plattsburgh. This decisive victory deprived British General George Prevost of support in his campaign to invade the United States by way of the lake and the Hudson Valley. As a result, Prevost's forces had retreated to Canada. Once again, as at Saratoga during the Revolution, the British had been stopped in the north.

On December 13, 1814, a local newspaper *The Plebeian* stated, "Capt. Peter Van Gaasbeek's company returned here on Saturday morning last. . .in good health and spirits, from a tour of three month's service in the defense of New York. They were the last of the troops from this county who were discharged. The whole are now again with their families and their friends. . ." (Schoonmaker, 402).

Proposals for direct negotiations had been made by the British as early as the beginning of the year, and President Madison had accepted. Even after the peace treaty was signed on December 24 in the Flemish town of Ghent, battles continued to be fought—most notably the defeat of the British forces at New Orleans by General Andrew Jackson in January of 1815. The war ground to a halt, and everyone on both sides of the Atlantic was relieved. On February 17, 1815, the day after the Treaty of Ghent was ratified, the entire village of Kingston was brightly illuminated. There was great excitement and a feeling of festiveness filled the air as the village inhabitants turned out dressed in their best. As the president of the village had decreed, it was a celebration "in demonstration of the general joy on the return of the blessings of Peace" (Schoonmaker, 402).

But peace did not bring prosperity to Kingston and Rondout at first. The war, in addition to other domestic problems, had created a financial crisis, and the country was deeply in debt. The United States Bank had ceased to exist in 1811, and its business had gone to state-chartered banks, whose notes were not backed by adequate specie. As a result, there was a bewildering number of notes, which fluctuated in value, and an epidemic of counterfeiting. In short, there was no reliable and uniform national currency, a severe handicap to the conduct of business. In Kingston, the village directors had even found it necessary to issue small bills of their own currency. Not until 1816, when a second Bank of United States was chartered by Congress and a sound paper currency issued, did the country begin to find a measure of fiscal stability.

Interestingly however, it was not a national legislative act which was to prime the economic pump of Ulster County and to bring forth the fruitful waters of prosperity to Rondout. It was, in fact, the simplest of events. In the autumn of 1814, as the ruins of the Capitol and the White House stood starkly against the sky, and as the militia from Kingston and Rondout sailed to New York in broad-beamed sloops, a Philadelphia merchant by the name of Maurice Wurts tramped in the mountains of northeast Pennsylvania. Every fall, leaving his brother William to mind the store, Maurice returned to this semi-wilderness of the upper Lackawanna Valley to hunt. His regular companion and guide was a local woodsman named David Nobles. In 1813, Maurice returned to the area as usual, and found Dave imprisoned for debt. Wurts promptly paid Nobles' debts, but in doing so quite shrewdly took title to his friend's mountain land. For back in Philadelphia, Maurice had purchased a basket of shiny, black stones, found in these mountains, which had fascinated him. Such "stone coal," as anthracite, or hard coal, was then called, was unpopular at the time. In comparison to bituminous, or soft coal, obtained from England, hard coal was thought to burn poorly. Nonetheless, Maurice reckoned that with the loss of the preferred English soft coal during the war, a market would be created for the hard. And so he viewed the upper Lackawanna Valley and the land of Dave Nobles with great expectation and interest.

Purchasing additional wild tracts of land in the valley at from fifty cents to three dollars an acre, Wurts hired Nobles to explore his new domain and to accompany him in finding and mapping anthracite coal outcroppings. A rigid Presbyterian, it is possible that Wurts believed that his success was preordained, for by 1816, he found what he sought. In no time he was prepared to mine the abundant coal reserves that were deposited there. Now, the problem was no longer a matter of discovery and acquisition, it was one of transportation. The question was simple: How could he get the coal to Philadelphia?

In succeeding years, Maurice Wurts attempted to raft his precious black cargo to Philadelphia by river, but without much success. In the first attempt, the raft struck rocks and broke up. It was during the infamous "Year Without Summer," when, due to the gigantic explosion of Mt. Tambora on the Indonesian island of Sumbawa the previous year, a dust cloud had encircled the globe, bringing snow in June and ice in July. Songbirds had frozen to death in the trees, and crops had been lost. In the second attempt in the following year of 1817, Wurts hauled coal over an old mountain road and then rafted it to the city, but in insignificant quantities and at great expense. Maurice and his brothers William and John (the latter was a lawyer) were not easily deterred, however. If reaching the Philadelphia market was not cost effective, then they would look someplace else. What about New York? they speculated.

As the Wurts brothers, rich in coal and opportunity, fatefully shifted their gaze, the spirit of enterprise was also being fanned into flame in Ulster County. In the fall of that year, John Tappen, the editor of the Kingston *Plebeian*, first articulated in print the need for local economic expansion. As if privy to the Wurts brothers' plans, prescient, or simply sensitive to the *zeitgeist*, Tappen advocated the importance of "cultivating commercial intercourse with the thickly populated settlements that border on the Delaware and Susquehanna Rivers." If this were done, he promised, Kingston and Rondout would become "the great emporium of that country" (Sciaky, 275).

Before this could happen, however, the link between these areas had to be established. To accomplish this, Wurts decided he must cross the Moosic Mountains of Pennsylvania by railroad, and then construct a canal through the New York State counties of Sullivan and Orange to Newburgh. In this way, he thought, coal could be brought from Honesdale, Pennsylvania, to the Hudson River, and then sent by water to New York City. Certainly, this seemed like a good plan, for numerous turnpikes and canals were being constructed throughout America at this time. The plan, however, had one substantial drawback. The Shawangunk Mountains were in the way, separating the proposed canal from the Hudson River. A tunnel could be bored through the mountains, it was true, but significant engineering problems were involved in the process. And so, for a time, Wurts' plans to bring coal to New York were stymied.

Then, Wurts met Abraham Cuddebac. Frustrated in his hopes for quick commercial success and searching for a solution to his dilemma, one can imagine how eagerly Maurice Wurts must have listened to what this man had to say. Suggesting that Wurts avoid the Shawangunk Mountains altogether, Cuddebac, who lived near what is now

Port Jervis, made the suggestion that would change not only the face of the Rondout Valley but also the destiny of Ulster County, Kingston, and Rondout. Continue north with your canal, Cuddebac proposed; take advantage of the natural terrain and the abundance of water. Use the route of the Old Mine Road, appropriately named and associated with legends of silver and copper mines and which follows, in part, the course of the Rondout Creek. As Cuddebac, in a few words, might have phrased his momentous advice: avoid Newburgh; head for Rondout at Kingston. To Maurice Wurts, this counsel made sense. And so the die was cast. A canal of a bit over 100 miles in length would be constructed from Honesdale to Rondout. At last, the Wurts brothers' anthracite coal would be transported from the mountains of Pennsylvania to the river and then to the great city at the sea.

During the first half of the nineteenth century, the country saw vast internal improvements made. For example, miles of roads and turnpikes were constructed by private companies. This, in turn, encouraged agriculture and stimulated development. By 1808, there were eighty-eight different turnpike companies operating three thousand miles of toll roads in the United States, most of them gravel-surfaced. In Kingston, for example, the Ulster and Delaware Turnpike Road had been incorporated in 1802. It ran from Columbus Point, near Rondout, to the Delaware River, passing through the towns of Hurley, Woodstock and Shandaken, to Delhi and Walton in Delaware County, and finally to Chenango County, some 104 miles away. A portion of this route was used in the late nineteenth and early twentieth centuries by the Ulster and Delaware Railroad, and it is followed today by New York State Route 28. The cost of building the U & D road—about $1,000 a mile—was significant, and the profits from the turnpike proved insufficient to pay expenses and the interest on the loan. By 1819, the turnpike was sold. Other local turnpikes were proposed, among them the Neversink Turnpike Road. This road, which later came to be known as the Lucas Turnpike, was privately financed by three-term Congressman Lucas Elmendorf, who invested $40,000 of his own money in the project. This turnpike, like the U & D, also began at the Hudson River at Rondout, but headed southwesterly through the towns of Hurley, Marbletown, Rochester and Warwarsing, and through portions of Sullivan and Delaware Counties, to Broome County near the Susquehanna River. The section of this turnpike which passed through the Kingston village limits is now called Lucas Avenue, in honor of its chief investor.

Privately financed turnpikes, however, generally proved unsuccessful; by 1825, most had been abandoned. The "turnpike craze" had been supplanted by "canal mania." Millions of dollars were invested. And although canals were more expensive to build than turnpikes, they were decidedly more lucrative. The Erie Canal, opened by Governor De Witt Clinton, the nephew of Revolutionary War General George Clinton, paid for itself in seven years. Begun in 1817 and built at the enormous cost of $7 million, "Clinton's Big Ditch," when connected to the Hudson River, formed a continuous waterway from one end of the state to the other.

On October 26, 1825, a fleet of boats carrying Governor Clinton and other dignitaries entered the canal at Buffalo. The news was relayed to New York City by cannon in ninety minutes. Clinton's boat was drawn by four handsome, gray horses. Another boat carried two Indian boys and wild animals from the West, including a bear and two eagles. Their journey was marked by a series of celebrations, where everyone who lived along the new canal rushed to its edge to see the strange procession pass. Finally, the entourage reached New York City, and a "marriage of waters" was proclaimed, when a keg of water from Lake Erie was poured ceremoniously into the Atlantic. Clinton and his Erie Canal had launched America into the Canal Age.

By 1830, forty canals were in operation or under construction in the United States, providing cheap transportation—less than one cent per mile per ton—for a wide variety of commodities of commerce, agriculture, and mining. By 1850, 4,400 miles of artificial waterways had been hand-dug. If joined together, these bodies of water would have formed a canal that could have stretched from New York City to San Francisco.

During the first decade of the nineteenth century, President Jefferson had suggested employing unexpended government money for internal improvements, but he had balked when he learned how much such projects would cost. After the War of 1812, which delayed the government from taking any action in this matter, demand for improvements, especially for the improvement of water transportation, grew. In 1816, President Madison urged Congress to finance projects using revenues obtained from the protective tariff of that year. Subsequently, however, he vetoed the bill passed by Congress which would have distributed $1.5 million to the states for such work. Not until after the completion of the two terms of James Monroe (the last president to wear a wig and cocked hat)—which brought to an end the long reign of the so-called Virginia Dynasty of presidents, with its deep commitment to the earlier agrarian tradition—did the era of government-financed internal improvements truly began. With the election in 1824 of John Quincy Adams, a president from the industrialized Northeast, and with the celebration of the fiftieth anniversary of American independence, as well as the commemoration of the deaths of both Presidents Jefferson and Adams a few hours apart on July 4, 1826, the course of the ship of state in the direction of economic growth, internal development, and cheap transportation was conclusively and irrevocably set.

Back in Philadelphia, Maurice Wurts and his brothers were hard at work, too, sympathetic and responsive to the changes that were occurring in American society. Now, not only would these thrifty Swiss brothers have to attend to their thriving dry goods business, they would also have to begin the preparations that would make possible the construction of a great canal. However, certain problems—technical, legal, and financial—had to be overcome before the work could begin.

With this in mind, early in 1823 the Wurts brothers hired Benjamin Wright, the famous chief engineer of the Erie Canal, then under construction, to survey the proposed route of their canal from the Delaware River to Rondout. The findings of Wright and his staff were favorable. Next, John Wurts, who had entered politics in Pennsylvania, gained authorization from the state for the brothers to "improve the navigation" of the Lackawaxen River, which would be utilized as the first section of the new canal. To this end, a company called the Lackawaxen Coal Mine and Navigation Company was formed, and would later be joined with the Delaware and Hudson Canal Company. A month later, John also obtained from the state of New York a charter for the Delaware and Hudson Company, giving it permission to construct a canal from Rondout to the state line on the Delaware River. Everything was falling into place. Only the consideration of money remained to be settled.

Surprisingly, the matter of finances at first proved to be no problem. For once the Wright report and map were circulated in 1824, interest in the project in financial circles in Philadelphia and New York ran high. A canal, four feet deep and thirty-two feet wide at the surface, would be dug at an estimated cost of a bit less than $1.25 million, stated the report. This bold plan soon caught the attention of Philip Hone, a rich and influential citizen of New York. Once Hone became committed, his name and unqualified support insured the success of the enterprise. Soon wealthy supporters begged to invest in the project.

The activities of Maurice Wurts helped, too. An energetic showman, this assertive person and leader of the three brothers, aware of the benefits of advertising, issued a descriptive brochure of the canal. Then, on a bitterly cold day in the winter of 1825, Maurice made a dramatic demonstration to a group of chilled financiers in the Tontine Coffee House in New York City. There, having earlier rafted and then transshipped a load of coal to the city, Wurts built, in a grate specially constructed into the venerable eating establishment's huge fireplace, a roaring fire. Warmed and cheered, as well as impressed by this brilliant act of salesmanship, the assembled potential investors were enthusiastic in their response. By early afternoon, the entire issue of stock was sold. On the same day, January 7, in both Goshen and Kingston, stock was also offered for sale.

Two months later, once again at the Tontine Coffee House, a board of managers of the Delaware and Hudson Canal Company was elected, and the company, which was to irrevocably alter Rondout, was formally organized. Philip Hone, then forty-four years old, was elected the first president of the company, and John Bolton, a respected New York financier, became treasurer. Thirteen others were made directors, among them Garret Abeel, John Hunter, Abram Hasbrouck, Benjamin Rogers, and Maurice Wurts. Their names, as well as others associated with the canal, can still be seen inscribed on street signs in today's Rondout.

Known as the "Famous Bean of Old Manhattan," Philip Hone was a "striking figure of a man, tall and spare, distinguished in bearing and courtly in manner." He was "a master of social graces and an intimate of the great men and women of his day," among them Charles Dickens, Daniel Webster, and Henry Clay (Dunshee, 58). His wife, Catherine, was beautiful and charming, and she and Philip made a handsome couple. They were bright lights in New York society.

Born in 1780 and descended from an old New York family, Hone was an intelligent and observing man. In a diary, still of great interest to historians, he recorded the important events of his life and times. Hone was clever, too. As a public relations strategy, once, during the construction of the D & H Canal, Hone shipped fifty tons of coal up the Hudson "to insure the comfort" of Governor-elect Martin Van Buren and the legislature. The D & H Canal project was in need of a loan at the time. Certainly, Philip Hone was a perfect choice for the presidency of the D & H Canal Company. Although he resigned a few months after his election due to the pressures of his duties as the newly-elected mayor of New York City, Hone continued to serve with effect on the D & H Board of Managers. Hone died in 1851 at the age of 71.

One of the first pieces of business of the board of managers of the canal was to hire a chief engineer who would oversee the construction of the canal. For this important job the services of Benjamin Wright, mentioned earlier, were engaged. With him, Wright brought John Jervis, who would succeed him two years later as chief engineer, and for whom the community of Carpenters Point was later renamed

Port Jervis. Jervis was an ingenious person, and his talents were of great assistance to Wright and to the company. After leaving his position as chief engineer of the D & H Canal, Jervis assumed the direction of the fledgling Mohawk and Hudson Railroad. It is said that in redesigning the heavy, English-made locomotives then in use, Jervis engineered one of the greatest advancements in the history of American railroading (Drago, 295).

In the summer of 1825, construction began on the D & H Canal. With the spadeful of earth turned by Philip Hone, who had spent the previous night with his family in the little village of Ellenville, and after speeches, singing, and the saying of appropriately hopeful prayers, the digging began in earnest. James Mc Entee (who also gave his name to a street in Rondout), the engineer in charge of the building of the first twenty miles of the canal, "proceeded with haste and precision" (Sciaky, 277). For the most part, the work went well. The terrain was not unusually difficult, and there were few extremes of weather. Near Rosendale, along the proposed route, a type of limestone similar to that used in the building of the Erie Canal was found, and thus was discovered what came to be known as Rosendale cement.

James S. Mc Entee, of Irish ancestry, is an interesting figure. Not only did he serve as an engineer during the construction of the canal, he also directed the building of the D & H company docks at Rondout. Without a doubt, Mc Entee's engineering accomplishments were legion. In subsequent years, he mined the first coal in the Lackawanna Valley, purchased and operated in 1832 the Mansion House in Rondout, built the first lighthouse in the Rondout Creek in 1837, quarried limestone for the Newark Lime & Cement Company, constructed the Island Dock coal depot in Rondout in 1845-46, and in 1865 made the initial surveys for the construction of what would later become the Ulster and Delaware Railroad. In a biographical sketch written and published in his later years, Mc Entee, the father of Rondout landscape painter Jervis Mc Entee, was described, somewhat inadequately it seems, as "a man of correct habits, sterling integrity, and. . .liberal. . .views " (Sylvester, 204).

Between 1815, the year in which the Napoleonic Wars ended, and 1860, just prior to the Civil War, immigration to the United States swelled. During this time, approximately five million people entered the United States looking for a more prosperous and secure way of life. Of this figure, the greatest number of persons were of Irish and German descent—80 percent, in fact. Two and one-half million, fleeing the famine of Ireland, and one and one-half million the conscription and disruption of German wars, faced the agony of separation from loved ones and the discomfort and perils of crossing the cold, stormy Atlantic to reach what was perceived to be a land of unlimited hope and opportunity. Understandably, some of these expectant and aspiring people, who entered America through the port of New York less than 100 miles to the south of Rondout, found work building the D & H Canal. Eventually, many of these individuals were to land in Rondout, and many were to stay.

As might be expected in the case of competing immigrant groups such as the Irish and the Germans, with different languages, religions, and ethnic backgrounds, misunderstandings, disagreements and grievances often occurred. Fights and brawls were not uncommon among the construction crews building the canal, disturbing the rural tranquility and outraging the local population. The Irish workers, said John Jervis, were "wild." He added, "I don't know what they've got to fight about. They don't need a reason; they fight just for the hell of fighting" (Drago, 93). One group of Irishmen was especially feared. They were the Irish from County Cork in Ireland, called "Corkonians." Truly, they were the terror of the countryside, raiding gardens and orchards, and destroying what was left behind. They even fought among themselves. German and Irish workers could not be housed together, and thus barracks, situated several miles apart, had to be constructed. Few weekends, however, passed without pitched battles occurring between them. In an effort to protect property and maintain order, the local sheriffs stationed men at suitable locations along the line. But even these deputized law officers were often unsuccessful at maintaining the peace.

Just as the undoubted violence and ignorance of this volatile immigrant labor force must be described, the blatant prejudice directed toward its members should also be noted. For just as their supervisors perceived the Irish as "wild," drunken and brawling, the Germans were seen as dumb and good-natured—both caricatures, to be sure. The image of the jolly, sentimental German was to be presented in a popular poem of the nineteenth century called "Vot I Like Und Don'd Like," composed by the old-line New Englander, Charles F. Adams (Handlin, 139). Similar to the satirization of the Irishman's brogue, German-accented English is derided in this demeaning poem. One stanza begins with the words, "I like to see a hand dot's brown,/ Und not avraid off vork." Quite appropriate sentiments, it could be suggested, for one whose labor was essential to the completion of the vast projects of internal improvement in progress at this time.

Certainly, the ridiculing and dehumanization of the immigrant laborer seems to be common in a society where the exploitation of large numbers of untrained and dependent workers, perceived as dangerous and infantile outsiders, ungrateful and improvident, is considered necessary and, therefore, acceptable. Such a practice, which continues to this day, is to be lamented.

Considering the frequently rowdy conduct of the workers and the mistreatment and exploitation which they suffered, however, it is surprising how rapidly work on the construction of the canal progressed. Although troublesome and uncontrollable, especially in their free time, these men were unrivaled as workers. In only sixteen months, they completed sixty miles of canal in the section between Rondout and the Delaware River—more than one-half its total length. And in only a bit more than three years, these tough and eager workers were to complete the job. When they were finished, they could feel very proud of themselves, indeed. For they had built 107 locks, 22 aqueducts, 110 waste weirs, 136 bridges, 16 feeder dams, 22 reservoirs, and most notably, 108 miles of canal, which stretched all the way from Honesdale to Eddyville, near Rondout.

5 : Natchez Under the Hill

Wᴴɪʟᴇ ᴄᴏɴꜱᴛʀᴜᴄᴛɪᴏɴ ᴘʀᴏɢʀᴇꜱꜱᴇᴅ along the route of the canal to the south, an unassuming agent of the D & H Canal Company stepped ashore at Rondout and quietly began to look for land. Keeping an especially low profile, since he did not wish to stimulate speculation and increase the price of property, the agent carefully searched for a proper site on which to construct the company's main office and depot. At first it was thought that the company should situate its base of operations as near the Hudson River as possible. So, after consideration, a tract of land in Ponckhockie was purchased. However, before this site could be used, the large farm of Peter Van Gaasbeek at the Strand came on the market unexpectedly. So the company changed its mind, abandoning plans for the Ponckhockie site. On April 6, 1826, it bought the Van Gaasbeek Farm. Although not located directly on the river, the docks and buildings of the farm, as well as its ample acreage, made it an even more desirable purchase. Situated in Rondout, on the southwestern side of the road leading from Kingston to the landing, this venerable, old farm dated back to the early days of Esopus. In addition to the Van Gaasbeek Farm, the company also acquired the sloop docks of William Swart, which had been used since the previous century by his transportation company. Swart subsequently moved his operation up the creek to Wilbur.

Abraham Hasbrouck, another major landholder and entrepreneur in Rondout, was also approached by the canal company's agent. Hasbrouck, however, refused to sell his land. A man whose French Huguenot descendants had come to Esopus in 1675 and then settled in New Paltz, Hasbrouck had conducted a profitable freighting and forwarding business since his arrival in Rondout in 1795 after the Revolution. In sloops, which he owned and had built, he carried grain and other agricultural products to New York, becoming wealthy and powerful as a result.

In 1801, while still in his twenties, the young and ambitious Abraham had purchased from his father-in-law, Henry Jansen, the parcel of land that was desired by the D & H Canal Company. Located on the northeastern side of the Kingston-

Rondout road, opposite to the Van Gaasbeek Farm, this property was not only important to Hasbrouck's business, it was also notable for its historic interest, for it contained the grave of Thomas Chambers and the ancient pear tree which marked the site. Hasbrouck was firm in his refusal to sell. For this reason, as Rondout grew and streets were laid out, the streets on either side of what would soon be called Division Street (today called Broadway) were not, at first, made to meet. In fact, as the population of Rondout mushroomed in the early years of the canal, immigrants and those who worked on the canal tended to inhabit the dwellings built on the southwest side of the dividing street in the old Van Gaasbeek tract, and the older, more established residents of the county gravitated to the northeast side of that line. Today in Rondout, interestingly, no Van Gaasbeek Street is to be found. Yet, until its virtual elimination during the recent construction of an arterial approach road to a new bridge, the eastern boundary of central Rondout remained Hasbrouck Avenue, named after the man who would not sell his farm.

Once the necessary land was purchased, the canal company began to establish itself in Rondout. During this process, an interesting bit of human drama occurred. John Bolton, the newly elected president of the D & H Canal Company, the successor to Philip Hone as well as the designer of the plan for the building of the first streets in Rondout, unexpectedly decided to rename the area Bolton, in his own honor. The response to this egotistical act was strong and negative, however. The canal company could put the roads wherever it wanted, thought Abraham Hasbrouck and other prominent members of the community, but it could not call Rondout "Bolton," and so their opposition to Bolton's plan was outspoken and firm. As a consequence, the Strand, or Kingston Landing as it was called, kept its old, familiar name, and Bolton had to be content with naming only his domain to the southwest of Division Street. Even this distinction was not to last for long, however. For when Bolton's term as president ended in April 1831, the new president, John Wurts, felt no responsibility to continue the use of his predecessor's name. Everyone, except Bolton, it might be supposed, thought the name was inappropriate, anyway. And so, quickly, the appellation was eliminated without regret. Bolton and Kingston Landing at the Strand would simply be called Rondout, as it had been in earlier days, and as it would remain. Ironically, nothing in Rondout today is named for John Bolton. Nonetheless, the Wurts brothers, as well as Hone and many of the other presidents, managers and engineers of the canal company, have found their names assigned, if not to an entire village, at least to its streets.

To the great many individuals who came to Rondout to find a job and to work, however, the question of the name of this new place did not matter all that much. Expressing this point of view, many newcomers might have asked the old question, "What's in a name?" Such a matter-of-fact approach to place is understandable. Yet, nearly one-half century later, during the fateful years of 1871 to 1873, when faced with another threat, Rondout residents, just as Abraham Hasbrouck had done, would realize how important the name of a community actually is. But by then it would be too late.

In the fall of the year in which the D & H Canal Company purchased the old Van Gaasbeek Farm, a strange flotilla sailed up the usually placid Rondout Creek to the Eddyville Falls. Here, George Eddy had established a saw and cotton mill in 1820 on the site of a previous mill built by Cornelius Delamater in 1739. It was late morning, and the sun shone brightly, which was a good thing, for it had been cold and uncomfortable for many days. On board the *Morning Star*, piloted by Captain Griffin, and followed by attendant craft, were to be found a select group of company officials and guests. Among these notables were Maurice Wurts, the infamous John Bolton, the engineers Jervis and McEntee, and "several ladies and gentlemen of the vicinity." Along both banks of the creek awaited workers and sightseers in wagons and on horseback. Many had traveled long distances, some by foot, to see the *Morning Star* and to view the ceremony that would consecrate the cornerstone of the recently completed Tidewater Lock No. 1 of the D & H Canal at Eddyvile. As one spectator reported in the *Ulster Sentinel* only a few days after the event, "It was a scene, which speaking without exaggeration, has never been equaled in this part of the country." As the *Morning Star* approached the lock, he continued, "the foam of the river. . .tumbled over the dam. . ." and "from the heights above the creek, cannons were fired to salute the *Morning Star*." At the lock, a band struck up "Yankee Doodle" and other happy tunes. Then, the boat entered the lock, passing beneath an arch of evergreens. With the gates closed and water flowing into the lock built by Sage, Farwell and Cook, the *Morning Star* "rose majestically to the level of the Rondout Creek above the Eddyville Falls, the multitude cheering enthusiastically. Here, Freemasons performed the ritual of "laying the perfect ashlar," which impressed everyone. Prayers were offered by Reverend Gosman.

Then, with towline attached to the boat pulled by "two noble, well-trained horses, gorgeously caparisoned," it was taken for a short voyage up the Rondout Creek. According to the *Ulster Sentinel*:

> Everywhere the old and young, the mother and the daughter, the husband and the wife, hurried forward to witness the sight. They smiled, they shouted, they shrugged their shoulders and stared with open mouths at the magic scene. . . .Some, attracted by the melody of the band, kept pace with the vessel, seizing the towlines to relieve the horses.

Finally, after a short inspection of the canal above Eddyville, the boat put about and returned to an old stone house situated near the banks of the creek. Here, the assemblage disembarked and enjoyed "an elegant cold collation," prepared by their host, Hiram Radcliff. As the excited reporter wrote, the participants attacked "the viands without further ceremony. . .their appetites having been sharpened by the pure air of the Rondout."

Not everyone in Ulster County, however, was so delighted with the location of the canal. Some disgruntled people had wanted the canal to pass through the old village of Kingston, not Eddyville. If Kingston was bypassed, they feared, prosperity would come only to Rondout, and this would prove a "death blow" to Kingston, draining away all its business (Schoonmaker, manuscript, 16). As usual in matters of this sort, the D & H Canal Company kept its own counsel and disregarded the entreaties of the good citizens of Kingston. Setting a pattern of conduct toward all municipalities and government agencies which it would follow scrupulously in the coming years, the company ignored public opinion and the public interest and simply did what was best for the company. It had decided that the canal would follow the Rondout Creek, and that was that. The first lock, therefore, would be constructed at Eddyville. And so it was here that the dedication ceremony had occurred.

When the canal was opened to traffic two years later in October 1828, Kingston citizens waited with a mixture of expectation and fear. What would be the effect of the canal? they wondered. Possibly, it would not be as bad as they had thought. As it turned out, their fears were unfounded; prosperity, in some measure, did result for most everyone in business, both in Kingston as well as Rondout. Nonetheless, these negative sentiments clearly exhibit the mixed feelings of envy and fear which the citizens of old Wildwyck (uptown Kingston) felt for the new, commercial community developing at the base of the Rondout cliffs. This initial suspicion felt toward Rondout soon would blossom into full-blown antagonism, a sentiment which would last for many years.

In all fairness, however, it must be said that there *was* some call for anxiety. For as Rondout grew, boisterously and out-of-control in those first years after the completion of the canal—when all manner of men and women flocked to Rondout from Europe and the northeastern United States, building wooden shanties and living in what would in any era be considered substandard housing—Rondout began to fulfill its detractors' expectations. Certainly, no one would have called Rondout genteel. A person thought drunk in the village of Kingston would have been considered sober in Rondout, it was said (Mabie, 12). In an area of only about thirty to forty square blocks, there were nearly fifty legal bars and saloons. On Division Street, from the creek to the top of the hill at Holmes Street (Mc Entee today), thirty-four establishments sold alcohol. Of course, numerous unlicensed and illegal places were hidden throughout Rondout, too. One could even expect to be offered a free shot of whiskey at most all stores as an inducement to trade.

Without a doubt, drunkenness was a distinct problem in Rondout, one about which the local newspapers and many socially conscious citizens constantly complained. Nonetheless, alcohol continued to be sold in Rondout, even on Sunday, despite the efforts of temperance activists, such as William Burleigh, who lectured in Rondout and read his poem, "The Rum Fiend." Even the "fairer sex," as women were euphemistically called, were not exempt from the depredations of alcohol. The *Courier*, a precursor of the Kingston *Daily Freeman*, reports on April 7, 1854, that a drunken woman, called a "virago," entered Canfield's tin shop in search of her husband. Loud and ill-tempered, scolding everyone in sight, she smashed the windows of the shop with her fists when she was told that her husband was not there.

Fights and brawls also were not uncommon, especially when the canalers were not at work. On July 9, 1852, for example, the *Courier* reported that Rondouters had found themselves once again "in a spreeing mood," one which "produced a belligerent feeling among them." The article concluded, somewhat sardonically, "the liquor in Rondout, we notice, almost invariably produces this effect." As a result, brutal beatings, stabbings and occasional murders occurred. On election days and after horse races, which were conducted in the streets, rioting sometimes broke out. Frequent combatants in these altercations were native-born locals and immigrant Irishmen.

Due to extended periods of famine in Ireland during the early nineteenth century, Irish had immigrated to America and settled in Rondout in unprecedented numbers. By 1855, in fact, despite an impressive influx of native-born Americans from nearby counties and towns, half of the population of Rondout and Kingston was foreign-born, with better than one-third of the total being Irish and one-sixth German (Blumin, 80). These immigrants were perceived by many locals to be a significant threat. It is not surprising, therefore, that conflict between these groups developed. On July 4, 1851, for example, a riot began when two locals got into a fistfight with three Irishmen. As the conservative newspaper, the *Ulster Republican*, reported the affair, the Irish easily won the first encounter, but afterwards boasted loudly, "in a most demonical manner," that they could "whip any American." Soon, the battle escalated when an Irishman stopped a passing wagon by grabbing the horse's bit and swearing that he would allow no American to pass. As a result, the native-born locals were aroused to a high pitch of "righteous indignation," and joining forces with assorted "rowdies," "loafers," and members of the Kingston gang, the Bumble Bee Boys, pelted the Irish with stones and brickbats. Finally, the sheriff arrived and order was restored, with fifteen persons being arrested.

The election riot of 1853 was much bloodier. While standing in line waiting to vote, an Irishman from Rondout accidentally stepped on the foot of "a Kingston rowdy of some note," named Bob Baggs. Bob was a leader of the Bumble Bee Boys and a man, reported the *Ulster Republican* on March 9, 1853, "notoriously quarrelsome when intoxicated." Although the Irishman apologized, the drunken Baggs nonetheless started a fight, which was quickly stopped. However, tensions mounted, and later in the day Baggs provoked another fight, and a furious street battle ensued. Although the sheriff and his men arrived in due course, it took the combined forces of both the sheriff and the local firemen, who had been summoned by the ringing of the village fire bells, to quell the riot. When it was all over, there had been numerous injuries; eleven men had been arrested, and one man had been shot.

The Irish even fought among themselves, especially if they came from different sections of their homeland. In his diary entry for May 21, 1850, Nathaniel Booth, local entrepreneur, amateur musician, and avid observer of the Rondout scene, wrote, "Today a regular Irish row. . .a great clan fight came off in Rondout. . . ." On an earlier occasion in 1848 Booth had noted, "There was a glorious Row in Rondout last evening. . .no small number of eyes darkened."

Violence also erupted within the German community. When a three-year-old German child was run over accidentally on Division Street by a wagon driven by a man from Kingston, the father of the child attacked the driver, hitting him on the head with a stick. Soon, a crowd of Germans gathered, and the driver was mobbed. Fleeing for his life, the man finally escaped by running through Metzger's Hotel.

Due to the frequent occurrence of unfortunate events of this sort, it was not long before a distinct prejudice developed against the newcomers, and the stereotype of the drunken Irishman or the foul-mouthed German was commonly accepted by the native-born. Soon, the area near the D & H Canal docks, where an Irish shantytown had sprung up, was given the name "New Dublin." And the derisive term, "Dutchman," meaning a German of low caste, was employed in Rondout and Kingston, as it was elsewhere in America (Blumin, 96). Clearly, anti-Irish and anti-German sentiment ran high.

Although most local newspapers promoted growth and expressed approbation of the economic progress which the canal had brought, increasingly their scrutiny was directed at immigrants in the interest of the establishment and maintenance of social order (Blumin, 79). J. P. Hageman, the owner and publisher of the Rondout *Courier* from 1847 to 1868, printed an editorial on November 17, 1854, which stated,

And so with the German and the Irishman from the Canal—or the dock. Accustomed to bawling at their horses, or their drivers, or their unruly wives and children at home, when they meet together in carnival scenes or on business matters, and have their modicum of lager bier or bad whiskey to deaden their senses—it is not to be wondered at that the peace of the community in the immediate neighborhood. . .should be disturbed.

Kingston's *Ulster Sentinel* was even more explicit in its response to these new inhabitants of Ulster County. This local Whig newspaper, later Republican, owned by William Romeyn, referred to the "fateful events which had awakened the creek from its centuries of slumber and peopled its shores with a population so alien to its old settlers" (Sciaky, 278). Even the local representative in Congress, Erastus Root of Delhi, felt it necessary to comment on the situation. Declaring that certain Rondout inhabitants were not up to "the requirements of Christian civilization," he likened Rondout to the infamous Mississippi River port of Natchez, calling Rondout a "Natchez under the hill" (Lindsley, 38).

6 : A Hive of Traders and Bargemen

THUS, RONDOUT OF THE 1830s, '40s and '50s differed in many significant ways from the more established and staid village of Kingston. In Rondout, a very different sort of life was taking shape, one driven by commerce and the clock rather than by the timeless round of the seasons and the cycles of planting and harvesting, as was the old Dutch village of Kingston. The men and women who came to Rondout after 1828 were not farmers or landowning yeomen. Most were unskilled laborers; 64 percent of Irish immigrants, in fact, worked as day laborers. Of this number, 20 percent were craftsmen; the rest were journeymen working in the stone trades. About 40 percent of German immigrants were also skilled craftsmen. They worked at shoemaking, tailoring, coopering, brickmaking, butchering, brewing and baking, as well as cabinet-, wagon-, and cigar-making.

Female immigrants fared no better. Just under 40 percent of unmarried women over the age of fifteen had occupations. The most common of these trades were those of seamstress, milliner, domestic servant, and schoolteacher. Unmarried German-born women were mostly servants, although a very small number worked as seamstresses, milliners, bakers, and jewelers. Of 254 Irishwomen surveyed in 1860, fourteen were listed as seamstresses; all the rest were servants (Blumin, 89).

As might be expected, therefore, immigrants found themselves at the bottom of the economic ladder, and poverty was common. "It is well known that there are many families in our village who are suffering for the necessary means of support," stated the Rondout *Courier* on February 10, 1854. Although fundamentally self-interested, concerned obviously with the issue of public expense, this newspaper, nonetheless, bemoaned what it considered to be the "inhuman treatment" of immigrants, who arrived in America "suffering disease. . .[and] penniless. . ." as it stated on June 23, 1854. In this regard, it is interesting to note that in the 1860 census, only one out of ten inhabitants as worth between $10,000 and $25,000 was an immigrant. And whereas one out of every four native-born household heads could report property in excess of $3,000, only one in twenty foreign-born households could do so. Only among household heads reporting $100 or less in real and personal property were immigrants the most numerous group (Blumin, 90).

Nonetheless, it was to Rondout that these expectant human beings came, transforming a place, as Schoonmaker puts it, where "Quiet ruled"(203), and where a large part had been "covered with pine, oak, birch, [and] chestnut," as the *Argus* reported on April 13, 1887, into "a maze of crooked, narrow streets." (Sciaky, 277). One could contrast the pastoral landscapes of the port of Rondout before the building of the canal, painted by Rondout artist Joseph Tubby, to the description of Rondout at the time written by historian and attorney A. T. Clearwater. In his *History of Ulster County*, published at the beginning of our own century, he writes, Rondout "bristled with masts and belching smokestacks" (Sciaky, 222).

Indeed, Rondout had become, in the words of fiction writer H. P. Lovecraft, "A Hive of traders and bargemen" (Sciaky, 340). As the gifted diarist Nathaniel Booth was to write in 1848, "Our village is all life and commotion...and the whole county hereabouts is like a nest of hornets stirred up with a crooked stick." Describing the canaler of the time, Booth wrote that the essence of his education was "first to swear well then to fight."

Certainly, Rondout was not, in these days, an easy or comfortable place in which to live. No school existed until one was built in 1832 at the foot of Wurts Street on a ledge of rocks. The first church, the Presbyterian Church of Rondout, which ministered primarily to the spiritual needs of the native-born (Hasbroucks were trustees), was not incorporated until nearly ten years after the canal company purchased the old Van Gaasbeek farm at the Strand. No Catholic church was erected in Rondout for the many Irish or German Catholic workers until the next decade.

Not only was Rondout, at this time, lacking in educational and cultural advantages, it was also crowded. From a gathering of stone buildings and a handful of souls in 1820, Rondout had grown in twenty years into a village of 1,500 inhabitants and 200 dwellings, including six hotels and twenty-five stores. In twelve years, Rondout had equaled the population of Kingston; by 1850 Rondout would surpass it in growth, reaching a figure of 6,000 in 1855. (Kingston, at this time, had a population of 4,000.) Amazingly, Rondout had more than tripled its population of 1845 in ten years.

And so, by 1849 Rondout was heavily congested, the houses appearing, as Booth wrote, as if they had been dumped from above and "stuck fast wherever they struck." By 1860, almost the entire core of the village was covered with buildings. Some, like the Mansion House, took up an entire block. Most of these buildings, however, were small and closely packed together. Sixty-three percent of these dwellings contained more than one household, and 33 percent held more than two (Blumin, 120). Space and privacy were scarce in Rondout, indeed.

Rondout was also noisy, dirty, and smelly. Heavy dust from the coalboats, the stoneyards and the cement mill filled the air. One heard blasting, steam whistles, and the clang of hammers and the rumble of wagons throughout the day. "We want quieter streets," stated a letter in the Rondout *Courier* on November 7, 1854. The same publication complained on August 6, 1858, of the "sickening odors and stenches" and "a rankness almost overpowering," due to the practice of depositing one's "slop and garbage" in the streets. This unhappy condition was aggravated by the lack of free circulation of air and by the fact that swine roamed throughout the village unchecked. The correspondent continued:

> swine, innumerable, of all ages and sizes, in all conditions of fatness and leanness, wallow in the gutters and stroll up and down the streets. . . . They are frequently seen standing on the steps of the houses of their owners, making their marks with the snouts on the doors. . .sometimes they may be seen in the houses, apparently forming a portion of the family.

These unruly pigs had even attacked the cemetery. Calling this desecration "A Stigma Upon Rondout," the Rondout *Courier* on December 8, 1848, urged the citizenry to "prevent the graves and their tenants from being washed and rooted down the hill."

In addition to the lack of a proper sewage disposal system, Rondout also lacked a public water supply. Streets, too, were ungraded and unpaved. A brook, which originated at a spring on Spring Street, ran down Division Street to Ferry Street and then to Hasbrouck Avenue. There was a stagnant mill pond at Mill Street and Hasbrouck Avenue. And Wurts Street remained but a sandy ravine, muddy whenever it rained.

Although Rondout could not be called a slum, like the notorious "Five Points" slum which appalled the English novelist Charles Dickens on his visit to New York and prompted him to write in 1842 in his *American Notes* that "All. . .is loathsome, drooping and decayed. . .here," it was a place where crime frequently occurred. Well-organized gangs of native-born youth roamed the docks and stole from the weak and the unsuspecting. "The fact that Rondout is infested by a gang of juvenile pilferers is well known," lamented the Rondout *Courier* in June 1854. One of these thieves, a child eleven years old, was caught by the night watch created by the citizens of Rondout to deal with this problem, and was sentenced to sixty days in the county jail. Kingston-based gangs, such as the anti-Irish "Bumble Bee Boys," referred to by the *Courier* on March 11, 1853, as an "organization of ruffians," often came down to Rondout and beat up drunken quarrymen, or were used in local elections to provide intimidation in support of non-immigrant, or "Native American" candidates. Objects were even taken from houses, such as a set of silver spoons which was stolen from the third floor of the home of Mrs. N. Anderson. It was rumored and reported in the *Courier* on March 10, 1854, that the brick that had been thrown through the window of the house of Mr. and Mrs. W. B. Crane, causing Mrs. Crane to be injured by flying glass, had been thrown by a member of a gang.

Certainly, life was precarious in Rondout, and serious injury and violent death were reported regularly in the local newspapers. Both on the job and in the home, horrible accidents occurred. There were explosions and cave-ins in the cement mine, ironically called the "Glory Hole." James Corcoran, who was married and the father of a child, was killed in a mine blast there. David Keefe was crushed to death when a mass of rock fell on him. And Thomas Smith, who worked for Elihu Brown, who operated a mill on Hasbrouck Avenue, was caught by his clothing and hauled into a machine that was grinding lime. Smith was found dead, entangled in the machinery, "every bone in his body crushed to pieces," according to a *Courier* article published on September 29, 1854. Even a young girl was nearly killed when, stepping out of a house on Hasbrouck Avenue, she was knocked to the ground by stones dislodged by a blast at the nearby cement mine. The Rondout *Courier* reported on August 27, 1852, with indignation, that this was an act of "culpable carelessness." Stating that "hair-breadth escapes" of the sort the young woman had experienced were almost daily occurrences, it called for a check of "this growing recklessness of human life." As if to prove the paper's point, five years later, a giant, spontaneous rockslide took place after heavy rain. Appearing to terrified observers like an avalanche or an earthquake, 600 feet of cliff above Hasbrouck Avenue fell away. Miraculously, when the cloud of dust, like a huge column of smoke, cleared, it was discovered that only three houses had been damaged and a child slightly injured. "Thank God for. . .deliverance against all human probabilities," wrote the Rondout *Courier* on July 22, 1859.

In domestic accidents, people frequently died as the result of infected cuts and wounds. Oil lamps exploded; hot liquids scalded; and people died horrible deaths from tetanus, or from "hydrophobia," caused by the bite of a rabid dog. The hapless often died of exposure, freezing in winter. And there were many drownings and other misadventures of tragic consequences. "Another man drowned near Rondout. . .making five in little more than a week," wrote Nathaniel Booth in 1848. Later in his diary, Booth was to record: "A young man named Sullivan drowned in the creek—he had been drinking and fell asleep on the deck of a canal boat—unfortunately he rolled off and sank immediately." Booth even chronicles how a man, who had lived "in peace and tranquility," had, by mistake, drunk poison. Before night, writes Booth in characteristically melodramatic, nineteenth century style, the man "was a corpse."

All of these gruesome events were covered by the press in lurid detail. Indeed, there seems to have been a public fascination with death. "Melancholy suicides" were particularly interesting to readers. People mourned in special, detailed ways and for unusually extended periods of time. Cemeteries were referred to as "cities of the dead," and people liked to visit them, frequently holding picnics and parties there. Every good hotel contained a "death room" as well as a bridal chamber. Even the hair of a deceased person was often saved; it was woven into pictures depicting graves and other morbid subjects.

The citizens of Rondout faced natural disaster, too, with little forewarning and insignificant aid compared to our own time. Fires would periodically sweep through sections of the village; significant property damage, and often loss of life would occur. On a freezing Monday night in February 1849, the day before Ash Wednesday, a great fire broke out, and as Nathaniel Booth describes the scene, it sent "a stream of light along the ice on the creek," which could be seen ten miles up the Hudson River in Saugerties. Quickly, an entire block was engulfed in flame. Soon, the fire spread to the decks of two sloops docked at the wharf. A "terrible state of confusion exists," wrote Booth, who, with others, valiantly fought the flames. When the fire was over, ten buildings had been completely consumed, most of them stores. In addition, the D & H Canal coalyard had been destroyed, and two locomotives stored in Rondout and originally brought from England to work in the Honesdale coal mines had been reduced to "a mass of old iron." Even the office of the Rondout *Courier* had caught fire. Although there had been no wind, the loss of property, if not life, had been great; Rondout was a highly inflammable place, with its many wooden structures, ships and lumberyards. In addition, on the night of February 19, all sources of water required to fight the great fire had been frozen. Most significant, however, was the fact that in 1849 Rondout could boast no fire department of its own, being completely dependent on Kingston, miles away, for its defense. This critical situation led the *Courier*, after this fire, to call for the incorporation of Rondout and for the creation of its own fire department, which was accomplished soon after incorporation in 1849, and immediately after the first village elections. Fire Engine Company No. 1 was organized as a result, as was another unit, Hook and Ladder Company No. 1, in 1857.

The next day after the fire, Booth returned to "the ruins," as he called them, and saw "a sad sight." Men and boys, "like birds of prey," were "working among the blackened remains seeking bits of iron nails." There was a great deal of looting, and fights broke out. In the paint stores, paint of many colors lay in heaps on the ground.

Certainly, fires were to remain a problem throughout the history of Rondout. In 1854, the barns of Jacob Derrenbacher and Dr. John Wales were torched, the work of an "incendiary" named Riley, reported the Rondout *Courier* on February 10. Into the first decade of our own century, devastating fires would continue. The Ferry Street fire ocurred in 1890. In the winter of 1904, a fire began in the Ormerod Hotel that took eleven hours to extinguish; the nightwatchman, named Gregory, roused the guests and helped them to escape in their nightclothes. In this fire, the entire stock of Philip Schuster's cigar store, Alonzo Terpenning's confectionery store, Guilford Hasbrouck's shoe store, as well as the stock of a Mrs. Heller were lost. The Kingston *Weekly Leader* on February 20 called this "Big Fire on the Strand" "one of the most disastrous in a long time." And in 1908 the Sampson Brothers Opera House (the site of Mary P's Restaurant today) burned , taking the First National Bank of Rondout, which was situated opposite, with it. The historian De Witt called this fire "very hot and destructive." (78).

Flooding, too, offered a continued threat to Rondout, as it had in Ulster County from the earliest recorded times. Especially in the late winter and early spring, when snow melted and heavy rains fell, but also at times in summer and fall, Rondout and other riverside communities faced the menace of inundation and extensive property loss. In his diary entry for July 15, 1854, Booth mentions how the Esopus Creek at Kingston had risen twenty feet over its banks, destroying the grain crop. This, of course, was an unhappy, yet familiar, occurrence to the farmers of these fertile, alluvial lowlands. In fact, earlier in the same year in which Booth recorded the loss of crops, three days of rain had swelled the Rondout Creek "fearfully," and flooding, greater than any in the memory of the oldest inhabitant, had taken place. Reaching its crest late on a night in May, the scene was "terrific." As the Rondout *Courier* described it on May 5, 1854, canal boats broke from their moorings and floated downstream, "roaring, surging" in the "mad and resistless flood." The "shrill whistles" of steamboats sounded the alarm, and moving "here and there" to get out of danger, these boats attempted to avoid the "crushing of breaking timbers" and the "tossing and heaving" of other boats. Downriver, the steamer *Erickson* had sunk, and in the Rondout Creek the *Santa Claus* had been beached. The damage at Wilbur, Eddyville, and along the D & H Canal was also extensive.

Certainly, 1854 had been a difficult year in regard to the weather. In March, for example, a northwest gale had roared down the Hudson Valley. It demolished the stone house of William Tremper in Ponckhockie, tore the roof and gables off Derrenbacker's brick building, devastated Hudler's lumberyard, and leveled the barn of Theophilus Elsworth in Esopus. The storm possessed such force that it knocked the steeples off many churches in the area, among them the spire on St. Mary's Catholic Church in Rondout. It is said that this turret rocked for two hours before crashing into the graveyard south of the church. Miraculously, the church's roof was not damaged, and the bell, which weighed nearly a ton, was uncracked in its fall. In response to this unusual event, the Rondout *Courier* reported on March 24 that the churches of Kingston looked like "dismasted ships."

One of the next important floods to hit Ulster County—one which was to generate interesting consequences—occurred during the early days of the D & H Canal. It was 1832 and the workers, management, and stockholders of the canal were awaiting, with great expectation, their fifth season. Things looked good for the canal, and hopes ran high. Then catastrophe struck. On the night of March 12, rising water and large blocks of ice roared down the Rondout Creek and blasted a breach in the canal at Eddyville, where Lock No. 1 had been dedicated only a few years earlier. A shiver of fear ran through Rondout. What would happen to Rondout if the canal could not be restored? the citizens wondered. Stockholders, who had delighted in unusually high profits, quickly developed second thoughts, and then panicked as the value of their once-precious stock dropped. Wishing to unload their plummeting stock before it became worthless, these wary investors made the decision which they would soon regret. Dispatching a special messenger to New York, because the Hudson was frozen and river travel had stopped, they sold all their stock below par, believing the canal would never operate again. Ironically, if they had waited, things might have turned out differently, for soon after the completion of this transaction the value of D & H stock began to rise. And then, disappointed and disgruntled, the impatient sellers watched with dismay as the canal was repaired and returned to full operation by May of the same year. Certainly, they could blame the flood of 1832 for their loss. But as many more optimistic Rondouters believed, it was due, in fact, to their own lack of faith.

Clearly, the inhabitants of Rondout regularly faced crowding, squalor, violence and natural disaster, to say nothing of long, hard hours of exhausting and often dangerous work. There was little protection of workers, and sparse compensation if they were injured or could not work. Nonetheless, Rondouters took their chances and hoped for the best.

As if these difficult conditions were not enough, the residents of Rondout constantly confronted the specter of pestilential disease. In 1832—the year of the flood—for example, the first of a series of cholera epidemics struck Rondout. Then, in the summer of 1843, another epidemic occurred. This time it was a mysterious and terrifying disease presenting peculiar symptoms, such as the vomiting of a dark green or black fluid, called "black vomit," and the development of yellow skin and eyes. Significantly, it seemed a schooner named the *Vanda* (there are variant spellings), carrying a cargo of salt and pineapples from the Indies, had docked at Rondout about the time of the outbreak. Without hesitation, it was blamed for the importation of this "tropical" disease. Panic quickly spread up and down the river, even reaching New York City. Here, on August 27, the mayor issued a proclamation prohibiting all intercourse between the city of New York and Rondout until the cause and disposition of the disease could be determined. Subsequently, an inquiry was conducted by New York's Resident Physician, Dr. Alexander F. Vache, who dispatched a committee of investigators to Rondout. In the report, submitted to the Board of Health of New York in October, Dr. Vache established that there had been forty cases of the disease in Rondout and its environs during August and September. Twelve of these cases had died—eleven men and one woman. Five were Irish laborers; three clerks; one each a boatman, a hostler, and a bootmaker, and the woman had been a domestic. It was also determined beyond a doubt that the disease had been indigenous, and was not brought by the *Vanda*, as many had thought. Local physicians, including doctors Manley, Forry, Jewett, Stringham, and Elting, had observed cases of this mystifying disease before the *Vanda* had arrived in port.

More difficult to establish, however, was the correct name of the disease. It was not tropical yellow fever, Dr. Vache was certain. But what was it? After the taking of extensive testimony and the development of detailed case studies, it was finally concluded, but probably not to everyone's satisfaction, that this disease was to be considered "a malignant remittent fever with a strong tendency to assume the typhoid type" (Forry, 347). Whatever its appellation, however, the disease and its causes remained, for the most part, a mystery. As a result, little of conseqence was done to ensure that such fearful and enigmatic diseases would not visit Rondout again.

And so, six years later, to the horror of everyone in Rondout, such a inevitability transpired. In 1849, the year of the great fire and the year in which Rondout was incorporated as a village, its most devastating plague occurred, with "fearful loss of life," as the *Ulster Republican* reported on June 6. So great and widespread were the effects of this cholera pandemic that people fled the area; the canal closed temporarily, and a general business depression resulted.

It all started in December 1848 in New York City, when steerage passengers, exposed to cholera below decks on the trans-Atlantic steamship *New York*, jumped quarantine and came ashore. Within a week the first cases of the dreaded disease began to appear in the crowded immigrant boarding houses of New York, where insects swarmed and filth and stagnant water festered. Americans had expected the disease; news of its appearance in London in October had reached the states. "As early as September, the Philadelphia Board of Health had communicated with the Boston City Council in regard to the impending epidemic," writes medical historian Charles E. Rosenberg (102). However, New Englanders were unresponsive, believing that they were immune to the disease because their area was underlain with granite rather than limestone. Many also felt that because the United States was a "prosperous, pious, and enlightened" nation, unlike India, the ancestral home of cholera, it would be protected (Rosenberg, 103).

In New York, in contrast, there was no such geological or moral certainty. In addition, New York was, without a doubt, one of the dirtiest cities in America. Nothing had been done to alleviate this condition since the previous epidemic of 1832. Therefore, unlike their more complacent neighbors to the north, New Yorkers were profoundly alarmed when they learned that cholera had broken out in their city. Newspapers, many of them printing the latest cholera remedies, were sold out within hours of publication.

Nonetheless, in January the city received a brief respite. With the coming of bitterly cold weather, no new cases developed. This, of course, offered an excellent opportunity for the board of health to make the necessary preparations to combat the disease, such as cleaning houses and streets and disinfecting them with lime. Sadly, although brave attempts were made in this regard, the work of the board was largely ineffective due to the general lethargy and inertia of the citizenry, their unwillingness to be taxed or inconvenienced in any way, even in the face of imminent disaster, and the total lack of any sort of public health legislation in New York State at the time. Poor people hid their pigs from inspectors. Contractors were prevented from cleaning the streets. The city was even unable to find a suitable structure to be used as a cholera hospital; finally, the second floor of a tavern was rented at an exorbitant rate, but only after an angry and fearful mob had been dispersed. Later, the city's public schools were converted into hospitals as the epidemic worsened.

In the spring of 1849 the disease reappeared. James Gilligan, a laborer who with four women lived in a room ten feet square, took ill. Within a few days, he and his roommates were dead. The disease spread as the weather became warmer. As a consequence, many people deserted their houses and headed for the country. Others attended prayer meetings and participated in days of fasting. Stores closed. Great bonfires were lit to purify the air. The city was even unable to bury its own dead; rats swarmed and burrowed into shallow, hastily dug common graves. In church-yards, coffins were buried two and three deep. It is not known exactly how many people died in New York City in this plague. However, board of health reports estimate that by August, when the plague for the most part had run its course, more than five thousand persons had died.

Other cities also were affected. St. Louis, for example, lost one-tenth of its population. There, carts and furniture wagons were used as hearses. Cincinnati lost almost as many citizens. Eager gold-seekers on their way to California carried the disease with them, and the "route westward was marked with wooden crosses. . .often bearing only a name and the word 'cholera', " writes the historian Rosenberg.

Steamboats also played their part in spreading the disease. Along the banks of many great rivers cholera flourished, especially where immigrants congregated. Forty percent of those who had died in New York were Irish; 80 percent of the dead in St. Louis had been Catholic; and better than 80 percent of those who had died in Cincinnati, Buffalo, Brooklyn, Boston, as well as New York, had been immigrants.

With cholera in New York City, it was not long before Rondout became infected. In his diary entry for May 28, approximately two weeks after James Gilligan and his female roommates had died, Nathaniel Booth wrote, "cholera is increasing in New York. . .it is terrible." Even more alarming was the fact that a man had died of cholera aboard a steamboat coming upriver. Soon, cases of cholera began to appear in Saugerties, although Rondout was mercifully untouched, and many concluded, or just hoped, that Rondout would be spared. As a result, the newly formed village government did nothing, and the general populace did not complain. Only the Rondout *Courier* responded to this lackadaisical attitude. In an article entitled "Cholera—Its Cause and Cure," the paper stated:

> The threatened approach of Asiatic cholera is contemplated with the most perfect calmness. . .almost amounting to indifference. . .and we are far from wishing to disturb an equanimity which may do something to avert, and a great deal to mitigate the evil. But, at the same time, it is best to familiarize ourselves with its features, however loathsome, and be prepared to recognize and grapple with it from the first hour it manifests itself.

This article, published on June 15, 1849, was followed by another called "The Charm of Cleanliness."

This was not a new view, of course. The prediction of the plague and the call for preparedness had been made nearly two years earlier, but in a very different fashion. On an autumn day in 1847, a strange man from the backwoods had walked into Nathaniel Booth's store in Wilbur. He was a "genius," states Booth, "decidedly original." This unusual man, Booth soon learned, was a collector of roots, herbs, and other wild plants, and he had come to Booth's store to barter. During the negotiations, the two men talked, and one thing led to another. Eventually, Booth had discerned that this interesting backwoodsman was not only an entrepreneur, he was also a naturalist and a seer of sorts. It seemed this man had been studying a group of plants very closely for a number of years, and his observations had disturbed him. He had noticed that the plants had not been doing very well; they were dying. This fact had prompted the woodland prophet to make a dire prediction. There would be a period of pestilence or famine in the near future, he stated. Once their transaction was completed, the woodsman left Booth's store and was never seen again. But less than two years later, when the cholera epidemic struck Rondout, Booth remembered his earlier meeting with this strange and disturbing man. So memorable had been the event that Booth had not forgotten anything that had been said. From memory, Booth was able to write down every word of the man's prophecy.

Certainly, Rondout was ripe for such an epidemic to occur. In 1843, Dr. Alexander Vache, Resident Physician of the City of New York, had remarked to the New York Board of Health that Rondout was "amply furnished with all the requisites for the engendering and continuing of various forms of fever" (Forry, 297). As in New York City, pigs still foraged in the filthy, crowded streets, and no sanitary source of water could be found.

By mid-June, Rondout's hopes that somehow it would be delivered from the plague were dashed. Folklore has it that the first person to die of cholera in Rondout in 1849 was a Reverend Paddock, who lived in a brick house on Hone Street. However, the Rondout *Courier* reports that on June 13 a Black named Tomas Humans had died first; then on June 18 Henry Kramer, a German; and soon thereafter a child who was Irish. The newspaper remarked in droll fashion that there was democracy in suffering and death. By July 6, the *Courier* stated, sixty cases of cholera had been recorded, and by July 13, eighteen more. In the previous year, there had been an outbreak of smallpox in Wilbur; a man named Haggadorn and a number of children had died. As a result, wrote Nathaniel Booth, "the neighbors are frightened out of their wits." But cholera was different.

So quickly did the plague spread throughout Rondout and so unprepared was the village for the epidemic that the number of local doctors was insufficient to care for the sick. In addition, as had been the case in New York, no hospital existed at the time. In response, the D & H Canal Company dispatched a Dr. Hallet from New York to minister to ill canal workers. He transformed a large, white storehouse on Ferry Street into a hospital. It became the first and only hospital in Ulster County until the Kingston City Hospital was dedicated in 1893. (The Sisters of the Order of St. Benedictine leased and equipped a brick house on West Chestnut Street, and opened it to the public in 1902 as Our Lady of Victory Sanitarium.)

In his diary, Nathaniel Booth chronicles the progress of the epidemic. On June 25, for example, he mentions that four people had died the previous night. Then he notes a man had been found dead, floating in the creek, and a woman had been discovered in a ditch along the road to Kingston, both apparent victims of the disease. "Nine today," he writes, compounding the horror he must have felt.

By July, a general sense of helplessness manifested itself in Rondout. One pessimistic person was heard to say that, if he contracted cholera, he expected his friend to hit him on the head with an axe. People rushed out to purchase dubious and exotic patent medicines. Some misguided souls believed that eating green vegetables, which Germans seemed to enjoy, caused cholera, or that staying drunk would prevent one from contracting the disease. A great swarm of flies, which had been unusually scarce earlier in the summer, hatched. It was even suggested that the old Revolutionary War cannon that had been trundled out to Columbus Point to warn away ships during the 1832 epidemic be pressed into service once again.

In the early nineteenth century, American physicians possessed few diagnostic tools beyond their own senses. In addition, disease was believed to be the result of physiological imbalance (Vogel, 7). Drugs, therefore, were used to adjust the body's internal "equilibrium," rather than to treat a specific disease. As a result, and as might be expected, patients often noted a great deal of diversity in treatment. It was a popular belief at the time that five different doctors would prescribe five different remedies for the same condition. This inconsistency, plus the decidedly unpleasant nature of the pharmaceuticals used—not infrequently unsuccessfully—did little to build trust in the contemporary physician. In fact, by 1849 medicine had advanced only a very short distance from where it had stood in 1832—at the time of the first cholera epidemic—and the public reputation of the physician had fallen (Rosenberg, 151). Patients were drugged, bled and purged in dramatic fashion. Calomel, a strong purgative powder, taken in conjunction with laudanum and cayenne pepper, was applied as a common therapy, not only for fevers, but also for a wide variety of complaints.

During the weeks in which the plague raged, from mid-June to mid-August, a number of courageous and selfless individuals labored ceaselessly to alleviate as best they could the suffering of the sick. Dr. Hallet, who had been sent to Rondout by the canal company, had proved himself worthy of trust, the Rondout *Courier* stated on July 6, even though the "class of cases coming under his hands were very unpromising." Local doctors, also, such as Crispell, Brown, and Elting, acquitted themselves well, answering all calls upon their skill with "unwearied attention." Dr. Crispell even contracted the disease himself.

Prominent among these dedicated physicians was Dr. John Wales. Dr. Wales had been born in Belfast, Ireland, in 1813 and had studied medicine in Ireland and in Scotland at the Royal College of Surgeons. In 1842, after his marriage in England to Maria Davy, he had come to Rondout, where he soon found his services in demand. A generous and charitable man, always cheerful and smiling, displaying "antique courtesy and knightly hospitality," Dr. Wales' work during the cholera plague of 1849, when he was thirty-six years old, was praiseworthy (*Commemorative Biographical Record of Ulster County, New York*, 45). Undoubtedly, without the compassionate and attentive ministrations of Dr. Wales among the poor of Rondout, many more people might have died. A Democrat and a member of St. Mary's Church, Dr. Wales in later years helped to found the Mutual Aid Society of Rondout, an important, early charitable organization. He died in 1870 at the age of fifty-seven.

With the plague finally abating by early August, Rondout attempted to return to a state of business-as-usual. In this regard, steps were taken to restore public confidence. In an article entitled "The Alarmists and the Alarmed," published on July 13, the Rondout *Courier* stated, "The current business of Rondout has been seriously deranged by reports in respect to the health of the place." Those exaggerated reports, complained the *Courier*, an avid Rondout booster, had been generated falsely by a rival Kingston newspaper, the *Ulster Republican*. "There is no danger. . .certainly none in a business visit," proclaimed the *Courier*. On July 27 it added, somewhat prematurely, "the prudent are as safe here as in regions of better popular repute," and the disease has "a feeble hold on the village." This, of course, was hopeful thinking and definitely untrue at the time. However, the number of cases of cholera soon declined, and by August 21 no new cases had developed. Thus, on August 31, the *Courier* could finally declare, "the general health of the village is good. . .the epidemic is over."

Yet, it was not until well into the next decade that civic improvements were made to the village, such as paved streets, sidewalks and culverts, and attention was paid to problems such as waste disposal, unsanitary water supplies, and wandering livestock in the streets. In fact, as late as June 1854, when cholera reappeared in Rondout, the *Courier* could complain that there were still "ditches and pools of filthy, green, stagnant water in the streets." Nonetheless, by late summer of 1849, the canal was operating to near capacity, and people were going back to work. Most definitely, things were looking up; it seemed that the plague was over and there was still lots of money for everyone, if so inclined, to make.

7 : The Hum of Active Business

IN THE EARLY 1820s, before the D & H Canal was built and all the activity just described took place, the uncle of a man who would one day make his mark and significantly shape the development of Ulster County came to Rondout. His name was Thomas W. Cornell. He had sailed up the river, as so many other hopeful entrepreneurs would in the coming decades, to establish himself in business. The Rondout area, it seemed to Cornell, would one day flourish.

In 1822, he opened a general store in New Salem, near Eddyville, across and up the creek from Rondout, buying and selling wood and shipping it to New York. Informed by an uncanny business instinct and blessed by good fortune throughout his long life, Cornell found himself in the right place at the right time. Shortly after the building of the canal in 1828, he purchased property at Eddyville. There he opened another store, situated in an even better location—for his new emporium was located quite favorably not far from tidewater at what had become Lock No. 1 of the D & H Canal. Here, Cornell could cater most efficiently and profitably to the many and various needs of the workers on the canal.

From these modest beginnings, Thomas W. Cornell would build a significant fortune, entering the cement as well as the merchandising and freight businesses. In these first years of growth at Rondout, Cornell would prepare the way for the arrival of his brother Peter (1780-1860), who would purchase a dock on the Rondout near Eddyville, and for the success of his nephew and namesake, Thomas Cornell (1814-1890). A "self-made man," as self-educated persons from ordinary, working class families were often called, Thomas W. Cornell offers a perfect example of the so-called nineteenth century "common man" who, during the presidency of that great "democrat" Andrew Jackson, began to exploit the vast economic possibilities of a free and expanding economy. Through a combination of hard work, persistence and luck, rather than wealth, birth and inherited position, ambitious and ruthless persons amassed huge fortunes and helped to create the economic forces that would irrevocably change, for better and for worse, the course of the nation.

Such was the case of Thomas W.'s nephew, Thomas Cornell, who came to Rondout in 1837, a year of severe financial panic in America. Disregarding the dark portent of widespread unemployment and the failure of over 600 banks across the country (triggered by the loose money policies of the Jackson administration), Thomas Cornell promptly made the best of his opportunities.

Without a second thought, Thomas purchased a sloop and plunged into the lucrative river freight trade. Within two years, his company, Cornell, Bidwell and Company (changed to Cornell and Bidwell in 1840), began representing various Rondout riverboat captains and became the agent for steamships such as the *General Jackson*, the *Victory*, and the former steamboat *Saratoga*. Five years later, Cornell joined his uncle Thomas W. and Asa Eaton in the purchase of the sidewheeler *Telegraph*, which they employed in their expanding freight, towing, and passenger business. The next year, the company, now called Thomas W. Cornell and Company, composed of Thomas and his uncle, purchased the *Norwich* (built in 1836 after designs by Robert Fulton), running it as a night boat carrying passengers between Rondout and New York. In 1850, the canal enlarged to permit the passage of boats which could carry over four times the amount of coal as previously, and the towing business boomed. Cornell and his uncle increased their activities in this area; now, not only was the quantity of coal to be shipped greater, but these larger canal boats could be lashed directly to sidewheelers, therefore eliminating the transfer of coal to barges in Rondout. Thus, the profits of Thomas W. Cornell and Company greatly accelerated. In 1851, with his fortune made and his work complete, Thomas W. withdrew from the business. From that moment on, his nephew assumed complete control, a proprietorship that he would hold through four decades. On May 2, 1856, an admiring editor of the Rondout *Courier* was to write about the dynamic younger Cornell, "may he continue among us for many years, and the smoke of his multiplying boats become so dense as to completely becloud the Rondout and the Hudson."

Only after writing an ironclad will, establishing a trust with trustees to administer his vast fortune, and naming his own successor in the company, did Cornell relinquish his own rule. When he finally died of heart failure complicated by pneumonia in Rondout on March 30, 1890, he left behind an estate of nearly $4 million and an empire which included the Cornell Steamboat Company, the Rhinecliff Ferry, the First National Bank of Rondout, the Rondout Savings Bank, and four railroads, among them the Ulster and Delaware. During his life Cornell also served two terms in Congress. In his tenure of wealth and power, there was little activity in Rondout, or in the Catskill Mountains for that matter, over which Cornell did not preside. Without a doubt, for much of the nineteenth century, Thomas Cornell was the best known and most wealthy and powerful man in Ulster County. So great was his prominence that during his funeral in early spring a rare phenomena occurred: Business temporarily ceased in Rondout.

The year 1837 marked not only the arrival of young Thomas Cornell in Rondout, it also heralded the inauguration of the first president from New York State. Born during the last year of the American Revolution in the sleepy Dutch village of Kinderhook, thirty-six miles up the Hudson from Rondout, Martin Van Buren rose from the humble position of country lawyer, through a series of political offices to become the eighth president of the United States.

Resigning his senatorial seat in 1828, the year the D & H Canal opened, and then winning election to the governorship of New York, Van Buren used his power and prominence as senator and then as governor of the most populous and most wealthy state in the country to insure the election of Andrew Jackson over John Quincy Adams. Eight years later, after serving under Jackson as secretary of state, vice president, confidant and phrasemaker, the "Red Fox," or the "Little Magician," as he was later called, became Jackson's hand-picked successor. In 1836, with Jackson's wholehearted support, Van Buren easily won election over the Virginian military hero, William Henry Harrison. Although Harrison would dash Van Buren's hopes for reelection four years later—defeating Van Buren and then serving as president for only thirty days until dying of pneumonia on April 4, 1841—Van Buren's election in 1836 nonetheless proclaimed the ascendancy of New York State and the Hudson Valley in the country, and reflected the shift of political and economic power from the agricultural South to the industrial and mercantile North.

By the 1830s, New York City had become the financial center of the country. Forty cents out of every dollar paid for southern cotton, for example, went to New York—for freight bills, insurance, commissions, and interest (Miller, *A New History of the United States*, 162). In 1807, Robert Fulton had sailed his *Clermont* up the Hudson River from New York to Albany, making the journey in only thirty-two hours and ushering in the "steamboat era" and a veritable revolution in transportation. Within eighteen years, New York State had completed and opened the Erie Canal. The longest and, arguably, the most successful and important canal of its time, the Erie Canal cut freight rates from $100 to $15 a ton, and travel time between Albany and Buffalo from twenty to eight days. Linking one end of the state with the other, as well as the East with Lake Erie and the western territories, the canal and others like it, such as the D & H, resulted in the creation of vast markets and the dramatic expansion of the commercial possibilities of the state. By 1840, during Van Buren's presidential term, New York handled the bulk of all western trade, thus tying both the West and the South to its commercial institutions. Without a doubt, both in fact as well as name, New York had become the "Empire State."

Rondout, not unlike other burgeoning ports in the state, soon assumed the appearance of an important inland harbor. Lillie Linden, a visitor to Rondout and correspondent to the *Courier*, would, on April 8, 1859, liken Rondout to the port of New York. Vessels from all parts of the Atlantic coast visited Rondout, bringing to the creek, as one historian describes the scene, "the tang of salt water" (Sciaky, 282). The mouth of the creek was continually crowded with ships coming and going. And it was estimated that freight movement on the creek, of which only two miles were navigable, was one-tenth that of the Mississippi River, fifteen hundred times its length.

It was the heyday of a new merchant-capitalist class. Due not only to the improvements in transportation and the development of wider markets but also to the increasing urbanization of America, with its concentration of population and its rising demand for goods, a different breed of middleman flourished. As a result, a new nobility developed, whose position was grounded not in birth but in wealth derived from commerce (Miller, *Jacksonian Aristocracy*, 31-32).

Some of this wealth, however, was not always obtained honestly. Nathaniel Booth, who had opened a grocery and dry goods store in Wilbur, up the creek from Rondout, in 1847, and in 1852 had entered the shipping business, sending bark and bluestone to New York, remarks in his journal on April 28, 1851, that making a living by fair means was almost impossible. There were no standards and no government regulation. Thus, both buyer and seller hoped that, in any transaction, fairness would occur as a result of combined dishonesty. Competition, too, was fierce, and merchants often became bitter enemies, employing dock monopolies and even slander at times in order to prevail. In this regard, Booth writes,

> the poor consumer ignorantly swallows beans and peas for coffee...chalk and marble dust for sugar....The retailer must suffer indeed if he takes for granted the weight in measure he pays....This mode is so well understood by business men that it is looked for as a matter of course....He who can do it best and with least suspicion is...the best business man.

Such widespread acceptance and tolerance of dishonesty in business may have been grounded not only in the assumption that everyone was doing it, but also in the commonly held belief that everyone, if he or she worked diligently, *would* get rich. In *Democracy in America*, for example, Tocqueville had already pointed out that Americans believed profoundly in the concept of unobstructed freedom of enterprise and "equality of opportunity" for all. Certainly, the pursuit of wealth was an activity that engaged the energies of many men and women of all levels of society at the time; and material success, which often engendered social status and respectability, was a goal which profoundly captivated their minds. This pervasive spirit of capitalistic enterprise was enthusiastically presented by the *Courier* on April 9, 1852: "The denizens of our village...have no time or disposition to yield to...melancholy.... What has reflection to do with the accumulation of wealth...? What has intellect...except in helping...to cast compound interest...?" the newspaper asked.

It is not surprising, therefore, that affluent merchant-capitalists whose business practices might be considered questionable today acquired a great measure of respect—even admiration—from their fellow citizens, being judged primarily on their wealth rather than their character. More correctly, one's character then was perceived in terms of one's commercial success, which, in turn, was considered to be one's just reward for industriousness and enterprise. "There is one trait in the character of our business men," the *Courier* boasted on July 9, 1852, "that contrasts very favorably with many other places. All are busy."

Such was the case of another Rondout entrepreneur, George Francis Von Beck. Von Beck, who came to Ulster County in 1834 penniless and with few prospects, was a man who pursued success with a zealousness that was quite impressive. He was "a man of great energy and business ability, who...did much to develop the wealth and great industries of Rondout," writes local historian A. T. Clearwater (*Kingston*, 38). Or as Catskill historian Alf Evers during a public lecture more succinctly stated, Von Beck was "a very able man."

Born on January 13, 1798, in Alsace to French parents who had fled to Germany during the French Revolution, Von Beck learned early the precariousness of life lived in troubled times. During his youth he lost his father, who perished in Russia during Napoleon's retreat from Moscow. As a young adult and popular mayor of the city of Kapsweyer, Von Beck was forced to resign his office and flee for his life: At a public meeting in the old castle of Hambach, the young mayor had spoken out against indirect taxation of the peasants. As a result, his property was confiscated, a warrant was taken out for his arrest, and a price was placed upon his head. Under cover of darkness and wearing a disguise, Von Beck escaped into the mountains, never to see his hometown again. With little money and a small box of engineering instruments, he finally reached the port of Maintz on the Rhine River 120 miles away in the late fall of 1832. He took passage on a series of steamers, and on his thiry-fifth birthday landed in New York. In his pocket he carried only thirteen shillings, but this did not deter the resilient and ambitious immigrant. Without hesitation, the former mayor took whatever manual work he could find, swallowing his pride and biding his time. One day, while walking along Chatham Street, Von Beck chanced to meet a countryman who had known his father. As a favor, this man sold Von Beck $50 worth of goods on credit. These Von Beck packed in a tin trunk. Then, placing his treasured box of engineering tools in pawn, purchased a show-box of panoramic views. With his trunk in hand and his show-box on his back, Von Beck left the city and headed for Long Island, and later Connecticut and upstate New York.

By the spring of 1834, this German peddler and showman had reached the town of Rochester in Ulster County. For the most part, his occupational endeavors had been unsuccessful, and he was destitute. However, as was frequently the case with Von Beck, his luck was good, for he happened to stop at the farm of John Hardenbergh, where he found work. Quickly proving his industriousness to his new employer, Von Beck once again secured a loan, and with these funds purchased a horse and the use of a boat on the D & H Canal. Hauling coal that summer and returning to Hardenbergh's farm to work in the winter, Von Beck made his start.

The following year, Von Beck's situation became even better. Making some suggestions regarding the more accurate estimation of the weight of freight to officers of the D & H Canal Company, Von Beck won the appreciation and confidence of canal founder Maurice Wurts. As a result, he was given a position as a weightmaster on the canal. It is at this time that Von Beck moved to Rondout, where the competent discharge of his responsibilities soon led to further promotions in the company—first as a shipping clerk and then as bookkeeper. By 1851 Von Beck had climbed high up the company ladder, becoming, finally, the paymaster-general.

While working devotedly for the interests of Maurice Wurts and the canal company, however, Von Beck was not inattentive to the pursuit of his own financial affairs. Receiving restitution for the confiscation of his European property in 1839—he had become an American citizen the previous year—Von Beck was quick to put his windfall to good use. Seeing the rapid rate of growth of this thriving commercial community, Von Beck invested his money in all the Rondout property he could afford. In a poem written in 1854 and reprinted in the Kingston *Daily Express* on November 25, 1895, John Horton wrote: "And the Market and the Hotel and Clinton Hall and the Mansion House/ and other things too numerous to/ mention are owned by. . .George F. Von Beck." Even John Hageman, the publisher of the Rondout *Courier*, describing Von Beck and his activities at the time, was moved to write on April 23, 1852: "so bustling in his character, yet so silent in his operations."

Among the many desirable residential and commercial properties which Von Beck accumulated during his lifetime—amounting to about a half million dollars in value—one of the most impressive was the Mansion House. Originally built in 1832 by James Mc Entee soon after the completion of the D & H Canal, the Mansion House was the first hotel in Rondout. It had been constructed from a large, old house originally owned by Major Swart. During the winter of 1847, McEntee had renovated the hotel and increased its capacity by a number of rooms. As the *Courier* described the hostelry on February 4, 1848, the Mansion House "now ranks as one of the best houses in the county. . .situated in the business part of the village near all steamboat landings." In 1853, Von Beck purchased the McEntee property, which he, in his turn, planned to refurbish. Von Beck changed his mind, however, and decided instead to tear the old hotel down. This he did the following year, and with the assistance of a most energetic mechanic, the builder E. T. Van Nostrandt, constructed the four-story, eighty-foot-long building which exists today, somewhat in front of the site of the old hotel, at the corner of Broadway and West Strand (or Division and Lackawanna Streets, as they were called then).

At first, Von Beck considered changing the name of this famous hotel. He would call his new hostelry the Chambers House, evoking the memory of Ulster's first settler. The more he considered the matter, however, the more appropriate the old, time-worn name seemed. Certainly, an establishment of some "100 sleeping compartments," "elegantly furnished" and gaslit, could not be considered a "house." It was a "mansion" in every sense of the word. Wisely, Von Beck retained the familiar name, and it has lasted to this day. During its long life, the Mansion House would change hands many times, see good and bad days, and undergo a number of transformations. After the Civil War, it would be owned and operated by its most popular proprietor, John E. Lasher, who in 1871 would also open the great Overlook Mountain House near Woodstock. Under Lasher's capable ministrations, the Mansion House would become an "admirable house," one which was a "model of neatness" (*Commemorative Biographical Record of Ulster County, New York*, 476). In its present incarnation, the venerable and historic building continues to provide accommodations on a long-term basis. In addition, it houses a distinctive restaurant and an interesting store.

The Mansion House, if admittedly the crown jewel of Von Beck's collection, was only one of his many properties. Even more important to him, it could be argued, were his holdings across the creek in South Rondout. Here, for a time, Von Beck in effect owned the town. In a community in 1852 of some thirty houses, Von Beck was almost everyone's landlord. And owning the major source of employment—a lager beer brewery producing "Von Beck's Lager Beer," possibly the first beer of its kind in the United States—Von Beck found himself in an enviable position. There was even talk in 1853 of finding iron ore on one of Von Beck's farms. Von Beck's acquisitions were so well-situated, and therefore so desirable, that he even had dealings with men such as Thomas Cornell. In 1859, for example, Von Beck sold the Clinton Market to Cornell, which the latter converted into a warehouse for storing freight. According to the historian Stuart Blumin, "No one in Rondout, not even the wealthy Thomas Cornell, could compare with Von Beck in the range and level of his leadership" (171).

Not only was Von Beck a real estate magnate of consequence, he was also a public figure and community leader. Not eschewing the limelight, Von Beck sought recognition, courted publicity, and delighted in pomp and ceremony. He loved military titles and parades, and wore elaborately decorated uniforms while riding a white charger through the streets of Rondout. He was especially fond of decorative swords, and as founder of the local militia company, the Harrison Guards, was presented by the governor with one of six swords given to New York State by the Marquis de La Fayette. Although Von Beck was commissioned in 1852 captain of the militia company which he founded, he preferred to use the title "major." Whether this was in recognition of an actual rank earned in his youth in Europe or conferred later in the United States is unclear. Nonetheless, it was a privilege which Von Beck definitely enjoyed using, and an honorific which he retained throughout his life.

Not satisfied with the creation of the Harrison Guards, Von Beck also founded two more military companies in subsequent years—one artillery, the other rifles. All three of Von Beck's companies ultimately became members of the Twentieth Regiment of New York State. The devoted patriotism of this immigrant and his profound interest in military matters was recognized by most everyone in Rondout, most obviously the *Courier*, which noted on February 17, 1854, the presentation to Von Beck of "a massive and elegant silver goblet," for service rendered to the Harrison Guards.

A truly public-spirited man and community leader, Von Beck was active in the fire departments of Rondout, donating the first engine to the first fire company, founded in 1849. He also served as the first village president, a position to which he was later reelected, and as village trustee and assessor. He was active in Democratic politics and was nominated to run for town supervisor in 1859. Physically a solid and muscular man, and a person who had experienced firsthand the reality of poverty and hard work, Von Beck was sympathetic to the plight of Rondout's working class. As a result, he served as president of the Laborer's Benevolent Society and participated actively in numerous charitable and philanthropic endeavors.

Although primarily concerned with commercial and civic matters and not deeply interested in culture and the arts, as were many German immigrants who played in Rondout's famous Brass Band, or joined German singing societies such as the Rondout Maennerchor Concordia, Von Beck was not without artistic aspirations. Good at math and the speaker of a number of languages, Von Beck was also an orator and essayist of some local reputation. Although political and military subjects predominate among his lectures and essays (collected and published before his death as *The Literary Essays of G. F. Von Beck*), nonetheless, his prose is not without strength, clarity, and interest. Titles such as "Napoleon in the Field" and "The Development of the Laws of Nations," typify his work.

The father of eleven children, five of them born in Europe and later brought to this country, Von Beck married his second wife, Jane Maria Denning of Eddyville, in 1837, although his first marriage in Bavaria in 1820 was not annulled until 1844. Of the six children born to Jane Maria, only one lived into the twentieth century, Mary Josephine Von Beck Gifford of New York City, their first born. Also interesting to note is the fact that Von Beck named his first son, born in 1840, Maurice Wurts Von Beck; it would seem that Von Beck, unlike many others, did not forget an early benefactor.

When George Von Beck died at the Mansion House on December 12, 1870, a few days short of his seventy-third birthday, Rondout mourned openly. At his funeral, a big crowd gathered. Masons, Odd Fellows, firemen, local dignitaries, friends, family, and townspeople attended. No expense was spared in the arrangements. The hearse carrying Von Beck's body was drawn by four jet black horses, each wearing large black-and-white plumes and sable trappings. On the way to the cemetery, this impressive cortege was accompanied by the Rondout Brass Band. Afterward, the Von Beck residence on Abeel Street was filled with mourners. Additional spectators stood silently in the street.

The story of George Von Beck does not end with his death and funeral, however. For, unfortunately, Von Beck, who died a very wealthy man, left two sets of heirs. Not only did little good feeling exist between the two families which Von Beck had fathered, there was actual antagonism. In addition, the will which Von Beck had written exacerbated the situation, and so it was inevitable that it would be contested—which it was, at great cost. Certainly, Von Beck's children were not new to litigation. About the time of the Civil War a few years earlier, when Von Beck had been experiencing a period of illness, his children had taken him to court in an attempt to have him declared incompetent. During the proceedings, which were lengthy, the Kingston *Weekly Leader* reported that "so much feeling was exhibited" a battle seemed imminent. Coats had been pulled off, and a "very rhetorical display" had been made. However, as the jury was unable to make up its mind (thus the petitioners lost their case), Von Beck retained nominal control of his property until his death. Ironically, however, when the children of Von Beck themselves died, there was trouble once again, engendered by a bequest of family heirlooms which had been made to a woman in South Rondout. Such a bequest, it would seem, was unacceptable to Von Beck's grandson Irving, who was to inherit the bulk of the estate. And so in 1896 this will too was contested.

While the foundations of the great Rondout fortunes were being laid and the commerce and industries of Rondout were expanding, the average worker profited little from such progress. Although many would aspire to wealth and prosperity, as had men like Cornell, Von Beck, and others, few would actually achieve it. Many worked out their lives barely making ends meet, finding a wider gap between hope, promise, and the hard reality of everyday life. When the Pennsylvania Coal Company built a depot in its company town of Port Ewen in 1851, and when William and Simon Fitch of Wilbur, who had entered the stone business in 1839 two years after Phillip Lockwood had made the first shipment of bluestone to New York, expanded their business, an increasing number of workers gained employment. But although the Fitch Brothers (its office building is extant in Wilbur) was to become the largest exporter of bluestone in the world in 1850, handling $2,000 worth of stone a day, with between 150 and 200 huge stone wagons trundling out of the hills of Hurley and Sawkill and down Wall Street to its yard on the Rondout Creek, its Irish immigrant workers for the most part earned inadequate and inequitable pay. Such was also the case with the ice industry. In the winter of 1853-54, one small company, the Union Ice Company, cut and stored 1,600 tons of ice; other larger companies, such as the Washington Ice Company and the Knickerbocker Ice Company, cut an even greater amount. Nathaniel Booth wrote in his journal in 1849 that 150 men and horses were engaged in cutting and filling three large ice houses in Rondout. They worked ceaselessly, "plowing long furrows up and down the creek, others sawing through, others conducting the blocks down a canal to the houses into which [the blocks] are hoisted by horsepower." By 1859, the Knickerbocker Ice Company itself would store 80,000 tons in the Rondout area and employ 750 men. These men, however, only received eighty-eight cents for working a long, cold, wet day. Nonetheless, those who worked on the canal or in the brickyards in warmer weather were usually unemployed in winter, and thus eager for any sort of work. And so, as the photographer Richard Lionel De Lisser stated in the late nineteenth century, one could still observe an "army of unemployed" and "needy men," who "anxiously awaited the thickening of the ice" (89).

As early as the seventeenth century, the Dutch had made bricks in small quantities in Kingston. However, with the discovery of large deposits of clay near the mouth of the Rondout Creek in the nineteenth century, brickmaking became big business. Supplementing its regular workforce of Irish and later Italian immigrants with Blacks from the South, the Cordts and Hutton brickyard, at one time the largest of over 100 brickyards spread along the Hudson River from Coeymans to Haverstraw, produced sixteen million bricks per year. In addition to Cordts and Hutton (the ruins can be found on North Street today), many other companies in the area also made brick. Among these are to be found the local names of Brigham, Goldrick, Rose, Shultz, Staples, Terry, and Washburn. Before mechanization, which occurred in most yards in the 1880s, a worker was expected to produce about 1,000 molded bricks a day. In a recent interview, James Polacco, who was born at the turn of the century and with his father and brothers worked for most of his life in a local brickyard, expressed the unspoken sentiments of many of his fellow workers: "I worked like a damn horse," he said, "when there was no union or nothing" (O'Connor, 26).

In both the brick and the cement industries, dust was pervasive and was breathed by the workers without protection except for a wet handkerchief held over the mouth. As a result, respiratory diseases were not uncommon. However, as with other Rondout industries, since cheap immigrant labor was plentiful and competition for jobs great, laborers flocked to the yards and mines to work, accepting the conditions and taking what pay they could get.

Thus, when Abraham Hasbrouck, who had refused to sell his farm to the D & H Canal Company in the 1820s, leased his quarry on the Vlightberg to the Newark Lime and Cement Company in 1843, the prospects for employment in Rondout vastly increased. Purchasing the quarry, its landing on the creek and the entire farm from Hasbrouck's trustees the following year, the company commenced mining operations under what is now Hasbrouck Park. At first the limestone, which runs in a strip some three miles wide by fifteen miles long, was extracted from layers of Niagara and Helderberg formations and then shipped to Newark, New Jersey for processing. The first workings were conducted upon the ledges high up the hillside. Subsequently, tunnels were driven into the hill, and soon it was honeycombed with galleries, some of them up to ninety feet below tidewater (Sylvester, 277). In 1851, as a result of the increased yield, a manufactory was constructed at the mines in Rondout, thus eliminating the necessity of shipping the stone to New Jersey. By 1855, therefore, the Newark Lime and Cement Company at Rondout became one of the leading manufacturers of natural cement in the country.

Capitalized at $85,000, the Newark Lime and Cement Company produced up to 1,200 barrels of cement a day at maximum production in the late nineteenth century, each paper-lined wooden barrel weighing 300 pounds. Limestone mixed with fine coal was burned to drive off all water, and was then turned in a hopper to insure uniformity. From the hopper it passed to the crackers, then to the mills, and from the mills to the packers.

In F.W. Beers' *County Atlas of Ulster New York*, an interesting engraving depicts the "Newark Lime and Cement Manufacturing Co's Works, Rondout" in 1875 (59). There, one sees many sheds and larger buildings, chimneys with black smoke pouring out of them, huge conveyor belts, ships docked at the wharf packed tightly with barrels of cement, the "Cement Office" in the center of the complex, and in the background, situated up against the base of the Vlightberg, a well-proportioned stone barn. To the far right of the engraving, on the edge of Ponckhockie, is the three-story building with large windows on the front ground floor that served as the company store. The barn, some of the plant's stone foundations, as well as the concrete Children's Church in Ponckhockie, built by the cement company, exist today. Situated on 250 acres, with two mills, twenty-three kilns, a giant storage space for 30,000 barrels of cement, as well as a cooperage and numerous shops and barns, the company became a major employer in Rondout, engaging the services of over 200 boys and men.

Going into business, nonetheless, especially for the individual entrepreneur, was extremely precarious. Although fortunes were made in Rondout, many were lost, and thus the names of many of these persons and their families are unknown to us today. Such was the case of Nathaniel Booth, whom we have met already. A close observer of Rondout life in the 1840s and 1850s, as well as an ambitious and talented person, Booth, who had been born in England in 1819, purchased a grocery store in Wilbur at the age of twenty-seven. Taking a second job as a part-time bookkeeper while he operated his own store, Booth saved every penny. Soon he was investing his hard-earned capital in tan bark, limestone and bluestone. By 1852, he could report sales of $12,000 in groceries and $50,000 in bluestone. So successful were his operations that he was able to construct a new store, build two additional docks and purchase the Jockey Hill Quarries, considered the best in the county. He even brought his two brothers into the business. At this time, he commanded the services of two sloops to transport his bark and stone to New York. He also employed over 100 men. In the contemporary ledgers maintained by the Merchantile Agency of New York, the predecessor of Dun and Bradstreet, the Booth brothers are given high marks, being praised for their industriousness and business acumen.

By 1870, Booth could take pride in the fact that he was a wealthy man, "with a solid reputation based on 20 years of unbroken success, prompt payment of debts, and personal reliability and character" (Blumin, 210). However, by 1872 the periodic fluctuations of the bluestone business, with its ruthless competition and its merciless dictation of supply and demand, overwhelmed Booth. He was "hard up," the Merchantile Agency reported. Although he was able to recoup his losses temporarily, by 1876 his time of prosperity had ended; Booth could no longer pay his debts. The following year he declared bankruptcy, and in 1881 he withdrew from business forever.

Nonetheless, although business opportunities for those possessing capital were unpredictable, if potentially immensely profitable, the economic situation of the average worker in Rondout was worse. Though jobs were plentiful, the work was difficult, at times dangerous, and the days were long and the wages small. Without a doubt, the unrestrained enterprise and *laissez-faire* policies of the first half of the nineteenth century had resulted in the development of new economic combinations and the concentration of power and wealth. As a result, although workers remained optimistic about their prospects, a deepening economic inequality and a widening gap between labor and capital became apparent.

In the old order of commercial capitalism prior to the American Revolution, a less exploitative relationship between the employer and employee existed. At least in theory, if not always in practice, the employer, like a parent, was responsible for teaching the employee, or apprentice, a trade, and also for attending to his general well-being. With the introduction of industrialization and the advent of nineteenth century capitalism, the responsibility of employer for employee declined, and eventually was eliminated. Competitive markets influenced employers to fire employees at will and to impose rigid "work discipline." These conditions were aggravated by the massive influx of immigrants who, fleeing the war and poverty of Europe, flocked to America's factories, mines, and mills. The new relationship that developed between employer and employee and the increasing divergence of interests between these two classes inevitably led to distrust, mutual antagonism, and conflict (Thompson, 56-97).

The first of a series of strikes which took place during the 1850s in Rondout occurred, as might be expected, in the mines of the Newark Lime and Cement Company. There, in May 1853, miners struck briefly and unsuccessfully for higher wages. The next month, boatmen working for the D & H Canal Company and for the Pennsylvania Coal Company struck, also unsuccessfully, for a raise in compensation from $1 to $1.10 a ton for transported coal. As early as 1851, handbills had been distributed in Rondout by agents of the rival Morris Canal Company to induce D & H Canal employees to abandon their boats and go to work on this New Jersey canal. In response, promises had been made by the D & H Canal Company, and almost all the workers had stayed. But wages and rates had remained the same.

However, as the demand for merchandise grew, and as the canal was enlarged and its holdings in Rondout expanded to meet this need, with increased tonnage passing through it every year and the company's profits rising correspondingly, dissatisfaction with the procrastination and tightfistedness of the company mushroomed. Although J. P. Hageman, the publisher of the Rondout *Courier*, could write in October 1849 about "capital's duties to labor," and in September 1858 could hope for the time when "the iron sway of capitalists will be broken. . .the moneyed aristocracy. . .a ruined institution" and laborers "well recompensed for their services," Hageman consistently took the side of the canal company during all labor disputes. Preferring to hear in Rondout the "never ceasing hum of active business" and to see "contented and well-paid laborers" filling the streets, Hageman wished to believe that the canal company always acted for everyone's benefit, "scattering funds among all classes," as he was to write on March 12, 1852. This, of course, was not the case.

In the same year in which Maurice Wurts, the creator of the canal, died, matters came to a head. On Tuesday, April 11, 1854, with the first coal shipments of the season coming down the canal, 400 laborers struck. These men, mostly Irish, demanded an increase in wages from seventy-five cents to $1 a day. They also called for a ten-hour day. Before mechanization, these "swarms of workers," some of them Blacks, removed the coal from the barges with big, iron tubs (Wakefield, 193). Although they had heard, undoubtedly, the popular canal song of the day: "Canaler,

Canaler, you'll never get rich/ You'll spend all your money and die in a ditch," they nonetheless believed fervently in the sentiments expressed in 1830 in the *Working Man's Advocate*, which declared: "we expect the reward of our toil, and consider the right to individual property, the strongest incentive to industry" (Sciaky, 283). With this in mind, they concluded that the "reward" for working on the canal was, indeed, inadequate, and the "incentive" weak. And so, they struck.

On April 12, the second day of the strike, a meeting was called, as the *Courier* stated two days later, "to consider, and adopt some measures in regard to the wages of laborers in Rondout." It was to take place in the evening at the Rondout Village Hall. That night, the hall was packed with angry workmen. Outside, a "dense mass" of laborers crowded the street. Feelings ran high, as Mr. Sykes, the new manager of the canal company, rose to speak. Fiery remarks were made by some of the assembled laborers; epithets were used. When the group finally settled down, Sykes repeated the offer he had made the previous Saturday, when the men had been paid: They would receive 87.5 cents a day until April 24; thereafter, the pay would be $1 a day. Sykes, however, did not address the question of a ten-hour workday. He simply sat down amid widespread grumbling from his audience. In response, the workers demanded an immediate raise and a shortened workday. Nothing less was acceptable, they said.

Although the average laborer could not quote the figures, he knew that the D & H Canal Company had done very well the previous year. At the annual meeting of the company on March 28, about two weeks before the strike, the company had reported earnings of $830,972. This was equal to 11.5 percent profit on the capital stock of the company. The company had shipped nearly half a million tons of coal, as had the Pennsylvania Coal Company, with sales amounting to over $2 million.

At the meeting, the next to speak was Rev. Madden, a Roman Catholic priest. He counseled the workers to accept the company's terms and to return to work. What would happen if the strike continued, he asked, how could they live without their pay? Some of the less-determined workers agreed, and Bernard Quinn reiterated Rev. Madden's view. Nonetheless, although most in the audience were Catholic and held their clergy in great respect, the group reached no decision on the company's proposal, and the meeting was adjourned. They resolved to meet again the following night to discuss, in addition to the proposal, the possibility of forming a laborer's "Protective Union."

The next day the strike continued, with workers assembling on the docks, and recalcitrant members threatened or beaten. However, as the company stood firm and there were no strike funds available, the workers' resolve soon began to weaken. Although small, local unions had been formed in America in the 1830s, for the most part they were without experience or financial resources, and in general the courts, as well as public opinion, were hostile to them. As a result, their efforts were usually unsuccessful.

Such was the case of the D & H Canal laborers, who grudgingly returned to work on the 24th, when the company gave notice that all workers not back on the job by then would be fired. This "did the trick," wrote Hageman of the *Courier*. It "had the effect of making all things right." Although Hageman would concede that $1 a day "at the present state of affairs" was "little enough," he nonetheless echoed the opinions of many of his fellow citizens when he added that there was "a right way and a wrong way to amend conditions" between employers and employees. The strike, he declared, had been the wrong way.

And so, the laborers, who lost nearly two weeks' pay, returned to work, and the so-called "Laborers' Protective Union" was never heard of again. In the following season of 1855, while food prices rose substantially, the company decreased wages back to 87.5 cents per day. And even though a brief strike occurred the next year, it was simply ignored by the company. As a result, this feeble protest sputtered and ended, without incident, in a single day. Although an organization called the Hudson River Health Association had been founded in 1852 to provide accident insurance for workers who were members, and the Rondout Laborer's Benevolent Association had been organized by German- born Rondouters in 1859, little was done to substantially improve the lives of laborers in Rondout. It was not until 1869, after the Civil War, that the first important nation-wide labor organization, the Knights of Labor, was formed. The era of the great labor strikes in America was yet to come.

8 : An Increasing Collective Awareness

 ALTHOUGH *Courier* columnist Lillie Linden was to write in 1859 that Rondout was "more a business than a literary place," not all Rondouters were exclusively dedicated to commercial enterprise and the pursuit of money. In fact, by the 1850s, Rondout had developed into a community of "increasing collective awareness," one whose identity was not based on the manner in which one earned one's living alone (Blumin, 165).

Certainly, Rondouters had much to be proud of. For example, one of the liveliest and most popular newspapers in the county, the Rondout *Courier*, had been founded there in 1845 as the Rondout *Freeman*. In addition, Rondout contained a number of good hotels. Among them was the Mansion House, a first-class hostelry which, when the William W. and J. M. Hague and Company constructed a gas works in Rondout in 1854, claimed the honor of being the first such building in Rondout, as well as Kingston, to use gas to light its commodious rooms.

Even more notably, the first telegraph in the Kingston area was installed in 1852 in Winter Brothers' store on the Strand. And when, on a Monday evening in August 1858, this telegraph, which had linked Rondout with England and the world, brought the news that the president of the United States had spoken with the Queen of England, the citizens of Rondout filled the streets, congratulated each other and shook hands. As cannons were discharged from the hill above Rondout, church bells were rung and bonfires ignited; a torchlit parade marched through the streets and ended at the Mansion House, where the Rondout Brass Band performed and speeches were delivered. All the houses in the village were illuminated, their windows bathed in light, and almost everyone participated, experiencing, as the *Courier* stated, a deep feeling of camaraderie and a profound sense of community.

Rondout gained notoriety, too, when Dr. David Kennedy, of "Kennedy Row" on Ferry Street, developed a patent medicine which was known and respected nationwide. Marketed as Dr. David Kennedy's Favorite Remedy and packaged in a bottle that carried Dr. Kennedy's picture on the label, this elixir purported to cure a wide assortment of ailments from kidney trouble to constipation. Dr. Kennedy became so rich and famous selling his medicine that in 1891 he was elected overwhelmingly as the mayor of the town. As Dr. Kennedy might have agreed, the creation of civic and cultural institutions, the addressing of social issues, and the flowering of art, music and literature, as well as the founding of political, fraternal and military organizations, would make Rondout an especially interesting place in which to be.

During the 1850s and '60s, numerous civic and cultural organizations were formed in Rondout. In 1853, for example, the Rondout Library was founded, and five years later a branch of the Y.M.C.A. During these socially active decades, the Rondout Lyceum, dedicated to "vigorous improvement," was begun, to the immense delight of many Rondouters. This organization advertised a very successful series of lectures and debates that were presented regularly on topics of the moment and were attended by enthusiastic crowds. Noted speakers and nationally known figures appeared in this series and in other forums held in Rondout's churches, and in its Clinton and Washington Halls. Among these celebrities and intellectual heavyweights were Mark Twain, the author; Henry Ward Beecher, the most famous clergyman of his day; Wendell Phillips, the abolitionist; Theodore Parker, the radical theologian and social reformer; Horace Greeley, the founder and editor of the influential New York *Tribune*, who said "Go West, young man, go West"; and William Henry Channing, the iconoclastic Unitarian minister, who spoke about the famous social experiment at Brook Farm.

These notables are only a few of the many lecturers and social activists who came to Rondout to share their frequently revolutionary and often disquieting ideas. Truly, in responding to the contemporary, national impetus toward popular education, collective action and reform, Rondout was not to be left behind. In this regard, speakers on spiritualism were sure to draw a large, if not always appreciative, audience in Rondout. For in the nineteenth century, interest in spiritualism, or the "voice from the other side," as it was commonly called, ran high. In a time characterized by a deep fascination with death, lectures such as those given by Miss A.W. Sprague of Vermont, who spoke in a trance state, were certain to generate a strong response. However, as the *Courier* reported the next day, "Spiritualists are not likely to gain any large accession to their numbers, in this quarter."

Adherents of health-food fadism, enthusiasts of Kickapoo Indian health shows, and disciples of John Humphrey Noyes, the founder of the Oneida Community in central New York, also surfaced in Rondout. The Perfectionists, as Noyes' followers called themselves, practiced the simple communism of the early Christian church, as well as complex, or "open" marriage, which the press labeled somewhat sensationally, but inexactly, as "free love." Such "free lovers" (the Rondout *Courier* in 1851 called them "unclean birds") fared poorly in Rondout, and were persecuted by the clergy and held in disdain by the ordinary citizen. George and Mary Cragin, for example, moved to South Rondout and joined a family of Perfectionists headed by Abram Smith. The Cragins, however, soon found Rondout an inhospitable place in which to settle down, and the liaison which developed proved to be a troubled and unsuccessful one. On July 25, 1851, Mar drowned in the Hudson River near Rondout. The sloop in which she had been sailing had capsized in a squall. The captain of the sloop had been Abram Smith. A few days later, Mary's body was recovered from the river and buried south of Rondout in an Episcopal cemetery in a pauper's grave.

Another topic sure to generate heated discussion in Rondout was temperance. One of the most intense reform crusades in the country before the abolition of slavery, the temperance movement and agitation against the excessive consumption of alcohol can be traced back to the colonial period and to the work of Dr. Benjamin Rush. In his *Inquiry into the Effect of Ardent Spirit Upon the Human Mind and Body*, written during the Revolution, Dr. Rush pointed out the negative effects of alcohol upon one's health. The reformers of the next century, however, such as Lyman Beecher and Timothy Shay Arthur, although inspired by Dr. Rush's work, directed their own attention not toward the health of the body but toward the moral and social consequences of drink. As a result of this different approach, Bible and tract societies were founded to address this widespread social problem, and by 1830 more than two thousand "T-Totaling" societies had been formed. In 1836, the American Temperance Union held its first national convention, and in 1840 the Washingtonian Temperance Society was founded, enlisting as members reformed alcoholics. During this time, the popular as well as the church press published copious amounts of anti-drinking propaganda. One of the most famous of these publications was Arthur's *Ten Nights in a Bar-Room and What I Saw There*, which sold extremely well. Temperance became a hot political issue when temperance candidates were run successfully for public office and enacted laws. In 1845, New York State passed a law, for example, which provided for local option. As a result, in 1846, 528 of 856 towns across the state—Rondout not among them—voted in favor of prohibition. Although the New York State Legislature repealed this law in 1847, by 1851 prohibition laws had been enacted in thirteen northern states.

In Rondout, concerned citizens enlisted in the Carson League, in reform clubs called Red Ribbon Clubs, or in either the Ulster County Temperance Society or the Ulster County Total Abstinence Society, which had been founded in 1831 and 1842, respectively. A Women's Christian Temperance Union chapter and the Delavan Temperance Union for Blacks were also established in Rondout, as well as a Law-and-Order League, which did not espouse abstinence, as did these other organizations, but nonetheless advocated the strict enforcement of laws regarding the sale of intoxicating beverages. In Rondout, as elsewhere in America, temperance dramas were produced, alternate, non-alcoholic Fourth of July dinners were held, and temperance lectures delivered.

One such speech was made in Rondout on July 8 at the dedication of the newly built St. Mary's Church. Upon this date, it was advertised, a famous temperance lecturer of the day, Father Matthew, would speak. As a result of this announcement, great excitement developed among Rondout's large Catholic population. In his journal, Nathaniel Booth records that on the steamboat trip from Wilbur to Rondout to attend the ceremony all talk centered on Father Matthew and his greatly anticipated sermon. Most passengers, reports Booth, intended to "take the pledge" of abstinence at the priest's hand. In preparation, remarks Booth somewhat wryly, these penitents had drunk heavily throughout the journey, attempting to build up their courage to take this drastic step. When the group finally reached Rondout, disembarked, and walked up the long, steep hill to the new brick church at the top of Division Street, they were shocked to be informed that Father Matthew would not appear. Exhausted, sweaty, and experiencing the effects of the alcohol they had consumed, these pilgrims were dumbfounded when they learned that they would still have to pay a dollar admission fee to enter the church. Believing themselves to have been duped, many of the faithful refused to pay, and, as Booth records, "much dissatisfaction was expressed."

Sadly, in a era when alcoholism was ubiquitous and flourished largely unchecked, temperance crusades were for the most part unsuccessful in Rondout. Due no doubt to the conditions under which so many of its inhabitants lived and worked, "demon rum" continued to play a significant role in the life of the community, no matter how active the "T-Totalers" were. And It was not long before new issues competed for the public's attention, inexorably turning its busy mind to other concerns.

Even more controversial than temperance was suffrage and the rights of women. In this regard, 1848 is important, for it was during this year that the state legislature passed a law that protected the property of a married woman and made it impossible for her husband to use it to pay his debts. Even more significant was the Seneca Falls Convention, which met on July 19 and 20 at the Wesleyan Methodist Chapel in Seneca Falls. Under the leadership of Lucretia Mott and Elizabeth Cady Stanton, this momentous gathering ushered in the modern feminist movement, adopting a number of important women's rights resolutions, among them the right of women to vote.

In belated response to this national convention, some five years afterward the first speaker of the season for the Rondout Lyceum series was the Reverend Miss Antoinette L. Brown. Rev. Brown, who was twenty-five years old at the time, spoke at the invitation of the library executive committee on the subject of "the mission and position of women." Expecting something outlandish, "unwomanly, and startling," wrote John Hageman, the editor and publisher of the Rondout *Courier*, who covered the story himself, the large and expectant audience was surprised when they heard Rev. Brown's presentation. For as Hageman describes Rev. Brown, she was refined and cultivated, "true-hearted and right minded," a woman of marked talent, acting from a high sense of duty. Nonetheless, reports Hageman disappointedly, people generally listened with the "skepticism of rusty conservatism." Men, said the editor, feared that women's rights would militate against their "creature comforts and pre-eminence." Two days later, on a cold Sunday morning in December, Rev. Brown spoke again in Rondout, this time preaching at the Methodist Episcopal Church. In her sermon, she advocated the radical equality of all humanity and women's right to vote.

Although women in Rondout were often idealized, or even objectified in the press (as in the poem "Rondout in the Fifties," in which John Horton asserts, "Rondout ladies look so sweet/They're almost good enough to eat"), it was the commonly held public perception that women functioned most appropriately and productively in the home. Few women at this time in Rondout—except some widows, who were forced to work, and others, who plied socially acceptable trades, such as Miss E. Lefever and Mrs. E.A. Hardenburgh, who were milliners—owned their own businesses, or were valued for what the *Courier* in 1856 called their "head work." It was not until the twentieth century that this deplorable state of affairs was to change, and according to Barbara Welter, a woman would no longer find herself "hostage in the home" (225).

In the Rondout village directory of 1871 to 1872, for example, which lists nearly 500 professional names and addresses, only twenty names can be attributed without question to women. Of these women professionals, most were dressmakers, grocers, or keepers of saloons. In the Kingston city business directory for 1885, which included Rondout, of nearly 800 listings, only twenty-five cite the names of women and their businesses. Even in 1892, when George F. Bacon published his *Kingston & Rondout: Their Representative Business Men and Points of Interest*, women were not afforded the equal recognition they deserved. In this directory, Bacon lists only the following businesswomen: Miss E.S. Wall, "dealer in and manufacturer of Fashionable Millinery" and Miss M.A. Keefe, who owned a "Millinery Parlor"; Mrs. Charles Stephan and Mrs. M. Symonds, who both operated confectionery shops; and Mrs. G. Frohlick and a Madame Rogow, who ran hairdressing salons. Of these six businesswomen, only Madame Rogow maintained a place of business in Rondout, the others operating in Kingston. However, in *The Freeman's Directory of the City of Kingston* for 1900, listing over 1,000 individuals and their services, women are finally abundantly represented. Not only do they dominate the trades of milliner, dressmaker and beauty parlor operator, as might be expected, women now pervade new categories such as boarding-house keeper, organist and nurse. Significantly, women began to enter the professions; by 1890, the first female physician had hung out her shingle in Rondout. Her name was Miss Sarah Mc Entee.

This is not to suggest, however, that women did not work outside the home or that they did not run businesses during the nineteenth century in greater numbers than these publications would indicate. To the contrary, the contribution of women to the professional, as well as the cultural life of Rondout, although inadequately and unfairly reported, was undoubtedly significant.

In this regard, the example of Julia Mc Entee Dillon is instructive. Although primarily known as an accomplished artist and painter of vivid still lifes of flowers, Mrs. Dillon's significance in this context rests in the fact that in 1873, upon the untimely death of her husband John, she temporarily put down her brush and palette and took up his work, successfully managing the family business, the iron foundry and machine works of Langworthy & Dillon, remaining a partner until 1895. Childless and a widow, in the years following this endeavor Mrs. Dillon was to resume her artistic career. With the support and encouragement of her cousin, the noted Hudson River School landscape painter Jervis Mc Entee, whose Rondout studio she used briefly, Mrs. Dillon studied in Europe, exhibited at the National Academy of Design, and at the Columbian Exposition in Chicago in 1893 won a prize for her *Peonies*. A productive and popular painter, Mrs. Dillon's work sold well, and thus she was able to support herself, in part, through her art as well as through her teaching.

In her sixtieth year, Mrs. Dillon closed her studio in New York City, ceased her travels, and returned to Kingston to stay, settling finally at 109 Pearl Street, where she is first listed in the Kingston directory of 1899 as "Mrs. Julia Dillon, artist." In her later years, Mrs. Dillon tended her flower garden, and authored a pamphlet entitled the *Old Gardens of Kingston*. She also helped to found the Kingston City Library and the Kingston City Hospital, even designing the nurse trainees' uniforms and graduation pins.

Born in Rondout in 1834 and spending her youth in the family home on West Chestnut Street there, Julia Mc Entee was the oldest of ten children born to Christina

Tremper and Charles Mc Entee. A self-supporting artist, professional woman and public-spirited citizen of note, one whose contribution to the life of the area is substantial, Mrs. Dillon died in Kingston in January 1919. According to Betsy Calhoun, who wrote a brief biographical sketch of Mrs. Dillon, "Those who knew her remembered her as a generous, cultured and charming woman."

Catherine A. Murdock is also of interest. Although it is unknown whether Mrs. Murdock "found women's traditionally passive role intolerable" and "wished to assert female worth and values in a heretofore entirely male world," as Carroll Smith-Rosenberg suggests was frequently the case in American society before the Civil War, it can be said that Mrs. Murdock rose handily to the challenge of professional life after her husband drowned in the Rondout Creek in 1857 (Smith-Rosenberg, 584). As a result of this tragedy, she took her husband's place as the Rondout lighthouse keeper and held this responsible post for the next fifty years (1857-1907). During Mrs. Murdock's tenure at the lighthouse (first constructed in 1837 by James Mc Entee and rebuilt in 1880; the present lighthouse was built in 1913 on a different site on the other side of the entrance to the harbor), many things happened which would test her ability and courage but afford her the opportunity to prove herself in a manner primarily reserved for men. Maintaining the light through all seasons and in every kind of weather, Mrs. Murdock was to see the river at its best and its worst. For example, in the time of the great flood of December 1878, when the Eddyville dam broke and the creek rose dangerously, Mrs. Murdock watched steamboats beach themselves on the tidal flats and ram the entrance channel dike near the light. On another occasion, during a raging storm in a dark night, she was awakened by the sound of a ferocious crash. Lighting a lamp and descending the narrow stairs from her bedroom, she was astonished to find the prow of a ship projecting through a downstairs window. None of these experiences, however, seems to have fazed the redoubtable Mrs. Murdock, and she performed her duties with skill and success. When she retired after one-half century of service to maritime Rondout, many citizens must have thought that no lighthouse keeper like her could ever be found again.

One area, however, in which women *were* exhorted to assert themselves was religion. For, as Barbara Welter suggests in her essay "The Cult of True Womanhood, 1820-1860," religious participation was encouraged because it did not take a woman away from her home or make her less domestic (226). Within a few years after the completion of the D & H Canal, places of worship began to sprout up all over Rondout, no doubt due to the efforts of many dedicated women.

The first church to be erected in Rondout was the First Presbyterian Church, completed on Abeel Street in 1834 and enlarged about 1861. This building was subsequently sold and a new and larger edifice built on the corner of Wurts and Abeel Streets. A prominent and founding member of this congregation was canal-builder Maurice Wurts. Prior to 1834, Protestants who wished to worship together either walked to churches in Kingston or attended small services held in private homes or boarding houses in Rondout.

In 1835, subscriptions were taken toward the building of a Catholic church in Rondout. By 1838, land had been purchased from Abraham Hasbrouck and a wooden structure built; two of the more prominent contributors to this project were Mary Giddy and Ann O'Reilly. Within a few years, however, this church became inadequate to hold the increasing number of Irish, who came to work on the D & H Canal. So in 1849 the present, more commodious building, which still stands near the top of the Broadway hill (Division Street then), was consecrated. It is said that until their own local churches were built, Irish canal workers from Rosendale, and quarrymen and their families from Jockey Hill and Stony Hollow near West Hurley, often walked the many miles to St. Mary's in Rondout to attend Sunday mass.

German and Polish Catholics also built churches in Rondout. Numbering about half the Irish Catholic population in Rondout, German Catholics, inspired by the example of St. Mary's and aided by that congregation, purchased a lot at the corner of Adams and Pierpont Streets in 1860, where they constructed a brick church. Then, in 1871, desiring to establish a school in the first church building, another structure, the largest church in Rondout for a time, was built of North River brick on the corner of Wurts and Pierpont Streets, to be called St. Peter's German Catholic Church. A much smaller community of Poles, numbering a few hundred at the time, constructed the Church of the Immaculate Conception on Delaware Avenue at the turn of the century.

Sometime after the abandonment of the Jewish colony of Sholam in the town of Wawarsing in 1842, visiting rabbis established, over a period of years, four Jewish congregations in Rondout: the Emanuel Congregation, incorporated 1853-54 by Rabbi Isaacs; Congregation Aushe Chesed; Congregation Agudas Achim; and the Congregation Ahavath Israel. Since the earliest days of settlement, Jews had played an important role in the life of Ulster County. As early as 1684, for example, a Jewish attorney named Assur Levy had practiced law in Kingston. And, throughout the colonial period, Jews had established themselves in business, some even peddling their wares by foot and horseback. By the mid-nineteenth century, Jews had taken their place along side the Irish, German and other immigrant groups in Rondout. Like Israel Sampson, who operated a clothing store and whose sons in 1875 would run the most sophisticated and up-to-date emporium in Rondout (they used monkeys to entertain children while their parents shopped, and built the famous Sampson Opera House, later the home of the *Freeman* and today the site of Mary P's Restaurant), Jewish citizens purveyed comestibles and spirits, and provided all manner of useful objects and necessary services.

Making a modest beginning in the 1880s as a butcher on Abeel Street, by 1890 Jacob Forst, descendant of horse-trader Henry Forst who came to Rondout in 1847, had become the manager and local agent for Armour's Chicago Dressed Beef. By the turn of the century, Jacob had built a local business of some size and significance, as had the Kaplan Brothers, who sold furniture, and Morris Yallum, Aaron Kaatz, and Barney Millens, who bought and recycled used items.

Anti-semitism, however, was prevalent in Rondout, as it was throughout the country, and Jews often experienced extreme hostility and prejudice (as did other non-native peoples, including the Italians and Blacks, who would come to Rondout in great numbers in later years). Although Jews and other immigrant populations would later make their way in significant numbers into the professions, as well as into the arts and civic life, at this time few non-natives seem to have enjoyed membership in this elite coterie because of strong discrimination. Of the fifty-seven professionals listed in *Boyd's Kingston & Rondout Directory 1857-8* who practiced the professions of pharmacy, dentistry, engineering, law, medicine, and veterinary medicine, thirty-one of these can be accounted for by local surnames, primarily Dutch, Huguenot, or English, reaching back to colonial days. Only four of the twenty-six remaining professionals possessed unquestionably non-native names.

In addition to the earlier Presbyterians, other Protestant denominations, such as the Baptists, Congregationalists, Episcopalians, Lutherans, Methodists, and Reformed Dutch, built and maintained places of worship in Rondout, many of these edifices being built on or near Wurts Street, which clearly might have been called the holiest street in Rondout, or the "Avenue of Churches." Most of this ecclesiastical architecture was created between 1840 and 1870, a number of years after these congregations first had been established in more modest structures, often in other locations. Such was the case of the Baptist congregation, whose first house of worship was constructed in 1843 on Post Street between Abeel and Union Streets on land donated by John Wurts, the president of the D & H Canal. However, in 1859, when Thomas Cornell, who had become a deacon of the congregation, donated a building lot on the corner of Wurts and Spring Streets near his own home, a new and more impressive structure, called the First Baptist Church, was built and completed in 1861. Nearby stood the Episcopal Church of the Holy Spirit, constructed on the corner of West Pierpont and Wurts Streets, and later purchased by Congregation Ahavath Israel; it was later sold by the congregation, becoming in turn St. Marks AME (African Methodist Episcopal) Church. About a block from Wurts Street and the First Baptist Church, the Trinity Evangelical Lutheran Church, called the German Lutheran Church, was completed in 1874 on the corner of Spring and Hone Streets; George Von Beck was a prominent parishioner there. In addition, dissatisfied members of the Trinity Church founded another congregation on Livingston Street about this time, and constructed their own church soon thereafter. Farther down Wurts Street, and two blocks up from the Presbyterian Church on Abeel Street, the Trinity Methodist Episcopal Church, now called the Trinity United Methodist Church, was constructed in 1867 on the corner of Wurts and Hunter Streets. Across town, on Hasbrouck Avenue, the Reformed Dutch Church of the Comforter was built in 1864 on territory occupied primarily by natives or locals. And in 1870, in Ponckhockie, on Abruyn Street, a Congregational church called the Union Chapel (or the Children's Church, because of its non-sectarian Sunday school) was erected by the Newark Lime & Cement Company for its employees. It was constructed entirely of cement mined locally, and originally boasted a spire 150 feet tall.

Although the practice of religion flourished in Rondout for many years, by the middle of the present century economic and social conditions had altered, and earlier populations had moved to other parts of the county. As a result, the original congregations either declined in numbers—some from the hundreds to less than a few—or the composition of their membership changed. Some congregations combined temporarily or merged with others; some sold their places of worship and either moved up the hill to Kingston to begin again or dissolved their congregations altogether. A few of the original structures were later abandoned and demolished. In addition, new churches came to Rondout, filling the void: In 1912, the Redeemer Lutheran Church was built on the corner of Wurts and Rogers Streets, the last such structure to be constructed on this boulevard; the New Central Missionary Baptist Church and the Riverview Baptist Church were established in the East Strand; the Seventh Day Adventist Church was situated on West Union, the street where the

Agudas Achim congregation had been; and in the old Temple Emanuel synagogue on Abeel Street, the Green Chapel House of Prayer is now maintained.

Related to the founding of religious congregations in Rondout was the establishment of schools. The first school in Rondout, which was soon replaced by another, was built not long after the completion of the D & H Canal on a ledge of rocks above the creek, near what was to become the intersection of Wurts and Abeel Streets. Previous to this time, in about 1812, New York State had been divided into school districts—Rondout in its infancy becoming District No. 7. With the rapid growth of population in Rondout after the construction of the canal, however, it became apparent that one school district and one school building were no longer sufficient to serve the needs of the many children who were being born. So in 1850 another district was formed—and this is when the trouble, which lasted for many years and was known as the School Wars, began.

Created out of District No. 7, District No. 3 became the setting for a series of bitter struggles that began during the first months after its creation. In this conflict, two factions fought for control. In particular, the location of the new school building became a major point of contention, for each group proposed its own site. One faction, which lived in the hollow between Hasbrouck Avenue and Division Street, wished the school to be built nearby for the sake of convenience, even though this area was a bit congested. The other faction claimed that the most desirable location existed on the apex of the hill above the village. Here, they claimed, it would not only be more healthful and spacious, but the view would be sublime. Other sites, such as the Seminary Lot and the Old Burial Ground, were also suggested. The community was clearly divided when John Hageman of the Rondout *Courier* entered the fray. Reporting in 1851 on the "discursive sort" of discussions that had been held on this issue, Hageman sided with the faction which had proposed the elevated site, although he added that the burial ground seemed acceptable to him, as well, for it possessed a fine grove of evergreen trees that would provide shade in hot weather. No site, he admitted, was utterly free from objections. Whatever choice was made, he wrote, someone would be dissatisfied. However, "for the sake of the public good," he averred, everyone must suffer some inconvenience.

Such public-spirited sentiments do not seem to have moved the two disputatious groups, however, and when the votes were counted it appeared that people had voted according to their own self-interest. As a result, the faction with the greatest number of members carried the day. Disappointed, Hageman wrote that through acclamation and the influence of the "orations" of Larry Clunen and others, a small frame building would be erected in what he called "the filth" of the hollow. Nonetheless, such a decision on the part of the citizens of Rondout, although democratically reached, *does* seem in hindsight to have been poorly considered. For the school was soon overcrowded and, as Hageman writes, "health and comfort and cleanliness were haphazard," an "experiment on human endurance." Added to these shortcomings was the undoubted fact that the dissension continued, and the district remained divided. Consequently, after a few years the school was closed, not to open again until the state became involved and the district was reorganized.

In 1868, a larger, more satisfactory brick building was erected. Yet, by the 1870s it too proved to be inadequate to the task of housing Rondout's burgeoning population of scholars. By 1875, it was apparent that something would have to be done to address this continuing problem. To accomplish this goal, an arrangement was made with St. Mary's Church, which maintained its own parochial school. Renting a St. Mary building known as the Franciscan Brothers' School and employing its resident clerical faculty, District No. 3 opened what was thought to be a temporary school. This interesting relationship between church and state appears to have continued for nearly two decades, however. Finally, in 1895, when the passage of legislation enabled the community to fund the construction of a new school building, and when strong, if belated public outcry over the sectarian influence in the school developed, the association between the church and District No. 3 was terminated. In effect, with a sort of unity achieved, Rondout's protracted School Wars were formally ended.

Not only did competition between factions in Rondout, as well as its population increase, promote the growth of education, so too did the long-standing rivalry between Rondout and Kingston. Since before the American Revolution, students from Ulster County's elite and affluent Dutch and French Huguenot families had availed themselves of the privilege of attending the prestigious Kingston Academy. Begun on the southwest corner of Crown and John Streets in 1774, closed by the British invasion of Kingston in 1777, reopened and later moved to Academy Park, between Clinton Avenue, Division Street, and Maiden Lane, Kingston Academy served for many years as the crown jewel of Ulster County education. During its 141 years of existence, Kingston Academy prepared many young people for college and for entrance into a world of position, accomplishment and affairs. Among the long list of noted students who attended the academy were the painter John Vanderlyn; De Witt Clinton, who would become the governor of New York; Clinton's cousin, Kathy, who would marry Major-General Pierre Van Cortlandt; several Livingston, Schuyler, and Van Rensselaer children; and Nicholas Roosevelt and David Colden. As Marius Schoonmaker, Kingston politician, attorney and historian, himself an alumnus of the academy, was to state, Kingston Academy was indeed an aristocratic and "high toned" institution.

In contrast, Rondout could boast no comparable educational heritage. In fact, it possessed no secondary or preparatory school of any type. So, by the second half of the nineteenth century, it became clear that Rondout needed its own high school, one that would not only fulfill the educational needs of this developing, primarily non-native community, but also one that could compete in excellence with the older and revered Kingston Academy. As a result of these aspirations, in 1870, near the far end of West Chestnut Street, overlooking the harbor of Rondout, Ulster Academy was established. Offering three courses of study, the classical, modern language, and English, Rondout students were prepared "to enter upon an intelligent discharge of the duties of citizenship," and were "taught to appreciate good literature," according to William Bunten, who was the principal of the academy at the turn of the century. Quickly outdistancing Kingston Academy in size, Ulster Academy graduated its first class in 1881, and by the 1890s was serving between 800 and 900 pupils. Well-respected academically and the largest school in the county, Ulster Academy could boast proudly of its impressive view, its many airy classrooms, its science laboratory, and its nearly 1,500-volume library. When it and its competitor Kingston Academy were closed in 1915 due to the opening of the new Kingston High School, situated on Broadway halfway between uptown Kingston and Rondout, Ulster Academy became an elementary school, while Kingston Academy was torn down, the property upon which it stood becoming a city park in 1918. Today, few people remember the academies or the rivalry that existed between them.

Nonetheless, the newcomers who came to Rondout and established Ulster Academy there can take limited satisfaction in the fact that it, or at least the building that housed it for forty-five years, still stands. Unlike the more venerable and august edifice of Kingston Academy, long absent from Academy Green, this three-story brick building, enlarged in 1886, continued to function during the twentieth century as a public school, and had the distinction of serving briefly in the 1960s as the first campus of the new Ulster County Community College. Even now, in a quiet way, this nearly forgotten historic structure continues to be employed in the interest of education—it serves, quite effectively, as a warehouse of the local Kingston city school system.

AN ALBUM OF

OLD RONDOUT

D & H Canal Company office and barge.
John F. Matthews Collection

George Clinton, general and statesman.

Maurice Wurts, canal entrepreneur.

John Vanderlyn, painter.

James S. Mc Entee, engineer.

Abraham Hasbrouck, farmer.

George Von Beck, entrepreneur.

Thomas Cornell, shipping magnate.

Dr. John Wales, physician.

James Lindsley, cement plant manager.

Mary Cragin, Perfectionist.

Division Street, 1850s and 1860s.
John F. Mathews Collection

Jervis Mc Entee Studio on West Chestnut Street.

Coal barges at the strand.
Courtesy Hope Farm Press

Henry Abbey, poet.

Julia Dillon, painter.

Col. Theodore B. Gates, 20th N.Y.S.M.
Seward Osborne Collection

Capt. Joseph Corbin, 20th N.Y.S.M.
Seward Osborne Collection

Anthony Coons Hotel, 28 Union Avenue, 1880s.
John F. Matthews Collection

Fitch Bros. office and stoneyard.
Robert Slater Collection

Looking down Rondout Creek from Sleightsburgh, 1880s.
Robert Slater Collection

Overleaf: East Strand, 1880s. John F. Matthews Collection

Left:
Bluestone cutters
at Wilbur, 1890s.
Courtesy
Hope Farm Press

Below:
The Strand at the
corner of Union
Avenue and Ferry
Street, 1890s.
John F. Matthews
Collection

Stock & Cordts Building, 82-86 Broadway, late 1890s.
Courtesy Hope Farm Press

Absalom Anderson, steamboat captain.   Jacob Tremper, steamboat captain.

Mary Powell in winter ice.
John F. Matthews Collection

Musicians aboard the *Mary Powell.*

The *Jacob Tremper* docks at Rondout.

Dayliner *Hendrick Hudson*, 1st Pilot Harry Kellermann at the helm, 1930s.
John F. Matthews Collection

Kingston Point, 1920s.
John F. Matthews Collection

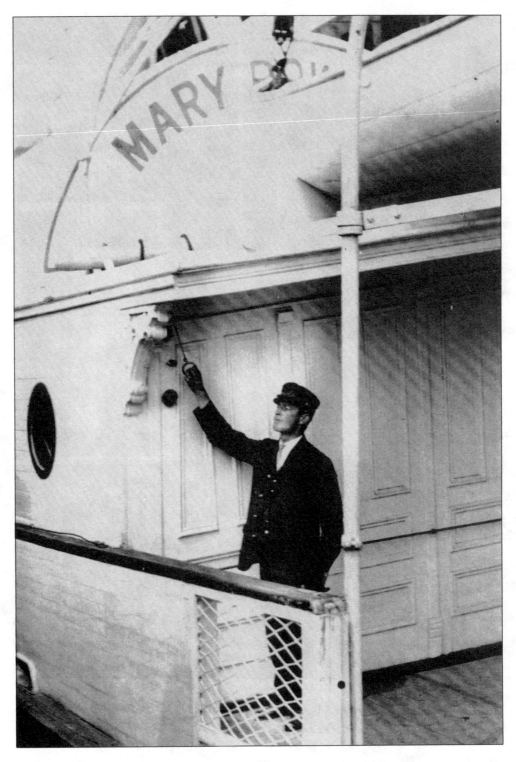

Capt. Arthur Warrington on the *Mary Powell*.
John F. Matthews Collection

Top: Looking down from the Vlightberg on the U & D rail yard and Sleightsburgh.
Above: The U & D rail yard in the 1920s.
Inset: Railroad magnate Samuel D. Coykendall
Facing page: U & D railroad employees.

John F. Matthews Collection

Left:
Mansion House,
early 1900s.
John F. Matthews
Collection

Below:
Main desk at the
Mansion House,
1890s.
John F. Matthews
Collection

Isaac Weiner, bookkeeper.

Dr. David Kennedy, patent medicine king.

D & H clerical force, 1880s. Henry B. Snyder (top left), Louis Hoysradt (bottom right).

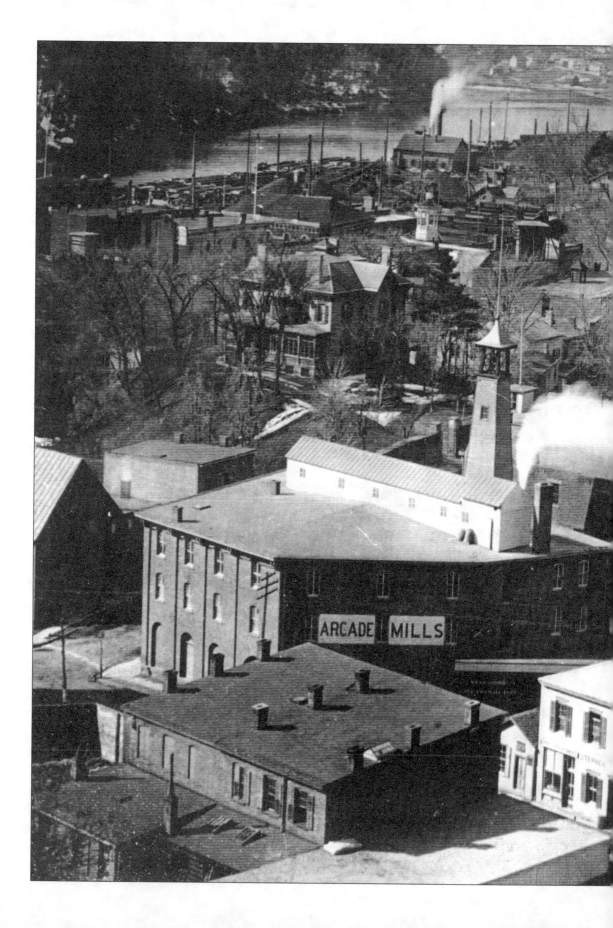

Ponckhockie and Kingston Point, early 1900s.
John F. Matthews Collection

The last trip of the *Riverside,* affectionately known as the *Skillypot,* early 1920s.
John F. Matthews Collection

Overleaf: Rondout looking south, 1880s. John F. Matthews Collection
Facing page: Cornell tug *A. E. Levy.* John F. Matthews Collection

Left:
Alton B. Parker, presidential candidate.

Below:
Looking up Broadway near Abeel Street, 1920s. John F. Matthews Collection

Above:
Rondout prior to urban renewal, early
1960s. Dan Shuster Collection

Right:
Half Moon, replica, 1993.
Monica Freer Collection

9 : The Veneration of Beauty

IN ADDITION TO THE CREATION of civic and cultural institutions, the addressing of social issues, and the establishment of churches and schools, the flowering of the arts in Rondout and the artistic contributions of Rondouters, often nationally recognized, also helped to engender in its citizens an increased sense of public pride and community. The Mickey Finn stories, for example, first published in the New York *Sun* and *Harper's Magazine* during the second half of the nineteenth century, were set in one of Rondout's ethnic neighborhoods, situated near a pond, a flour mill, and a stone quarry (possibly near Hasbrouck Avenue). Written by Rondout-born writer Ernest Jarrold and depicting the adventures of a lovable and mischievous young boy, these widely circulated sketches of local pranks and highjinks helped to give Rondouters a sense of identity and place. It was not difficult to empathize, or even to identify with Mickey and his gleeful spiritedness, a sensibility believed by most to reflect accurately Rondout and its inhabitants at this time.

The poet Henry Abbey, who was born in Rondout in 1842 and published his first book of poems, called *May Dreams*, at the age of 20, might be considered the first professional poet from Ulster County. In poems such as "The River-Side," "By Hudson's Tide," and "On the Rondout," collected in *The Poems of Henry Abbey*, Abbey describes Rondout and its environs. Although his poems seem to us today dreamy and sentimental, typically Romantic and not to our contemporary taste, they represent nonetheless the first attempt by a practicing poet to respond to the local landscape. Even though his work appears inconsistent in tone and sensibility with the pragmatism and materialism of the Rondout in which Abbey lived and worked as an editor, merchant, and banker, these poems undoubtedly were important to his fellow citizens who, it would appear, read and enjoyed them immensely. In the countless letters of appreciation which this genteel poet received throughout his career of approximately fifty years, the praise and gratitude of local readers is volubly expressed. The poet's openly professed love for the Hudson River, where, as he writes in "By Hudson's Tide," he spent many "careless hours," endeared Abbey to his admiring public. Although his critics were less than appreciative of his work—among them the poet Walt Whitman, and Abbey's acquaintance John Burroughs, who wrote that *May Dreams* "contains no performance but only promise" (*Life and Letters*, I: 70)—his poems, such as "May in Kingston" and "On the Rondout," where he describes the hills along the creek, which "loom" high "on either side," are read with pleasure by some in Kingston still today.

A somewhat retiring figure, strangely reminiscent in demeanor and lifestyle of the modern American poet and insurance executive Wallace Stevens, Abbey captured in his popular and widely published verse something of the longings and idealistic aspirations of persons like himself, who found themselves caught up in the rough-and-tumble life of making a living. Although most of Abbey's poetry is unconcerned with Rondout, being set in exotic and imagined locales, the example of dedicated artistry which he set until his last days continues to inspire us. A recognized and successful poet, Abbey published more than ten books of poetry, among them his collected poems, *The Poems of Henry Abbey*, which he edited and expanded three times, the last edition being published in 1904, seven years before his death. In poor health after 1900, Rondout and Kingston's first poet was forced to spend his last moments away from his beloved home. Sadly, he died in Tenafly, New Jersey, in a sanatorium. His final book, appropriately called *Dream of Love*, was published in 1910. A portrait of Abbey, painted by a nephew of John Vanderlyn, hangs in the Kingston Area Library.

Artists, too, directed the attention of Rondouters to the local scene, deepening their sense of place. In their landscapes—like the work of John Vanderlyn and Julia Dillon discussed previously—these talented artists portrayed Rondout and its environs with a vividness and clarity hitherto unseen. In an era before the widespread use of photography, they shaped and defined the public vision of what Kingston and Rondout had been like before the profound changes that were occurring in their own time. Painters such as Joseph Tubby, who was primarily self-taught and who worked much of his life as a house and sign painter, as well as his friend, the better-connected and -trained, and ultimately more successful Hudson River landscape painter Jervis Mc Entee, depicted in their canvases the beauty and tranquility of early Rondout, the Hudson River, and the Rondout Creek.

In his oil paintings, some oval, some painted on cardboard, Joseph Tubby, possibly as well as any other painter, captured the atmosphere of old Rondout—its water, its shipyards, and the terminal of the recently completed D & H Canal. In his views of Rondout and the creek and river from above Ponckhockie and from other Rondout promontories and vantage points, of Hussey Hill, and also of Kingston and the Esopus Creek, of the Catskill Mountains and other distant scenes, Tubby most simply and poetically communicated his experience of place.

Born near London, England, in 1821, Tubby immigrated in 1832 with his siblings and parents to the United States and ultimately to Rondout, where he joined his Quaker father in the building trades, having left school at the age of eleven. Taking evening classes in art after spending long days painting houses, church interiors, railway bridges and business signs, Joseph Tubby nonetheless persevered in the pursuit of his true vocation, studying for a time with a local portrait painter by the name of Black and making extended sketching trips to the Shawangunk, Catskill, and Adirondack Mountains. Marrying Ella Hopkins, the daughter of the minister of the First Baptist Church on Wurts Street in Rondout in 1858, Tubby fathered six children between 1859 and 1878. This circumstance assured that Joseph Tubby would continue to work as a house painter and contractor for most of his life, and even prompted him to make a financially disastrous investment with his father in the construction of the Tubby Row House, still standing on the corner of Hone and Spring Streets, which advertised white marble fireplaces, pale parquet floors, and a view of the Rondout Creek.

Most active as a landscape painter and member of the National Academy of Design from 1851 until 1860, Tubby was raw-boned and angular. Possessing clear gray eyes, a mass of jet-black hair, and sporting a neat, close-cropped beard at the time, Tubby traveled with Mc Entee to the Adirondacks on a sketching adventure in 1851. A bachelor until his late thirties, Tubby wrote a letter to his friend Gosman from the mountains, penned on August 3, 1851. In it, in characteristically good spirits, he states, "we shall be home in about a month and if we don't see you before then we will have a long yarn to spin."

Spending his final two years in painful invalidism, Tubby died in Montclair, New Jersey, on August 6, 1896, nearly completing his seventy-fifth year. It is possible that had Tubby received the formal education in art that he lacked, and had he had the leisure to pursue his art unfettered by the necessity to earn a living and support his family, Tubby might have achieved the success he deserved. Be that as it may, he and his large family are now buried in the Montrepose Cemetery (Mount Repose) above Rondout, a setting where Tubby had painted and which he had once called "the sweetest spot on earth."

Jervis Mc Entee, the affluent and gifted friend of Joseph Tubby, was born in Rondout in 1828, the year of the completion of the D & H Canal. Cousin of Julia Dillon, Mc Entee was the son of James Mc Entee, discussed previously, the exceedingly successful Rondout citizen who served as a resident engineer on the D & H Canal, supervised the construction of its terminal docks at Rondout, and owned the Mansion House for a time. A student of one of the most famous Hudson River painters, Frederic Church (who later built a Moorish-style estate high above the river near Hudson) and friend of other noted painters such as Worthington Whittredge and Sanford Robinson Gifford (with whom he traveled in Europe in the 1860s) Mc Entee and his work today are known widely and have been collected by the finest museums.

Named for the chief engineer of the D & H Canal, John Jervis, who had employed his father, Jervis Mc Entee worked for a time in Rondout during the 1850s in the flour-and-feed business, but soon abandoned this job and moved with his wife, Gertrude Sawyer, to New York City, where he pursued his painting career. There, he established a studio, painted, and was soon elected to the National Academy, subsequently exhibiting his work, among other places, at the Paris Exposition of 1867 and the Centennial Exposition at Philadelphia in 1876.

Exhibiting what he called in a letter written from Rondout in October 1874 "a preference for the soberer phases of Nature," Mc Entee was inspired early in his life by Henry Pickering, a poet who had boarded at the Mc Entee home, and by the poetry of William Cullen Bryant, whose poem, "Death of Flowers," provided

Mc Entee with the title of one of his many autumnal landscapes, *The Melancholy Days*. Called a "poet among painters" by Whittredge, Mc Entee even wrote a few poems, including "The Trailing Arbutus." Diabetic and melancholy in temperament, Mc Entee eschewed the sublime subjects of Thomas Cole's paintings as well as the emphasis on topography of luminist Gifford. Mc Entee found autumnal and winter landscapes most appropriate to the rendering of the effects of light, climate and season to which he was greatly attracted. Though them, according to one art historian, he could "channel his own depressed thoughts into avenues of esthetic expression" (Avery, 279). "I don't care for what is known as a 'fine view'. What I do like to paint is my impression of a simple scene." wrote Mc Entee (Sheldon, 52). A man "as modest as he was gifted," according to Frederic Church, soft-spoken, restrained in conduct as well as in his interpretation of nature, Mc Entee was to write in his diary in July 1872, "It saddens me to find that I am looking forward to the Autumn. Some spirit of unrest and melancholy has hold of me and controls me against my will." In October of the same year, he added, "I get so lonely and melancholy when I walk alone that I dread to go. . . ."

Endeavoring, as is stated in a sale catalog of his oil paintings prepared in 1888 by the auctioneers Ortgies & Company, "to note the changing of Nature as observed in our own land, and to express something of the sentiment which distinguishes our landscape from all other," Mc Entee maintained close ties with his native Rondout throughout his life. Constructing a picturesque cottage with attached studio on West Chestnut Street, Mc Entee and his wife spent summers and falls there from the early 1850s on, wintering in New York. Designed by his brother-in-law Calvert Vaux, the noted architect and author of the influential book *Villas and Cottages*, this ornamental, board-and-batten cottage, with projecting eaves, tin roof, complex hips, cross gable, and exterior chimney, was, according to one visitor, "most romantically situated" (Aldrich, 623). Inside, the cottage was airy and bright, with the rafters left visible. According to Vaux, the edifice had an "extended view of the Kaatskills and the Hudson" (Aldrich, 153-155). Mc Entee even improved this prospect by having some trees removed. "From my home in the Catskills," Mc Entee boasted, "I can look down a vista of forty miles, a magnificent and commanding sight" (Sheldon, 52- 53). Painting a number of his landscapes of Rondout and Kingston from this site, among them *On the Rondout, Morning on the Rondout*, and most notably, *View from the Studio Window*, which is owned by a Kingston resident, Mc Entee expressed both his love and his loyalty to this area. "Since my earliest recollection I have had 'studios' here," responded Mc Entee in an 1866 interview (Alrich, 625).

Predeceasing his less-successful and almost forgotten Rondout friend Joseph Tubby by approximately half a decade, Jervis Mc Entee died in 1891 of Bright's disease. In his "Memorial Address," delivered at the Mc Entee home in Rondout on January 30, the Reverend J. G. Van Slyke noted Mc Entee's refinement and charm, and added that the painter had "lent a lustre to this town which would not be conferred by any measure of wealth or any eminence of political position." What Mc Entee had accomplished, he said, was to divert our minds "from too gross an absorption in material achievement and turn it toward the veneration of beauty." John Hageman, of the Rondout *Courier*, had rendered a similar sentiment forty years earlier at the beginning of Mc Entee's career. Mildly questioning progress and the mercantile spirit which animated Rondout, Hageman, in reviewing in November of

1851 an exhibition of Mc Entee's work, noted the experience in himself of "an ennobling feeling rising superior to the wrangling and jarring world." Such was the effect of the work of this talented and prolific landscape painter from Rondout. Today, like Joseph Tubby, Jervis Mc Entee rests in Montrepose Cemetery, a short walk from the locale he painted in his lovely, melancholy landscapes and which he loved so much.

10 : Forever Forming Associations

IN THE SECOND HALF of the nineteenth century, although the earlier pattern of informal activities, such as songfests and serenading, sleigh riding and ice-skating on the river, house visits and picnics, continued, Rondouters exhibited a new willingness, even an eagerness, to associate formally in groups (Blumin, 150). They began to make music in organized societies, such as the Social Maennerchor, a German singing society. They formed baseball clubs, like the Rondout Base Ball Club, founded in 1861, which competed successfully with other teams from up and down the river. They traveled in large parties on steamboats to experience the delights of New York, such as Castle Garden, where Jenny Lind, the "Swedish Nightingale," first sang on September 11, 1850, an appearance arranged by the infamous P. T. Barnum. Many from Rondout made the journey to see and hear this modest and gentle person, unremarkable in voice and beauty, but in presence completely captivating, it would seem.

The Rondout *Courier* notes that in 1853 many people visited the Crystal Palace Exhibition of the Industry of All Nations, called a "world's fair." Some attended the newly-opened Hippodrome, which offered chariot races and could seat 4,600 spectators. In July 1860, members of the Rondout Y.M.C.A. took an excursion to New York harbor on the steamboat *Thomas Powell*, piloted by Capt. Anderson, to see the gigantic ship the *Great Eastern*. Others, like Alfred Snyder, age twenty-five, voyaged even farther afield, becoming one of about a dozen hopefuls from Rondout to die in California in search of adventure and gold.

Popular entertainment took new forms, and a new social calendar, responsive to changing economic and social rhythms, was being created (Blumin, 151). Even the traditional Fourth of July celebration became a "complicated, carefully organized affair," with thousands attending late dinners hosted by the local fire companies, and viewing fireworks displays after dark (Blumin, 157). Committees for this important patriotic event were organized months in advance, and according to the Rondout *Courier* only "the right kind" of people were put in charge.

The inhabitants of Rondout also formed an effective village government, participated avidly in politics, and joined fraternal and military organizations. After a shaky start in 1849, when a quorum could not be raised and few candidates wished to run for office in the first village elections, Rondout gradually developed a healthy and active government. New village charters in 1851 and 1857 subsequently expanded the powers of this government, and concomitant with this development an increase in voter turnout occurred—from the beginning to the end of the 1850s, it nearly tripled. In addition, the party that was repeatedly elected to the village board ran on a platform of vigorous public works initiatives such as the draining and grading of streets and the erection of lighting. Significantly, this party referred to itself as the "progress and improvement ticket."

During the second half of the nineteenth century, immigrants became involved in the activities of all major parties; however, in Rondout, they manifested no apparent pattern of allegiance. Although one might think that the large ethnic populations of Rondout would have voted solidly Democratic, it appears that Whigs and later Republicans were just as likely to carry Rondout as uptown Kingston, or any other place (Blumin, 183). In the census of 1855, for example, the Irish polled were for the most part Democratic, but only by a ratio of seven to four, and the Germans were evenly divided. This same balance, it would seem, continued through 1860, despite the rise of the Know-Nothing Party, which dominated Kingston but not Rondout politics from 1855 to 1858. A so-called "Native American" political organization, the Know-Nothing Party advocated law and order, strict enforcement of temperance laws, tougher criteria for citizenship, and most significantly the belief that "none but the American born" should obtain government jobs. When this party was finally defeated and swept from office in 1858, the editor of the *Republican* expressed his delight that Kingston had seen the last of what he called "grimmer days." Possibly in response to such sentiments, the Rondout Wide Awake Club was formed in 1860; it was an organization created by enthusiastic supporters of Abraham Lincoln to assist in his first Republican presidential campaign. These Friends of Lincoln held torch-lit marches through the streets of Rondout—one to the top of the Vlightberg, where a seventy-foot "liberty pole" was raised. They gathered together in mass meetings where more than one thousand people attended, demonstrated in public places, and founded additional clubs in support of Lincoln and the Union. In general, in Rondout as elsewhere, political activity consisted of a blend of social consciousness, compassion, self-interest, and prejudice.

With commerce flourishing and wealth increasing in Rondout, an attempt was made to facilitate business and to provide a means of better managing accumulation of capital. In the interest of providing these services, three banks were organized over a period of years: the Bank of Rondout, founded in 1848 by Jansen Hasbrouck, the son of Abraham, which became the National Bank of Rondout and later the Rondout National Bank; the First National Bank of Rondout, established in 1863; and the Rondout Savings Bank, opened in 1868. Both the First National Bank and the Rondout Savings Bank were established by Thomas Cornell.

In other civic developments, fire departments were organized, which not only protected the growing community but also provided entertainment, such as festivals, dinners, parades, balls, and the extremely popular concerts given by their uniformed brass bands. In 1860, for example, a spring festival was held in Rondout which 400 firemen attended.

In addition, a jail, or "lock-up," was considered, and a village clock installed in the steeple of the Presbyterian church. It rang upon the hour, proclaiming proudly the existence of Rondout to its rival Kingston.

Americans are "forever forming associations," wrote the French traveler and observer of American life, Alexis de Tocqueville, in 1835, and he was correct. By mid-century, this passion had reached dramatic proportion. In Rondout, for example, old organizations were expanded and many new ones created. In 1854, the Free Masons opened a Rondout lodge, with George Von Beck and Thomas Cornell serving as prominent members. In rapid succession, other social, fraternal, and benevolent organizations were formed, among them the Odd-Fellows, the Knights Templar, the Knights of Pythias, the Knights of Honor, the Ancient Order of Hibernians, the literary society called the Humboldt Verein, as well as the Social Turner Association of Rondout, dedicated to gymnastic exercise and physical culture. In addition, Catholic aid societies and the German Sick and Aid Society of Rondout were established, as were the Royal Templars of Temperance, the Law- and-Order League, and the Red Ribbon reform clubs. It seemed that in a time before radio and television had conspired to keep people at home, the level of participation in these multitudinous and diverse groups was extraordinary.

Rondouters also assimilated the martial spirit of the time, catching what one historian has called "military fever" (Blumin, 158). Joining the 20th Regiment of the state militia, organized in 1851 and called the Ulster Guard, and creating independent units such as the Jefferson Dragoons, established in 1854, or enlisting in one of the newly-formed infantry regiments during the Civil War, such as the 120th and the 156th, the men of Rondout and Kingston avidly entered military life. These regiments at full complement were divided into ten companies of approximately 100 individuals each. Many of these companies were ethnically oriented, or specifically local in membership, as were the 20th Regiment's Harrison Guards, sponsored by George Von Beck and composed primarily of Rondout German-Americans; the Jackson Rifles, formed by Irish-Americans and called by the *Courier* "Rondout's especial company"; and the Washington Rifles, in which the artist Jervis Mc Entee served as first lieutenant. During the 1850s, these and other companies from the area held innumerable musters, inspections, encampments, contests of marksmanship, presentations of colors, balls, excursions and trips to other river towns, where they were received formally and feted.

The expenditure of money on food and lodging at these encampments and other events could provide a financial bonanza for the village in which they occurred. In 1855, for example, over 10,000 troops assembled in Kingston, greatly assisting the local economy. At these festive occasions, the uniforms worn were flamboyant and personalized, like the green costume of the Jackson Rifles, and the blue frock, gold-laced pantaloons and plumed cap of the Jefferson Dragoons. Officers were particularly fond of impressive titles; they carried ornamental swords and rode in parades on white prancing horses. Before 1861, participation in military organizations afforded Rondout's male population the opportunity to gather, to dress up, to march, and to use firearms in a spirit of patriotism and solidarity. For many, being a part-time soldier was simply great fun, and the support and public approval of these activities was profound.

This safe and secure, even naive, communitarianism, however, was to continue for only a relatively short time. Little did these enthusiastic young men know that one day soon their martial skills would be called upon in engagements other than parades and balls.

11 : This Hand For My Country

WHEN RONDOUT LEARNED in early spring of 1861 that Fort Sumter in Charlestown harbor had surrendered to Confederate forces and that the War of Rebellion, as it was called, had finally begun, excited citizens gathered everywhere in the streets. Although a war between the North and the southern secessionist states had been expected since the election of Abraham Lincoln, and some preparations had been made in Rondout, the effect of the news of its actual beginning was, according to the *Courier*, "electric." Quickly, a mass meeting was organized at the court house in Kingston and a rally was held at Washington Hall in Rondout in support of the Union. Patriotic speeches were delivered, resolutions passed, committees appointed, and donations and monthly subscriptions collected to aid the families of the soon-to-depart fighting men. Thomas Cornell donated $100. Soon thereafter, the "Ladies of Kingston" met to form a relief committee to provide "articles of comfort and necessity" for the troops.

In 1861, nearly seven thousand people, comprising some twelve hundred families living in about 730 dwellings inhabited Rondout. From this population, by the most conservative estimate made in 1865 by the *Courier* from incomplete census records, at least 180 to 200 men from Rondout would be recruited to fight in the Civil War. Of this number—about 3 percent of the total inhabitants of Rondout, and possibly 5 to 10 percent of eligible males—20 percent would not return, although the actual figure could have been much greater, as it was for Ulster County regiments on the whole.

The first to be called up by the newly elected president were the state militia. On April 15, Lincoln directed all state governors to provide 75,000 men for three months' service, as was allowed by law. At this time, U.S. Army strength only amounted to 16,367 officers and men, with 198 line companies so scattered on the western frontier and the Canadian border that it was impossible to mobilize them. Even this regular army was divided by what Lincoln called the "insurrection." Of 1,036 officers on active service, 286 resigned and fought for the South. Most regular army enlisted men, however, remained faithful to the Union.

The militia, although some three million strong, was, for the most part, untrained and led by politically appointed and inexperienced officers. One military historian describes these state militia as "a huge unorganized mob" (Dupuy, 6).

Nonetheless, among the militia regiments called up was the 20th Regiment of New York State Militia, whose members had so happily and proudly paraded through the streets of Rondout in the decade before the war. The regiment was commanded by Col. George W. Pratt, the son of a wealthy tanner and congressman from Greene County named Zadock Pratt (Prattsville is named for him). A well-educated, widely traveled man who had been elected in 1857 to the state senate and had settled with his wife on a farm in the town of Esopus, George Pratt had originally named the 20th Regiment the Ulster Guard. He had also written its motto: "This hand for my country." Capable and effective as a leader, Pratt was trusted and liked by his men. And so, a bit more than two weeks after Major General Pierre Gustav Toutant Beauregard, commanding secessionist forces at Charleston, had opened formal hostilities between the states, the 20th Regiment, approximately 800 infantrymen in number, assembled willingly (for the most part) in front of Col. Pratt at the Academy Green in Kingston. Here, in the early morning of Sunday, April 28, they prepared for a formal leave-taking and departure.

During these "public exercises of separation," as the Rondout *Courier* described them, hands were shaken, farewells exchanged, prayers rendered and divine blessings invoked. Each man, no matter what his religion, was given a Bible, with which, held aloft, he took the oath of loyalty administered by Col. Pratt. Following this solemn and moving ceremony, the regiment, accompanied by a sizable escort of firemen and a "mammoth array of citizens," marched toward Rondout. So large was this procession that it stretched from St. James Street in Kingston to the hill above Rondout. Both sides of Division Street, renamed the Union Plank Road, were filled with well wishers. So great was the mass of people and so densely packed the streets of Rondout when they reached the village that the escort could move no farther than the Mansion House at the corner of the Strand. "Windows were alive with faces," and the tops of all the buildings were "occupied." The docks, too, were covered with people seeking a last glimpse of the departing men. "With resolution in their eyes"—and one might think tears—the militia "poured" on to Thomas Cornell's steamboat *Manhattan* and a barge attached to its side, and with great whistle-blowing, waving of handkerchiefs, and the playing of martial music, the 20th Regiment embarked ceremoniously for New York.

In New York, however, it appeared as if the expectations of the 20th would be frustrated and it would have to return home without seeing action. For although Ulster County banks had agreed to advance the regiment up to $8,000 for supplies and equipment, this amount was sufficient only to partially uniform recruits and to supply the regiment's most pressing needs. Many soldiers of the 20th wore their old uniforms; some wore none. And most of their weapons were old and out-of-date. Requisitions for arms and equipment had been made to the state, but none had been forthcoming.

When the regiment reached New York, therefore, its lack of uniforms became a subject of remark in the newspapers. Embarrassed by this unfavorable publicity, the governor of the state, Edwin Morgan, called for the return of these troops. However, through the efforts of one of Pratt's officers, Major Theodore Gates, the matter was resolved to both the satisfaction of the governor and the relief of the regiment, and the 20th continued on to the war, where it spent its three-month enlistment guarding the railroad between Annapolis, Maryland, and Annapolis Junction, along the main trunk line between Baltimore and Washington.

During their tenure in Maryland, the 20th established Camp Reynolds, named by Col. Pratt after a generous Kingston supporter and called "a very pretty canvas village" by Major Gates. Here, they received mail and parcels from home, including Greene County butter from Zadock Pratt, medical supplies from Rondout sent by Dr. Wales and druggists VanDeusen and Deyo as well as others, and underclothing from the ladies of Wilbur. The duty, however—maintaining picket posts to protect the railroad—was neither interesting nor dangerous, and soon the members of the 20th became dissatisfied and bored. Seeing other troops passing south on the railroad daily, the 20th requested orders to remove to Virginia and into battle, but these were rejected. About this time, Hiram Schoonmaker of Rondout resigned his commission, and Theodore Gates was promoted to lieutenant colonel, becoming second-in-command under Col. Pratt. The first deaths occurred, too: Dunbar Schoonmaker of Company B accidentally shot himself through the heart, and John Elmendorf, a thirteen-year-old drummer boy attached to Company F—a "great favorite" of the regiment—died in Kingston while on sick leave.

By late July, when their three-month service had expired, the men quite naturally were anxious to return home. But this was not to transpire on schedule; the disastrous loss of Union troops under McDowell at Bull Run near Manassas, Virginia, rendered such a return temporarily impossible. As a result, dissension broke out in the ranks, with many soldiers avowing that they would not stay in Maryland any longer. In response to this lapse in discipline, Col. Pratt called the men together and addressed them: "If there are any here in favor of going right home step three paces to the front," he said, and then he quickly added, "but be careful that no one shoots you in the back. Anyone going home shot in the back will be justly considered a traitor."

Almost needless to say, no one stepped forward, and the regiment remained at its post. Soon thereafter, however, the 20th was released from duty, and on a Friday morning in early August its men disembarked at Rondout and marched back up the long hill they had descended in April to the Academy Green. Here, after speeches and the consumption of a hearty breakfast, they were finally dismissed, many never to fight again.

Within three days of its return to Ulster County, however, the 20th New York Militia, soon to be officially designated the 80th New York Volunteers, advertised for recruits, and a camp was established on the parade ground to the west of the Union Plank Road between Kingston and Rondout. It was called Camp Arthur, after the Quartermaster General of New York State, who in 1881 would become the twenty-first president. This time, volunteers would enlist for a term of three years, or for the duration of the war. By late September, more than 500 men had enlisted and were living in this camp, and the number of recruits was growing bigger every day. Finally, on October 25, 1861, the camp was struck and nearly 1,000 men marched to Rondout in the second of three enlistments of the Ulster Guard.

This time, however, no special sailing was arranged and no lengthy ceremonies conducted, for the novelty of war had passed. Nonetheless, the regiment would see much action, fighting in many bloody encounters, among them the battles at Fredericksburg, Antietam, South Mountain, Chantilly, Gettysburg, and Manassas, called the Second Battle of Bull Run, where the unit's commanding officer, Col. Pratt, and many others would be mortally wounded. Not until the end of January 1866, long after other Ulster County regiments had returned, would the Ulster Guard finally be mustered out of service and come home to Rondout for good. This would occur nearly ten months after Lee's surrender at Appomattox and almost five years after the first men from Kingston and Rondout had sailed off to war. In difficult and distinguished service in Virginia, Pennsylvania and Maryland, the Ulster Guard would loose approximately 284 men (Phisterer, 2860).

On July 2, 1862, however, while the Ulster Guard was camped near Fredericksburg, Virginia, in an unusually cold, summer rain, President Lincoln issued a call for the recruitment of another 300,000 men. The war had continued for more than a year, and the South had not been brought to its knees as many had expected, even though the ratio of available combat manpower was about five to two in favor of the North (Dupuy, 8). Clearly, Southern successes on the battlefield presaged a prolonged struggle, unless something was done. In response to the president's summons, two new volunteer regiments—the 120th and the 156th—were formed in Greene and Ulster Counties. In these two regiments, as in the 20th and others, additional Rondout men enlisted.

The 120th was organized in Kingston by Col. George H. Sharpe, and was mustered into service August 22, 1862, returning to Rondout in June 1865. Commanded by Col. Sharpe, who had acted previously as Captain of Company B of the Ulster Guard and who would later serve on the staff of General Grant as head of the Bureau of Military Information, the 120th, known as the Washington Guards, left Rondout in haste in the last week of August 1862. Consisting at the time of some 906 poorly prepared, green recruits, the 120th found itself in battle by the final days of the fall. Fighting primarily in Virginia, and engaging in some of the most sanguinary battles of the war—at Chancellorsville, the Wilderness, Cold Harbor, and other sites, as well as Gettysburg—the 120th sustained heavy losses. By the end of the war, nearly 340 Washington Guards were missing or had lost their lives. In short, in more than twenty engagements over three years, approximately one-third of the regiment succumbed to wounds, disease, exposure, or deserted. Sixty-nine of these men died in Confederate prisons (Phisterer, 3410).

In Company H, the number lost was even greater. Recruited exclusively in Rondout and commanded by Capt. Charles Mc Entee, a relative of the painter Jervis Mc Entee, Company H left Rondout with eighty-nine men. Of this initial complement, twenty-one died in battle; eleven were discharged for injury or physical disability incurred in service; nine deserted; ten were transferred to other units or to the reserve; and only thirty-eight of the original group of infantrymen served in this company to the end of the war. Of the eight officers who were mustered into service in Rondout in July and August 1862, five died in action of disease or as a result of wounds received in battle; one was discharged for physical disability. Only two others, Capt. James Holmes, who assumed the command of the company upon the death of Capt. Charles Mc Entee on December 21, 1862, at Falmouth, Virginia, and

Warren Kemble, who was later transferred to Company G, survived the war. Lieutenants Michael Creighton and William Cockburn died at Gettysburg, falling on the second day of battle, July 2, 1862. John Lockwood was killed in the battle of the Wilderness while commanding Company K, and William Dederick died at picket duty near Petersburg, Virginia, in September 1864. In total, by one reason or another, Company H from Rondout lost a shocking 46 percent of its men (Van Santvood, 297-305).

The 156th Infantry Regiment was also organized in Kingston. It was commanded by Col. Erastus Cooke and mustered into service on November 17, 1862. Containing a significant number of recruits from outside Ulster County and the area, the 156th, or the Mountain Legion, as it was called, was the last local regiment to leave Rondout for the war and the one which was to fight farthest from home. Serving briefly along the east coast, the men of the 156th spent most of their three-year enlistment in the Deep South fighting in Louisiana and losing 231 men (Phisterer, 3819).

As with the 20th and 120th, the hardship encountered by the 156th was great. Ordered to New Orleans in early December 1862, the regiment sailed from New York City upon the steamer *M. Sanford*. About eighty miles east of Key West, Florida, their ship sank after running aground on a reef. It was not until Christmas morning that the 156th finally reached New Orleans. By early spring, the 156th was engaged in battle up-country, loosing its first men. In two days, in heavy humidity and heat, the men marched ninety miles, many dropping from exhaustion. In June, they crossed the Mississippi River and participated in the siege of Port Hudson, and in the spring of the following year, 1864, the 156th became a part of the "ill-starred" Red River Campaign. That summer, it was sent by ship to Washington, D.C., this time without mishap, where it joined the forces of General Sheridan in clearing the Shenandoah Valley of Virginia of Confederate troops, participating in fierce fighting. In the final days of the war, the regiment was transferred to Georgia, and later to North Carolina with the army of Gen. Sherman. Finally, on October 23, 1865, the 156th was mustered out of service.

Of special interest to students of Rondout is the fact that in this regiment, a man, unknown and in his late twenties at the time, would, upon his return to Rondout, profoundly influence the life of the village in the years following the Civil War. His name was Samuel Decker Coykendall, and later in this narrative we shall meet him once more.

Although it has become fashionable to assert that the North did not fight the Civil War to end slavery, evidence exists to suggest the contrary, or more exactly, to indicate that slavery and its spread across the country was one of a number of complex and intricately related issues that motivated the North in its actions toward the South. Admittedly, this does not mean that most northerners fought to free the slaves, for preservation of the Union and the restoration of law and order, as one recruitment poster proclaimed, were undoubtedly the dominant concerns in the mind of the average citizen. In general, Blacks and Whites in the North did not mix, and stereotypical and prejudiced views of Black culture abounded, with Blacks such as Shanghai Bob, who ran the Turkey Buzzard Saloon in Rondout during the 1850s, being referred to as "coons." Some Whites, notably in southern Illinois and in New York City, even blamed Blacks for causing the Civil War, and refused to fight. When war broke out in 1861, northern Blacks attempted to enlist but were rejected. Even after the Militia Act of July 1862 authorized the president to use Blacks as soldiers, Blacks were not welcomed into the ranks, ultimately acting as cooks and nurses, or fighting in one of the segregated units commanded by Whites. Although by the end of the war some 200,000 Blacks had served in the Union Army and Navy, and about 68,000 had been killed or wounded, their position was ambiguous and the attitude of most Whites toward them was at best ambivalent.

In Ulster County in 1860, only 2 percent of the population was Black. For the most part, Blacks lived at the bottom of the socio-economic ladder, almost unnoticed, and few if any Whites complained about this deplorable condition. A telling statistic regarding the general lack of local understanding of or sympathy for Blacks is found in the fact that after the Civil War the Black population of Ulster County declined within fifteen years some 14 percent.

Nonetheless, if not a matter of active, local political debate, it can be averred with assurance that many northerners, and certainly some Rondouters, were sincerely concerned about the life of their fellow human beings enslaved in the South (Blumin, 145). By the fifth decade of the nineteenth century, all reforms previously mentioned had been subsumed within the anti-slavery impetus, and if abolitionists seemed more concerned with the concept of slavery than with Blacks, there were undoubtedly people who viewed the issue as essentially a moral one.

In 1848, for example, New York gave former President Martin Van Buren 26 percent of the popular vote in his run for the presidency as a Free Soil, or anti-slavery, candidate. Although some of this figure can be accounted for by the fact that the old Red Fox was a hometown boy, he did receive the second highest number of votes in the state, some six thousand greater than his Democratic rival, Cass. If not avowed abolitionists, "radical" Republicans, or activists like John Brown, who in 1859 attempted to seize the Federal arsenal at Harper's Ferry, Virginia, with the intention of arming the slaves and inciting an uprising in the South, there seems to have been sufficient public sentiment in Rondout against slavery before the war to prompt the editor of the *Courier*, John Hageman, to compose an impassioned editorial in 1854 in response to the passage by Congress of the Kansas-Nebraska Act. Sponsored by the Democratic senator from Illinois and soon-to-be Lincoln-competitor Stephen A. Douglas, this legislation created two new territories in the American West and called for "popular sovereignty," or the right of settlers to decide for themselves whether their state would become slave or free.

Infuriated by this "temporizing," as Hageman called it (for this act, in effect, repealed the Missouri Compromise of 1820, which had prohibited the spread of slavery north of the southern boundary of Missouri, except for Missouri itself), seventy-three prominent Rondout citizens, "disapproving" of this act and "opposed to the perpetuation and spread of slavery," signed a petition and called a mass meeting at the Rondout Village Hall. Expressing their sentiments, no doubt, Hageman, whose paper regularly published a column called "The Slave Trade," wrote, "The Anti Slavery people of the North are actuated by an irradicable principle of repugnance to slavery as a gross violation of natural and immutable rights. No rightly constituted mind will view slavery in any other light than as wrong."

The names appended to this statement are worth noting. At the head of the petition is printed the name of L.A. Sykes, the agent of one of the major employers in Rondout, the D & H Canal. Below his name, Hageman had signed. Also in the document are, among others, the names of George Von Beck, financial supporter and brigade inspector of the 20th Militia; George H. Sharpe, who would serve in the 20th and later command the 120th Regiment formed in 1862; and Erastus Cooke, judge advocate and later commander of the 156th Regiment. In addition, one sees the names of Hiram Roosa and John Griffiths, who served as quartermasters during the Civil War, as well as the names of many other Rondouters who would also enlist in the infantry. Among the list is the name of Charles Mc Entee, the commander of Company H from Rondout, mentioned earlier, who, within a few years of signing this document, would lay down his life in Virginia for this cause.

Members of the Rondout Wide Awake Club, mentioned earlier, and a considerable portion of Rondout had supported Lincoln strongly in his candidacy for the presidency in 1860. In fact, Lincoln had carried all of New York State's thirty-five electoral ballots, winning by some 50,000 votes. And when Lincoln made his triumphant inaugural journey by rail from Illinois to Washington, D.C., in February 1861, Rondouters had crossed the ice-filled Hudson River to Rhinecliff to wave and to cheer their new hero with the "heartiest spirit," reported the Rondout *Courier*. Although Lincoln took a conciliatory attitude toward the South at first, not wanting to panic the pro-Union, slave-holding border states, stating in his First Inaugural Address of March 4, 1861, that he would not interfere with the legitimate exercise of a state's right "to order and control its own domestic institutions," and although he had been reluctant and slow to use his wartime powers to abolish slavery during the first years of the war, Lincoln was nonetheless firmly associated in the public mind with the anti-slavery wing of the Republican Party, which he, if somewhat tentatively, represented.

Many in Rondout had read Harriet Beecher Stowe's sensational novel of slave life, *Uncle Tom's Cabin*, as well as the *Narrative of the Life of Frederick Douglass, An American Slave*, and they had been shocked. The first book to treat Blacks as individuals and not as stereotypes, *Uncle Tom's Cabin* inspired the actor and playwright, George Aiken, to dramatize the novel. His play was first performed on September 27, 1852, just up the river from Rondout in Troy, not far from the location where, 200 years earlier, Rondout's first settlers had left in search of their own freedom. Anti-slavery speakers such as Carl Schurz, who would become a Union Civil War general, senator, and founding member of the Liberal Republican Party, spoke in Rondout, as did many others, like Professor W. Johnson, a Black from the New York Institute of the Blind, who presented an illustrated lecture on the topic, "Scenes in Slave Life." Exhibitions of paintings inspired by the horrors of slavery were hung in Rondout, one at the Presbyterian Church on Wurts Street. And Rev. Felix. H. Farrelly, the pastor of St. Mary's Roman Catholic Church from 1859 to 1864, according to one historian, "did not hesitate to show his disgust for slavery." A trip to the South had convinced him of its "immoral results," and he regularly expressed these strongly anti-slavery views from his pulpit (Clearwater, 433).

Not everyone in Kingston and Rondout, however, disapproved of slavery, or approved of the war, for that matter. There were pacifists who, on principle, stood firmly against all war; there were those who believed that the war was unnecessary because a compromise between the North and the South could be reached; and there were individuals, referred to as Copperheads (a reference to a local poisonous snake) who, according to one local historian, were not sure the Union was "worth saving" in the first place. "Some of the most prominent citizens," he writes, "were openly opposed to the plan of coercion adopted by the administration, and they labored against it" (Clearwater, 240).

Horatio Seymour, who favored the war only as long as its aims seemed readily attainable, was elected governor of New York State in November 1862, as were other Democrats in congressional elections, suggesting that many New Yorkers by this time wished to repudiate the policies of Lincoln and the Republicans. By the dark years of 1863, when optimism about the war had declined markedly as Union losses multiplied, casualties mounted, and the horrifying conditions in the hospitals were depicted in illustrated magazines and in books such as Louisa May Alcott's *Hospital Sketches*, it became clear that the glamour that earlier had been associated with military life was definitely gone.

In some areas of the country, but not in Ulster County, it became necessary to pay men a bounty of between $300 and $400 to join the army. And so difficult did it become to raise troops in some places that Congress passed the Union Conscription Act of 1863, which not only permitted the government to draft all eligible males in areas not meeting their quotas, but also allowed individuals to avoid service by hiring a substitute, or by paying a fee of $300. The passage of this act sparked widespread draft evasion and protests, and ignited four days of bloody and destructive rioting in New York City, as well as trouble in Troy and at the far end of the D & H Canal in anthracite coal country, where Irish immigrant miners became aroused over the discriminatory nature of the draft, compounded by the oppressive labor practices perpetrated against them by the owners of the mines. General disaffection with the war was also furthered by the president's assumption of near dictatorial powers and his incarceration in military prisons of anyone critical of his policies. In addition, Lincoln also initiated an income tax and authorized the printing and distribution of "greenbacks," or paper money, to finance the war. As a result, inflation developed and prices skyrocketed. When Lincoln ran for reelection in 1864, although he carried New York State once again, he did so this time by only a margin of seven thousand votes.

Nonetheless, although sympathy for the federal government's policies and support of the war wavered during the long years of the conflict, New Yorkers, among them Rondouters, served in great numbers. From a population of four million people, New York furnished the equivalent of 400,000 three-year enlistments, or about 17 percent of the total Northern forces. Thirty percent of these men were foreign-born, among them 41,000 Germans; 40,000 Irish; 12,000 English; 3,600 French; 2,000 Welsh; and 2,000 Swiss. Five thousand Blacks also served in New York regiments. By the war's end, about 40,000 New Yorkers had given their lives to the cause—that is, 1 percent of the general population and 10 percent of those who served. Significantly, this was to be the same number that would be lost in World War II. However, at that time, the population of the state was four times as great (Rayback, 69-70).

12 : This Bugbear War

THE LIFE OF THE SOLDIER was not at all as the recruitment posters described it—not the enticing picture of constant, heroic activity painted against a background of patriotic flag-waving and comradeship around the campfire. In reality it consisted of days of inactivity, waiting, and boredom, relieved only by drink, gambling, and the dubious pleasures offered by camp-following prostitutes. In addition, there were tedious hours of drill, long marches, often during inclement weather, and finally, the fear and horror of battle.

The foot soldiers, or infantry, who made up the greater part of the Union and Confederate armies, were, for the most part, male adolescents in their late teens and early twenties, although older men, as well as women disguised as men, served too. Invariably, these soldiers were called "boys" (the word infantry is derived from the Italian *infante*, meaning youth). In 1861, at the beginning of the war, for example, the largest single age group recruited was eighteen-year-olds. As a result, homesickness reached epidemic proportions in the ranks, since many of these young recruits had left home for the first time.

When John Brown went off to war from Iowa , he took his eleven-year-old son Eden with him. Becoming ill soon thereafter, John was shipped home, but Eden remained with the regiment, acting as its drummer boy. In the years that followed, Eden saw many difficult battles and marched with General Sherman through Georgia to the sea. In all that time he did not grow an inch, a relative reports. The clothes he wore when he left fit him when he returned. Later, however, "he made up for lost time and grew to be six feet tall," and lived to become an old man (Brown, 146).

Hardtack (flour-and-water crackers) and coffee were the staple diet of both armies, supplemented by what could be obtained by foraging. Thus it is not surprising that young people like Eden Brown remained the same height during their tour of duty. Scurvy was a common complaint, with soldiers often writing home for onions and other fruits and vegetables. Sutlers, or civilian merchants permitted to serve the troops, charged very high prices for the goods they purveyed in tents and covered wagons. Sweets and soft drinks such as ginger ale were great favorites, yet few privates could afford them, since they drew wages of only about $15 per month. One molasses cookie, for example, could cost as much as twenty-five cents. By 1864, inflation had risen so high in the South that it took fifty Confederate dollars to buy a single, scrawny chicken.

The uniforms these soldiers wore "varied in comfort, quality, and appearance," and there was a great variety of them (Sutherland, 5). Some Northern regiments wore grey and some Southern regiments blue in the early stages of the war, until uniformity of dress was made possible. Each soldier carried a knapsack in which he placed his possessions, two blankets, and an oiled groundcloth which he strapped to his pack, the whole kit weighing fifteen to twenty-five pounds. Battle-hardened troops merely stuffed essential items into their pockets and carried a single blanket, rolled lengthwise in the oilcloth, thrown over the shoulder and pulled across the chest.

Although in 1863 some seventy-nine different models of rifles and muskets, twenty-three types of carbines, and nineteen models of pistols and revolvers were in use in battle, by 1864 Union soldiers, like those from Rondout, shouldered for the most part Springfield rifled muskets, muzzle-loaders of .58 caliber, which fired a lead bullet weighing about an ounce, effective up to 100 yards. The bullet, which "mushroomed on impact," according to one military authority, "inflicted atrocious wounds," shattering bones, and making amputation almost always necessary (Dupuy, 461-63). Discipline in the Union army was enforced often ruthlessly and without mercy, with insubordination, a persistent problem during the war, punished by hanging the perpetrator by his thumbs. Tens of thousands of men were disciplined during the war, 267 were executed, about half that figure for desertion.

Soldiers spent most of their time in camp or in bivouac, fighting less than 5 percent of the time. Some of these men left behind wives, families, and careers which were well advanced. Such was the case of Rondout landscape painter Jervis Mc Entee, who served with the 20th Regiment, New York State Militia, in its first tour of duty in Maryland. From camp at Annapolis, on May 17, 1861, Mc Entee was to write to a friend and associate that he was grateful for his and others' assistance in conducting the painter's business affairs while he was on duty. During this time, an exhibition of Mc Entee's painting *Indian Summer* had been arranged in New York, and the painter had been elected *in absentia* to the American Academy. Not without some resentment and a touch of self-righteousness, Mc Entee wrote, "I came to serve my country. . . . I left behind everything that could make life pleasant. . . . I gave no head to my affairs."

Other younger men with fewer responsibilities, however, wrote more optimistic, good-spirited letters while in the army, obviously excited about their participation in the war and the many possibilities which it offered. Lieutenant John B. Krom of High Falls, age twenty-two, serving in the 120th Regiment, composed a series of letters home from Virginia to his favorite "Uncle John." In these bright and sparkling missives, written between February 14, 1863, and March 10, 1864, Krom remarks cheerfully, "I never felt better in my life. . . . I cannot play sick to get a month's furlough." In another letter, he states, "No army was ever better fed better clothed and better equipped. . . We are all enjoying good health and getting fat on Hard Tack and salt junk." In early March 1864, after being promoted to captain and taking command of Company I upon the death of its commander at Chancellorville the previous year, Krom wrote to his uncle in characteristically good humor, "Your namesake is still O.K., doing his best to put in his three years in Uncle Sam's service..."(Krom). That fall, Krom would be discharged by special order for wounds received in action.

John Burroughs had always thought that, if drafted, he would make a good soldier, basing his judgment on his love and knowledge of the outdoors and the conventional view of military life held before the war. In 1863, at age twenty-six, while teaching school near the United States Military Academy at West Point, Burroughs wrote to his friend Myron Benton, "I am seriously contemplating going into the army....I am getting dissatisfied and crave action. I do want to get near this bugbear, War!" (*Life & Letters of John Burroughs*, I: 80). Resigning his teaching post that fall, Burroughs journeyed to Washington, D.C., where he obtained a position as a clerk in the treasury department and joined the treasury guards, wearing a blue uniform and drilling on his days off. In the summer of 1864, Burroughs finally got the opportunity to see the action for which he yearned. With Confederate General Early threatening Washington—his troops stationed only seven miles from the Capitol—Burroughs walked to the front. There, spending the night in the rifle pits with veteran soldiers of Grant's army, who were rushed up from Petersburg to defend the Capitol, he actually "saw and heard the firing." "Many bullets came close to me," he noted. "How the soldiers did laugh to see me dodge!" (96). Although excited by his first taste of war, Burroughs admitted later that he had drunk his fill of battle that night; he had experienced a sickening feeling and he confessed that, "if they had ordered me to go that night, I should have collapsed—I couldn't have gone if they were to have shot me for the failure" (96). As Thomas Wentworth Higginson, the commander of the first Black regiment in the Union Army was to say, "military glory is a fitful and uncertain thing," and "courage is cheap."

Most soldiers, however, were also terrified as they marched into battle, and the first time was always the worst. One veteran remembers, "the shock to the nerves was indefinable. . .one stands, as it were, on the brink of eternity." Another Confederate soldier, recalling his initiation into combat, stated, "I never saw the like. . . . The men fell like grass. . . . I saw men running at full speed stop suddenly and fall on their faces with the brains scattered all around." (Sutherland, 21). Wounded soldiers, laying in the battlefield with bullets whistling overhead, experienced a particular anguish. "I am alone with my thoughts," said an injured soldier. "I think of home, of the seriousness of my condition; I see myself a cripple for life." (Sutherland, 22).

John Flynn, of Rondout, a member of the 63rd Regiment and the famous Irish Brigade, described the battle for Fredericksburg in a December 1862 letter home to Edward O'Reilly. In that communication he depicts the devastation and destruction of war and its effect on the soldier. "A great portion of the city is laid in ruins," he writes, "while scores of houses are riddled and pierced with shot, grape, and shell." He continues,

> the cannonading is terrific. . . . Poor James Boylan from Rondout, was the first man of our Regiment wounded. He was hit by a shell, and I fear he will lose his right arm. Sergeant Patrick Carroll, from Port Ewen, was the next. He was hit by a Minie ball

in the right hand. . . . We move by the flank through the streets. . . . All this time a deadly fire. . .is poured into our ranks as we advance. . .being greatly thinned by the enemies shells, and by sharp shooters. On reclaiming the summit of the hill, we find ourselves in front of the rebels' first line of breastworks. . . . They open a terrific fire of musketry. . .and many a poor soul bit the dust.

Flynn ends his letter by stating, "Thank God your worthy correspondent is among the lucky ones which escaped unhurt." During the four years in which about three million soldiers and sailors fought, close to 690,000 died. In the battle at Shiloh alone, in two days more Americans fell than in all previous wars. And at Cold Harbor in June 1864, seven thousand troops died in only twenty minutes.

Those less fortunate than John Flynn, such as Col. George Pratt and Capt. Charles Mc Entee, were just a few of the Rondout soldiers who would not return home, bringing sadness and suffering to their families and friends. Col. Pratt was thirty-two years of age at his death. He left behind a wife and two children; nearly 400 people sailed up the river to Albany to attend his funeral. His bereaved father, the tanlord Zadoc Pratt, paid an itinerant stonemason to carve his son's bust above Prattsville on Pratt's Rocks; it can be seen there to this day. In response to the death of this prominent, affluent young man, the Rondout *Courier* was to write: "A brave officer has gone."

The body of Capt. Charles Mc Entee, age twenty, was returned to Rondout in the winter of 1862-63 from Falmouth, Virginia, where he had died in camp of "brain fever." In contrast to the interment of Col. Pratt, Mc Entee was buried in a private ceremony at Montrepose Cemetery with "no military display," as requested by his parents and intimate friends. A "broken column," however, was erected "to mark his resting place" (Van Santvoord, 298).

Joseph S. Corbin, who had been a teacher in Rondout before the war and had earned the love and respect of his students and the community, died on the first day of battle at Gettysburg. The principal of Rondout's District School No. 3, Corbin was considered by the *Courier* to be one of Rondout's "best known citizens." The first principal to be chosen after the acrimonious School Wars,' mentioned earlier, Corbin was known for his "ability, fine physique and personal beauty, together with his prowess in athletic sports." (De Lisser, 72). When the Civil War broke out, this patriotic teacher was quick to enlist, resigning his teaching post. "A most energetic and efficient officer," Capt. Corbin served with the Ulster Guard, Company F, the Irish Jackson Rifles, in two enlistments. Ironically, a few weeks before his death, Corbin had returned to Rondout temporarily on a brief leave. A "vigorous and manly person," Corbin had sported a thick, full, black beard at the time of his death at age thirty-four. Sadly, Corbin's body was never returned to Rondout; so today he rests where he fell. When President Lincoln delivered his famous address at Gettysburg there after the battle, one imagines that the spirit of Joseph Corbin must have been present.

The Ulster Guard, in which Capt. Corbin served, during what the *Courier* on July 10, 1863, labeled the "fiercest fight of the war," offered up what was called "a disproportionate contribution" to the list of killed and wounded. During the first day of battle, the guard engaged the enemy and was driven back through Gettysburg to high ground south of the city. As a result, its commander, Col. Gates, reported in his diary that many men were lost, and his own horse had taken "four bullets in him" (91). Late in the afternoon on the second day, the guard advanced against the enemy once again, and by night had occupied the battlefield. However, inspecting the field the next day, Col. Gates, who had been slightly injured by a spent rifle ball, remarked that the "groans of the wounded" were "heart rendering" (91). On this final day of the battle, the enemy opened "a terrific artillery fire" on the center of the guard for two and a half hours. "The air was filled with shot and shell and the earth groaned and trembled under the terrible concussions. The fire was from 75 to 100 guns and was directed principally at our Infantry," noted Gates (93). Although the Confederate forces soon advanced "directly upon" them, the Union Army ultimately carried the day, taking a large number of prisoners. "Our loss was heavy," though, wrote Gates, "especially in officers" (93). When the count was finally taken, Gates' estimate proved correct. For the guard had lost forty-four, and an additional twenty-four were missing (Phisterer, 2860). In 1888, at the dedication of a monument erected at this battlefield to the memory of the exploits of the Ulster Guard, Rondout poet Henry Abbey read a poem called "Gettysburg." In this long and sentimental elegy, he wrote, "Give pause. . .and weep for them/ all who died,/ In the three days' fight on the ridges, that the Union/ might abide. . ." (*The Poems of Henry Abbey*, 284).

The 120th New York State Volunteers from Kingston and Rondout, known as the Washington Guard, was also present at Gettysburg, and it, like the Ulster Guard, fought in the front lines. During the third day of battle, near the infamous Cemetery Ridge, the 120th absorbed the opening attack of Confederate General James Longstreet's forces and "held the line," as it was called, sustaining the loss of 203 of its 440 men, with fifty-one killed and seventeen missing in action (Phisterer, 3410). A monument was also erected to the 120th; it stands in the Old Dutch Churchyard, at the corner of Main and Fair Streets in Kingston, the birthplace of the regiment. Created by the sculptor B. M. Pickett and unveiled by the regiment's commander, Gen. George H. Sharpe, at a reunion of the survivors of the 120th held on October 17, 1896, this statue of Patriotism, the Daughter of the Regiment, as it was named by Gen. Sharpe, was the only such work of art at this time raised by a general to his men. Interestingly, although situated in a church cemetery, the few feet of land on which this memorial stands is actually deeded to the regiment.

More than 2,700 books have been written about the battle at Gettysburg to date, more than have been written about any other battle in American history. Every year, more than a million people visit the Gettysburg National Military Park in the verdant hills of Pennsylvania. With 51,000 casualties as a result of this three-day engagement, which might be considered the turning point of the war, and with Lincoln's memorialization of the event in his immortal Gettysburg Address, it is no wonder that this event, in which soldiers from Kingston and Rondout participated and lost their lives, should transcend its repeated recitation today, and become in the minds of Americans not mere history but myth.

Not all fatalities, however, occurred on the battlefield. Soldiers like Rondout's John Flynn, who escaped death at Fredericksburg, could still die by accident, disease, or even in hospital. Horseplay with weapons could be dangerous; typhoid (called "camp fever") and diarrhea (known as the "quick-step") were even bigger killers. More than 100,000 fighting men died of these two diseases alone, and another 300,000 or more to other sicknesses. One of Robert E. Lee's men remarked that it was "a very rare thing to find a man in this army who has not got the diorreah" (Sutherland, 20).

The Union hospitals in Washington, D.C., which John Burroughs visited with his friend and mentor, Walt Whitman, the author of *Drum-Taps*, poems inspired by the Civil War, were horrible, crowded and dirty, with sick, wounded, and dying soldiers propped in makeshift beds or sitting on the floor. During these trips of mercy, Whitman carried a great haversack in which he brought tobacco, apples and oranges, reading material, and even flowers, distributing them free to the suffering men. Whitman, who would visit Burroughs a number of times in West Park near Rondout after the war, would do errands for these soldiers, writing their letters and reading to them. Most movingly, the poet would clean and dress their wounds. As he states in his poem "The Wound-Dresser," "Bearing the bandages water and sponge/ Straight and swift to my wounded I go. . ./ not one do I miss,/ An attendant follows holding a tray, he carries a refuse pail,/ Soon to be filled with clotted rags and blood, emptied, and fill'd again."

Not unlike his contemporary and fellow ministrant Clara Barton, who, after nursing thousands of Americans during the Civil War went on to found the American Red Cross and become known as "the angel of the battlefield," Whitman's efforts on behalf of these men took its toll. After the war was over, Whitman's health was never strong again; at the age of sixty-four, the poet suffered a paralytic stroke.

Burroughs was shocked by what he saw in these hospitals—the piles of amputated limbs, the disturbing odors and appalling sanitary conditions, the hordes of desolate and hopeless men. On one occasion, Burroughs offered his services in a field hospital to the busy surgeons. His biographer writes: "The operating tables were full. The wounded lay in long lines on the floor, or sat crouched by the wall waiting their turns, some groaning, some joking, some in apathetic silence" (Barrus, 240). At first, Burroughs was able to help, holding vessels and passing instruments, but after a time the sight of so much blood overcame him and he felt faint. Noticing his condition, the surgeon yelled at Burroughs and shoved him out the door. There, Burroughs crawled into some hay and attempted to sleep, listening to "the clatter of hoofs and sabres" throughout the night (241).

C. B. King of Kingston, a hospital steward attached to the 20th Regiment, describes in a letter to his wife published in the Rondout *Courier* in September 1862 the removal of sick and wounded from a field hospital near Falls Church, Virginia, to Philadelphia. King, himself ill, writes,

> The tents were taken down. . .and all those who were able to walk, went to a platform on the Rail Road. . .and sat on the ground baking and frying in the hot sun. . .some seven hundred sick men set on their knapsacks and did the best they could. . . . We arrived in Washington about 9 o'clock. . .but we sat there in the rain till a quarter to three in the morning.

Finally, these men were taken to a place called "The Retreat" near the Capitol. Here they were given something to eat, but later were forced to sleep on the bare floor in their damp clothing. At the end of the next day, they were loaded into freight cars with no heat, the train containing about twelve hundred men jammed into fifty cars. Reaching Philadelphia at last, King was taken to the Cooper Union, where he writes, "I had a mattrass laid on the floor and had a good night's rest."

Some men had the misfortune to be captured by the enemy and incarcerated in dreadful prisons. During one battle on October 10, 1863, at James City, more than 100 members of the 120th Regiment were taken. Among this unlucky group were James Doyle, William Roots and Wilbur Hale from Rondout. These men were sent to the infamous Confederate prison at Andersonville, Georgia, where an encircled stockade housed 45,000 Union troops in tents. Although this prison only operated for fourteen months, during that time some 13,000 prisoners died of malnutrition, exposure, and other more direct forms of mistreatment. After the war, Union forces hung the camp's commandant, Capt. Henry Wirtz. Interestingly, he was the only person to be executed for war crimes after the Civil War.

Although James Doyle and William Roots died at Andersonville, miraculously, Wilbur Hale, who had been wounded in the hand, cheek, and hip three months earlier at Gettysburg, survived. Imprisoned for a year at Libby Prison, Belle Island, and finally at Andersonville, Hale described his harrowing experience in two newspaper articles published many years after his repatriation and return to Rondout. At first, wrote Hale, Andersonville seemed an improvement over Belle Island, for it was warmer in Georgia than Virginia. But as summer advanced, his opinion changed, since "No protection of any kind was provided from the sun. Men grew sick and died from contact with the almost torrid glare. At first we crouched along the stockade. . .but that was stopped by a line erected a rod inside the stockade, to pass beyond which was sure and certain death" (Van Santvoord, 98). "With no protection from the elements," continued Hale, "every change of weather resulted in a higher death rate. If hot or cold or wet, the result was all the same." (100).

In his articles, Hale describes the cruelty of some of his captors, especially that of the Confederate doctor, Dr. McVeigh of Salem, Virginia, who was in charge of attending to the sick. When asked for permission by Hale to go outside the stockade in order to obtain pine boughs to make a bed for Richard Johnston, a friend from Kingston who was suffering from severe diarrhea, the doctor responded arrogantly, "Damn the Yankees, let them die! Each one that dies is one less...for us to kill" (100). As a result of this lack of attention, Johnston died soon thereafter, on May 16, 1864. At the time, he had reached the age of twenty-five.

In addition to his duties as "sergeant of the floor," distributing the meager rations allotted to his men, Hale was also appointed "master of the gangrene ward," where he observed with horror Dr. McVeigh at his grisly work. Hale reports that the doctor would often remark that this ward was "an excellent place to learn surgery." He would "cut and haggle at the limbs of the poor wretches" who had been wounded, states Hale, their bodies rank with gangrene. He adds that these patients "were sure candidates for the trench, where in rows of fifty, the dead were laid," many of them "carried naked to burial."(101).

Finally, in September 1864, Hale was moved with other prisoners back to Libby Prison in Richmond, Virginia. On the trip, Hale states, seven men "literally starved to death" (104). In Libby, on October 20, after much waiting and great uncertainty about his fate, Hale was exchanged, his imprisonment of one year and ten days finally ended (105).

From May 1865 until the 120th Regiment was mustered out of service in June, Hale served as acting sergeant major. Upon his return to Rondout, Hale, then in his mid-twenties, embarked upon a business career. In the *Gazetteer & Business Directory of Ulster County, N.Y. For 1871-72*, Hale is listed as partner in a store selling groceries, which was called "Wilber and Hale." By 1874, Hale had struck out on his own and was in business for himself. Taking out a half-page advertisement in the *Kingston, Ellenville and Saugerties Directory for 1873-1874*, Hale proudly proclaimed, "Wilbur L. Hale, Dealer in Growseries, Prouvisuns, Kole, and C., Corner of Union Avenue and Chester Street."

Although Hale had fought in some of the bloodiest battles of the Civil War, been wounded at Gettysburg, and had survived, he never forgot his imprisonment in the South. Writing articles and speaking at numerous occasions about his experiences, Hale, although successful in the burgeoning world of Rondout commerce, marked his release from Confederate hands as one of the happiest days of his life. While a prisoner at Andersonville, he had "confiscated" a piece of cotton cloth from his captors; this he used to cover himself during the cold winter nights (103). Hale carried this flimsy and tattered rag with him throughout the rest of the war, and afterward brought it home. It remained with him, a stark reminder of his days as soldier and prisoner, for the rest of his life.

The jubilation occasioned by the surrender of Confederate forces in Virginia and the prospect of the return to Rondout of soldiers like Wilbur Hale, however, was dampened by the death of the president who had led the Union throughout the terrible years of this difficult war. Just five days after Lee and Grant signed the paroles at Appomattox, while attending a dramatic performance in Washington, D.C., at Ford's Theater, Lincoln was shot in the head by the actor and Confederate supporter John Wilkes Booth. Although the president survived the night, he died the next day, and funeral services were held four days later. On April 21, the casket containing President Lincoln's remains was placed on board a special train, and the long, slow trip back to Springfield, Illinois, which would not be completed until the first week in May, was begun.

Although report of the assassination reached Rondout by telegraphic dispatch soon after the shooting, most Rondouters were asleep at the time. The town, therefore, awakened to the sad news on Saturday morning, and was struck, wrote the *Courier*, with "dumb amazement." In his eulogy, published the following Friday (the *Courier* was a weekly), the editor, John Hageman, described the act as an "utter atrocity" and communicated "an indignation which knows no bounds." "At the very moment when sweet Peace with her white wings seemed brooding over a people already stricken with. . .loss," wrote Hageman, this "melancholy event has plunged the nation into mourning." That night, a meeting was called at Washington Hall by S. L. Stebbins and chaired by Dr. Chrispell. A committee was appointed to draft "appropriate resolutions" and to "take measures and make arrangements" for a local funeral observance. Thomas Cornell served on this committee. It was resolved that all places of business would be closed during the funeral services and that the village of Rondout would be united in this "expression of sorrow." "We record our testimony," they stated, "to the sterling worth of Abraham Lincoln. . .statesman, patriot, and man."

Throughout the funeral trip, wrote Hageman in his article published the following week on April 28, 1865, entitled the "Funeral of our late President," "along the whole hundreds of miles of railway. . .through 7 states. . .the people thronged to the humblest station." Some individuals from Rondout had even boarded the steamer *Thomas Cornell* on Monday, April 24, and sailed down the river to City Hall in New

York City, where Lincoln's body lay in state before continuing its westward journey. Others waited in Rondout for the train, which would pass on the evening of April 25 across the Hudson River at Rhinecliff.

Finally, after prolonged waiting, it was learned that the cortege would reach Rhinecliff at 8:40 p.m. In response to this news, more than 200 Rondouters crossed the river to the little railway station at the base of the cliff—just as many had done four years earlier on a happier occasion, when Lincoln, newly elected to the presidency, had made this journey in the opposite direction. In Rondout, the streets were shrouded in the deepest black of mourning, and flags were flown at half mast. On the promontory above Ponckhockie, soldiers commanded by Capt. P. J. Flynn, the Civil War veteran mentioned earlier, loaded a battery of cannons in preparation for rendering a military salute to the departed president.

At 8:20, across the river to the south, the presidential train was sighted, crawling like a glow-worm up the far side of the river, its dull light reflected on the dark waters. In response, the cannons were fired, and all the churchbells in Rondout were tolled. At Rhinecliff, the train slowed as it passed the riverside platform crowded with mourners, and the "reverent crowd," wrote Hageman, "saw indistinctly" the train roll "through the lines of light." A solemn dirge was played by the German Band of Rondout, breaking the silence; then, in a moment, the cars had swept past and "were lost in the deep gloom" of the night. Concluding his report of this sad and momentous event, Hageman wrote the people of Rondout "have done themselves honor. . . . Now let them do the rest of their duty by carrying out the great work of regeneration for the nation to which he has given his life."

13 : The Bonds of Municipality

 IT WAS WITH A "BLESSED" SIGH OF RELIEF that Rondout returned to peacetime activities after the "Rebellion." Gone were the fretful days of recruitment and enlistments and the loss of friends and loved ones in the long, bloody war. "May we never be tried by a like affliction," wrote *Courier* editor John Hagemen, expressing admirably, as he often did, everyone's hopes and fears. It was time to return to business as usual, and Rondouters did so with a determined and dedicated spirit.

Yet, life had gone on in Rondout even during the darkest days of the war. Even before the troops had come home, marching under a huge arch erected on Union Avenue, topped by a live eagle and trimmed with evergreens and flowers, people had continued to attend concerts and strawberry socials, had taken vacation trips on river steamboats, and had engaged themselves in all manner of recreational and entrepreneurial activities. George Von Beck and Thomas Cornell had pursued their financial interests avidly during this difficult time: Cornell had expanded his transportation empire and in 1863 had founded the First National Bank of Rondout; Von Beck, in addition to purchasing a number of choice Rondout properties, had cleared away the old Mansion House stables and had constructed new ones made of brick.

In fact, Rondout had entered, despite the war, what John Hagemen had named in June 1862 the "age of brick," with "dwellings constantly rising" and the business section along the Strand "rapidly being built up" with four-story brick buildings replacing the old one- and two-story wooden structures. In short, Rondout had been "busy as a hive" all along, and the "regeneration" which Hageman would call for upon the end of the Civil War was already well underway.

As early as the 1850s, suburbs had begun to spring up between Kingston and Rondout, and the ferry crossing the creek to Sleightsburgh by 1852 had proven itself inadequate to the needs of the growing community. As if to indicate the increasing "social and economic interdependence" of Kingston and Rondout, the two villages began to converge, with the new streets laid out in the southern end of Kingston and the northern section of Rondout (Blumin, 116). Here emerged a new community that would transform Union Avenue, in effect, from a "commercial highway into a central city street" (116). On the 1858 map of the area, for example, large sections in each village were set aside for suburban development. Along Greenkill Avenue and Cedar Street, a fashionable neighborhood, which would contain fine homes, a church, a female academy, and flower gardens was planned by the local real estate developer, Abijah Smith. Below this subdivision, in a wild and beautiful locale known as Jacob's Valley (Wilbur Avenue and South Wall Street today), entered by a road edged by pine trees, was to be constructed a picturesque rural cemetery and a public park for the use of Smith's suburbanites. Here, Smith would create groomed walks, a carriage drive, and an artificial lake that would provide water to the homes in his new suburb. With characteristic vigor, Smith attempted to sell both house lots and cemetery plots at promotional parties where sweets and lemonade were served. Although "Smith's Folly," as this ambitious project was known, was only partially to be realized—the fashionable suburb becoming a working-class neighborhood and later a railroad right-of-way, the lake and water system never built, and the valley incompletely transformed into a city park—nonetheless two cemeteries did materialize, and for a time the beautiful scenery of this intermediate territory was enjoyed by hundreds of citizens from the area, thus drawing attention to the increasing interrelationship of Kingston and Rondout.

Although in Rondout's early days both worker and employer, rich and poor, tended to prefer to live as near to their place of employment as possible, a slow but gradual movement by those with money out of the smoke and clamor of the central commercial area also began. As early as August 1851, the *Courier* reported that "Lands on the hill" above Rondout had been "brought into market." The newspaper called these lots "desirable locations for residence as found anywhere." and suggested that "high places can be made low and. . .rough places smooth." Two years later, the *Courier* stated proudly, these locations were being "ornamented" with houses, indicating an increase in good taste as well as prosperity. Seeking pleasant views, as well as desiring to separate themselves from those below them, Rondout's more affluent citizens constructed new and substantial homes on the Vlightberg, on Rockcliff near Hasbrouck Avenue, and on West Chestnut Street.

Regarding West Chestnut Street, the most prestigious address in Rondout, the *Courier* stated in 1856, "within a year or two. . .the whole length of the ridge will be crowned with good-looking houses." On this street, whose very name evoked pastoral and poetic associations so different from those of the urban center below, the commercial gentry of Rondout spent lavishly, creating great Gilded Age mansions of brick, bluestone, and granite. It was an era when ostentation and conspicuous consumption were considered fashionable, when American capitalism and industry had triumphed, and when one could accumulate vast, untaxed fortunes and spend them as one pleased, unfettered by government intervention. Here, for example, the cigar magnate George J. Smith built a home whose huge elliptical ceiling was painted with angels. Samuel Decker Coykendall, who, after the death of Thomas Cornell would become the wealthiest and most powerful man in Rondout, a personal friend in later years of Governor Charles Evan Hughes, constructed a massive house of red stone, similar to that used in the palatial mansion of "robber baron" Henry Clay

Frick in Pittsburgh. The house of his son Edward, built nearby, remains in use as an apartment house today. Other impressive residences were also erected on this street. Among the outstanding were the homes of tanner and politician Henry Samson (still in existence), for whom the Catskill mountain community of Samsonville is named, as well as the house of brick manufacturer George Washburn, which possessed three-story Corinthian columns and was made of yellow stone. One of the most notable West Chestnut Street houses, called "Cloverly," with mansard roof and tower, was originally built by James Van Deusen, one of the owners of the Van Deusen Brothers' drugstores in Rondout and Kingston. In later years, this property was owned by the Dwyers of Rondout, a family of noted boatbuilders. It still may be seen standing at the crest of the hill on this historic Rondout street.

Although rivalry and distrust continued to exist between the citizens of Rondout and Kingston in the years following the Civil War, the two communities, if somewhat reluctantly and suspiciously, nonetheless gradually began to extend their arms toward one another, symbolized by the development of mass transit between the two in 1866 in the form of a horse-drawn streetcar. What had seemed an unbridgeable gulf in history, values, and physical distance in 1828, when the D & H Canal had been built, in the early 1870s appeared less discernible. It was not long, however, before this new perception was severely tested.

The 1870s were momentous years in the history of both Rondout and the country. On the national scene, the long, sad years of Reconstruction in the South finally came to an end. And as if to atone for the many lives sacrificed during the Civil War, the persistent corruption and scandal which infected the two administrations of war hero and President Ulysses S. Grant, and the unbridled greed of robber barons such as Jay Gould and Jim Fisk, religious revivalism and public repentance swept across the eastern portion of the country. The inevitable thrust of railroads had joined both coasts, and further construction was driving vectors of settlement deep into the great open lands hitherto held by the indigenous peoples. In 1876, for example, the same year in which the Centennial Exposition opened in Philadelphia, Gen. George Armstrong Custer and his Seventh Cavalry were killed by Sioux Indians at the Battle of Little Big Horn, and the government, ironically, accelerated its policy of pacification and, at times, extermination, of these Native Americans. In this centennial year, the United States also discovered that it had increased its population tenfold, New York City reaching one million. Clearly, the country was undergoing profound social, political, and economic changes.

Rondout, of course, participated in this national transformation. In 1870, the village contained some 10,114 souls, a number significantly greater than Kingston, whose population was only 6,315. Out of a total county-wide population at the time of 84,075, no less than 12 percent of that number lived in Rondout (Beers, 4). For the children of this growing populace, two new schools were built at this time—Ulster Academy and No. 2 School. In this same year, when the movement of coal on the D & H Canal had reached its zenith, with nearly three million tons traveling from the mines at Honesdale to tidewater, up one million tons from the previous decade, and when it was said that the commercial traffic on the creek was so thick that one could cross to Sleightsburgh on barges without touching the water, things looked very bright in this thriving community, indeed (Hickey, 70).

In this year also, two of Rondout's most notable citizens passed away: the redoubtable George Von Beck and the brave and dedicated physician Dr. John Wales, who earlier had nursed the fledgling villagers through the difficult days of the plague. Both of these prominent citizens died within a month of each other—Von Beck at the Mansion House, and Dr. Wales in the Rondout Creek, his body not found until the following June. Finally, two years later, in December 1872, the first passenger train from Rondout rolled into Stamford, linking Rondout with the far side of the Catskill Mountains, and heralding the beginning of a new and promising commercial era.

Recognizing the rapid growth, increased prosperity, and improved prospects of Rondout at this time, it seemed to many of its inhabitants appropriate, even necessary, to make certain changes in the ordering of the village. Taking the first step in 1871 toward "improving" the village charter, Rondout petitioned the legislature in Albany to redesignate it as a city. At first, the response to this appeal in Kingston was noncommittal. At best, it was thought, this act would absolve Kingston of the obligation to provide Rondout with certain public services; in short, the change would save Kingston money. But soon the magnitude and implications of Rondout's petition became clear: Rondout, it was realized with shock and surprise, wanted to go it alone. If Rondout became a city in its own right, the effect on Kingston could be profound. Kingston might, eventually, be absorbed by the burgeoning village of Rondout; it might even, as in the distant past, lose its revered English name. As a result of these and similar speculations, the old fear and dislike of Rondout by Kingstonians, first expressed early in the century and then allayed for a time, surfaced once again.

In swift and strong reaction, therefore, Kingston presented its own case before the legislative committee which was to review Rondout's application. Whereas Rondout requested city status in its own right, with Seymour Stebbins speaking warmly in behalf of this position, a spokesman for Kingston shrewdly presented a counter argument: He suggested that, rather than designate Rondout a city and maintain Kingston as a village, it would be more efficient to merge the two communities into one city. Although both views were presented vigorously, by the end of this session of the legislature no decision had been reached. In the next session, however, as one observer reported, "the contest was renewed," with local assemblyman Robert Loughran, of Kingston, leading the fight for merger (Lindsley, 42). Although extended debate and discussion followed, in the end Rondout's petition was denied, and Kingston's case carried the day. Outmaneuvered and outvoted by the proponents of consolidation, Rondout lost its bid for a city charter. In due course, a bill was passed by both houses of the legislature and was sent to the governor for his signature. As a result, the villages of Rondout and Kingston were united and incorporated on May 29, 1872.

The name of this new municipality, however, was not the City of Rondout, as might have been expected and as fitting, considering the fact that Rondout had filed the first petition and could boast the greater population. A compromise appellation might have been the City of Rondout-Kingston, or the City of Kingston-Rondout, or even, the City of Rondout & Kingston, or the reverse. These longer and somewhat cumbersome titles, however, had not been considered. With neither apology nor accommodation to Rondout, these two very different communities would be designated hereafter simply as the City of Kingston.

As a consequence of this act, the name Rondout was removed from the official list of New York State villages. Eventually, it could be found only in directories as a post office site called Station Rondout, City of Kingston. And as the new city was divided into sections, or wards, interestingly, Rondout, in a sense, became a ward of Kingston. Clearly, the connotations of this term are highly suggestive of Rondout's abruptly changed political situation. For in time, Rondout, which had lost not only its name but also the power of administrative self-determination at the height of its size and affluence, would be absorbed into the very community which had dreaded the same situation.

In this regard, the perception of this event voiced by Alphonso T. Clearwater, the prominent attorney and historian from "uptown" Kingston (Rondout became known as "downtown"), is illuminating. "A sort of sub-acid antagonism" existed "between the two localities," he states with undisguised emotion more than a half century after the merger. "It was apparent that this divergence of view would prove disastrous," and so, he writes emphatically, "the villages of Kingston and Rondout were united." (*Kingston*, 20).

Nonetheless, there *were* advantages to the merger, and many in Rondout could see them. So, swallowing their pride and putting on a brave face, they accepted this irrevocable reality. In their turn, the politicians who had opposed so strongly the joining of Rondout and Kingston now made impassioned speeches of brotherhood and extolled vociferously the benefits of this new condition. "May God bless the new city," wrote Edward O'Reilly, president of the village of Rondout, to E.M. Brigham, president of the village of Kingston. "May the union ever be happy." Earlier, the Rondout *Daily Freeman*, on March 27, 1872, had written that consolidation would result in "better government, a more cordial feeling between the respective populations, and an enhanced prosperity." The newspaper even suggested that the two communities take the opportunity to celebrate together an "old-fashioned house-warming," in which each village would bury "old hatchets" and forget "old discords." Certainly, these statements illustrate how quickly politicians and the media forget the bitter battles and profound lessons of the past.

With boisterous and prolonged "bell-ringing, cannon-firing, bonfires and illuminations," reported the Rondout *Daily Freeman* on April 5, 1872, the two villages celebrated their union in what was called, continuing the use of the marriage metaphor, "the bonds of municipality." In due course, a meeting was held at Schwalback's Grand Central Hotel in Rondout. There, hearty handshakes and congratulations were exchanged by the representatives of both villages, speeches delivered, and arrangements made for the holding of elections. The meeting ended on a humorous note when Seymour Stebbins, who had presented Rondout's original petition for a city charter to the state legislature and who would become the first city corporation counsel, remarked that what had been accomplished this day between Rondout and Kingston might now be called the "Schwalbach Treaty."

On Tuesday, April 16, elections were held, with aldermen from the nine wards, supervisors and other municipal officers, and a mayor elected. Although city historian Clearwater was to write that James G. Lindsley of Rondout had been chosen the first mayor of Kingston because it had been "concluded that as a matter of delicacy and policy, the mayoralty should go to Rondout," this was not quite the case (*Kingston*, 20). Acceptance of the merger in Rondout, ending twenty-three years of village government, did not mean that Rondouters were oblivious to the implications of the electoral process, nor that uptown Kingston was willing to relinquish the benefits of its recently won victory in the legislature. Strongly aware of the necessity of a "balance of power," Rondout had cast its ballots "more solidly" than uptown Kingston (De Witt, 169). According to one local historian, downtown took pride "in electing a downtown man" (De Witt, 173). As a result, in the seventy years between this first city election and the beginning of World War II, eleven of the twenty individuals elected to the office of mayor were from Rondout.

This figure, however, is misleading. For when one realizes that Rondout was generally Democratic during this time and that the Democratic Party held the mayoralty for only eighteen years, the fears expressed prior to the merger that Rondout would lose its identity, influence, and importance, seem not without substance. James Lindsley, who was to hold the mayor's office from 1872 to 1877, was a Republican. And although a popular candidate, garnering some 71 percent of the vote, Lindsley doubtless felt sympathetic to the issues and values of his Republican colleagues uptown. Thus, it could be argued, from the point of view of the old money in uptown, James Lindsley was an ideal candidate. He lived in the more populated section of the city, Rondout, and thus could be expected to get elected; yet he *was*, in fact, a Republican.

Kingston's first mayor was born in 1819 in Orange, New Jersey, into a modest family of merchants. His father wanted him to become a hatter, so James worked at this trade obediently until the depression of 1837 forced him to seek other employment. Within a few years, Lindsley joined Calvin Tompkins, whose daughter Sarah he would marry, and began to learn the intricacies of the cement business. With the demand for cement increasing, James was sent to Rondout in the spring of 1846. Here, he took charge of Tompkins' Newark Lime and Cement Manufacturing Company, developing the quarries under the Vlightberg and extending facilities. This time Lindsley would later call the "best years" of his life (Sylvester, 310).

A temperance man, "ardent" Whig and later Republican, James Lindsley was active in public affairs throughout his lifetime (310). Interested in learning and literary pursuits, he was to write articles on geology, which he saw as "picturesque or beautiful," and on the history of Rondout (De Lisser, 25). Having served as both trustee and village president of Rondout, Lindlsey was well qualified to assume the duties of mayor in 1872. Attentive to the public works needs of Rondout, Lindsley had been responsible earlier for the grading of streets, the flagging of sidewalks, and the building of sewers. In 1884, after serving his terms as mayor, Lindsley finally won election to the United States Congress. Known for his energy, prudence, and sagacity, he died in December 1898, the year in which the D & H Canal closed, having lived during the greatest years in the history of Rondout.

One more event in the story of Rondout's surprising reversal of fortune during its highpoint of commercial activity needs to be told. When the new city hall was completed on a hill along Union Avenue halfway between uptown Kingston and downtown Rondout—the location was decided upon by compromise—a ceremony was planned to lay the cornerstone and to dedicate this new public building, the visible symbol of the wedding of Rondout and Kingston. According to the preparations, half of the dignitaries who would participate were to be from Rondout and half from Kingston. The building itself had been designed by Arthur Crooks of New York City. Large and impressive, it had been modeled after the famous Palazzo Vecchio in Florence, Italy, and could boast a spacious council chamber and large windows commanding sweeping views of the Catskill Mountains to the west. Whether due to conscious insult, oversight, misunderstanding of the time, or simple tardiness, when this important ceremony was conducted and the cornerstone laid, the representatives of Rondout were not present. More significant forces than rivalry and civic pride, however, were at work in the country and Rondout at this time.

14 : Railway Fever

As IF TO PROPHESY IMPENDING CHANGE, in the year following the merger a great fire swept through lower Rondout, destroying many buildings along the Strand. Then, three years later, in the summer and fall of 1876, a severe drought held the area in its grip. As John Burroughs wrote, "For nearly three months there was no rain. . .forest trees withered and cast their leaves" (*Locusts and Wild Honey*, 81). So low became the level of water in the Rondout Creek and the Hudson River that salt water from the sea, which normally moved up the river only about forty miles, reached Rondout. From the hills above Rondout, one could see scorched spots on the mountains, as if they had been burned by fire. The air was yellow and dirty, the sun red and dim at midday. The smoke from "innumerable fires" stung eyes and "smarted the nose." "Some malevolent spirit seemed abroad," wrote Burroughs from his home a few miles south of Rondout along the Hudson River (82). Then, two years later, the parched land was inundated by a raging flood, which at Eddyville demolished the D & H Canal locks. It was as if nature was trying to tell Rondout something.

Few Rondouters, however, entertained fatalistic thoughts. For what was on the minds of the people were less the unpredictable ways of Mother Nature and more the fluctuations of the business cycle. Precipitated by overspeculation and fueled by the unparalleled corruption and pervasive acquisitiveness of the Grant era, a panic, or economic depression, resulted. Seeking continued high profits, investors had risked capital carelessly, entrepreneurs had expanded production facilities unrealistically, and bankers had extended credit beyond the margin of safety. As a result, even the leading brokerage firm of Jay Cooke, a personal friend of the president, failed on September 18, 1873. Within a year, five thousand businesses closed, and three million laborers lost their jobs (Blum, 389).

President Grant himself had visited Kingston just prior to the failure of Cooke & Company. He had sailed up the river in July and been met at Rondout by local

Civil War commander and Republican boss, General George H. Sharpe. Grant was taken to Woodstock and driven up to the Overlook Mountain House. Although his sojourn had been enthusiastically awaited for many months, in actuality the experience seems to have been viewed as something less than anticipated, for by mid-summer, Grant's reputation had been deeply tarnished by scandal. In addition, it was reported with sadness and dismay that on his trip to Ulster County the president had been drinking heavily (Evers, *The Catskills*, 474).

In Rondout, times were difficult, but in contrast to other sections of the country things could have been worse. Although long-term investment had dried up, over-production and the resulting falling prices in actuality had facilitated commerce. Consequently, the level of employment in areas dependent upon trade, such as Rondout, remained relatively stable, and with the price of goods, in general, declining during this otherwise troubled decade, real income rose over 60 percent (Wiebe, 2). However, the development that was to most profoundly impact Rondout at this time was not, as might have been expected, this "strange depression," as it has been called, but something very different: It was the coming of railroads to the area. (1)

As early as 1866, Thomas Cornell had foreseen the importance of railroads. Although commanding a successful fleet of steamboats, among them the longest craft on the Hudson River, the *Thomas Cornell*, and the most famous, the *Mary Powell*, Cornell nonetheless invested in the fledgling Rondout & Oswego Railroad and directed its operations for the next four years. By May 1870, twenty miles of track had been laid, a tunnel dug under Hasbrouck Avenue, and the first regularly scheduled passenger train had left Rondout for Mt. Pleasant. In September of that year, Cornell resigned his directorship of the Rondout & Oswego, but promptly organized the Rhinebeck & Connecticut Railroad as well as the Delhi & Middletown Railroad. By this time, it seems, Cornell had become convinced that railroads would become the most popular form of transportation in the future, and he proceeded to increase his position. He had even sold the coveted *Mary Powell* and her route to the Hudson River Day Line the previous year.

In 1871, Cornell became involved with the Wallkill Valley Railroad, which in 1873 became the first railroad to enter Kingston. In 1875, after the foreclosure and auction of the Rondout & Oswego Railroad (renamed the New York, Kingston & Syracuse Railroad), Thomas Cornell once again assumed control, this time of a reorganized company called the Ulster & Delaware Railroad. Until the end of the decade, Cornell expanded and consolidated his holdings, changing the Wallkill Valley Railroad, which terminated at Rondout, to standard gauge, building repair shops in Rondout, and adding milk cars to the Ulster & Delaware.

At the beginning of the next decade, Cornell determined that the Wallkill Valley Railroad was operating at a loss. Hearing that another railroad planned to lay track to Albany, Cornell announced that his Wallkill Valley Railroad would do the same. As a result, he was able to sell the Wallkill Valley Railroad to its competitor, the West Shore Railroad, at a profit.

In the early 1880s, Cornell entered the burgeoning Catskill Mountain hotel business by backing the building of the Grand Hotel near Pine Hill, one of three large tourist hotels that could be reached by train. In 1881, the Stony Clove & Catskill Mountain Railroad was organized by Cornell, and the following year the Kaaterskill Railroad, to serve the mountain houses situated at North and South Lakes near Haines

Falls, which hitherto could only be reached by stage. In 1884, continuing his building of Catskill Mountain railroads, Cornell created the Hobart Branch Railroad. Finally, in 1890, the year of his death, Cornell divested himself of all steamboat passenger and freight assets, selling them to the Romer and Tremper Steamboat Company of Rondout.

Certainly, Thomas Cornell had been right: In the second half of the nineteenth century, railroads were transforming the country. It was a time of "railroad imperialism" (Cochran, 130). Some people even suggested that the railroads had become the "real government" (Sterne, 15). Between the end of the Civil War and the beginning of the depression in 1873, more than 30,000 miles of new track were opened. By twenty years later, 150,000 miles had been laid. The capital invested in this period was nearly $10 billion (Cochran, 131). In the process, stockholders were hoodwinked, judges and legislators bribed, and enormous profits were obtained. When Cornelius Vanderbilt, the creator of the New York Central Railroad and one of the most famous robber barons of the time, died in 1877, he was worth some $100 million, a shockingly great amount of money at the time (Chamberlain, 144). As Henry Adams would write in his autobiography published in the early twentieth century, it was clear that Americans had "mortgaged" themselves to the railroads (240).

Although many critics of the railroads existed—and with good reason—no one could deny their great importance. For creating markets, stimulating production, and moving people and products quickly and cheaply, no other means of transportation could beat, or even equal them. This fact seemed vividly clear in Rondout.

Since the arrival in Rondout in 1829 of the Stourbridge Lion, interest in the possibilities of the steam locomotive had never completely waned. Although this English engine had proven itself to be too heavy in tests and was subsequently abandoned, there were some Rondouters who remembered fondly the day in July when the Lion, with bright red beast painted on its front, had been transferred from the steamboat *Congress* to the canalboat that would transport it along the newly built D & H Canal to the mines. As early as September 10, 1852, the Rondout *Courier* pointed out that railroads could compete successfully with steamboats, especially in view of disasters such as the sinking of ships like the *Henry Clay*. People no longer expected "floating palaces," the newspaper stated, preferring quick transportation to entertainment. In addition, the vexation of not being able to sail in winter, when the river froze up, inclined many prospective passengers to consider seriously this new means of transport. And so, in Rondout and Kingston by the end of the Civil War, "railway fever" was already well advanced. Clearly, the actions Thomas Cornell undertook between 1866 and 1890 bespoke a bold and decisive response to this impetus.

Of all the railroads that Thomas Cornell owned in his some quarter century of involvement with the "iron horse," it could be argued that the Ulster & Delaware was his favorite, for in the years following the reorganization of the Rondout & Oswego Railroad in 1875, Cornell lavished attention on the U & D. Driving the line farther and farther to the west year after year, building a railroad complex in Rondout—containing facilities such as a yard, round house, turntable, shops, and station—and constantly improving and modernizing its rolling stock, Cornell displayed his strong belief not only in the viability of railroads in general, but also the significance and value of the U & D.

In short order, the U & D became the railroad of the Catskills as well as Rondout. Throughout the year, it kept the economy of the region going. Only five years after the reorganization, Nathaniel Bartlett Sylvester, in the first published history of Ulster County, was to write that the new railroad had been "of great value," not only "affording ready means of travel and freighting," but also "opening up a channel" through which a stream of summer visitors could enter the area (151). More recently, Catskills historian Alf Evers has underscored this fact. "The U & D built up the central Catskills," he writes. "It carried foodstuffs to feed the visitors, and building supplies. . .to be worked into boardinghouses and hotels." It hauled "hides and leather, ice and milk to the Hudson." Trains "carried people from the upcountry to circuses and wild west shows in Kingston; they carried others into the Catskills bound for camp meetings, Sunday school picnics set in shady groves" (*In Catskill Country*, 135-36). Without a doubt, Cornell's railroad "had been a powerful force in shaping the fortunes of one of America's most scenic and romantic regions."(132).

Although it was Thomas Cornell's intention to link the U & D with the Delaware & Hudson Railway in Oneonta, this dream was not to be realized in Cornell's lifetime. It was not until 1900 that the line was completed, making it possible for coal from Pennsylvania—shipped by the D & H Railroad to Oneonta and transshipped by the U & D to Rondout—to reach the Hudson River. In 1913, the U & D registered its peak year in passenger transit with 676,000 people traveling along its rails; in the 1920s, its greatest tonnage in freight was hauled.

Optimism regarding the long-range prospects of the U & D, however, was soon to disappear. For by this time three other railroads met the U & D at Kingston: the New York, West Shore & Buffalo Railroad; the Wallkill Valley Railroad (operated by the New York Central Railway Company); and the New York, Ontario & Western Railroad, which first reached Kingston in 1902. With increased competition, the development of the internal combustion engine, decreased government support, as well as changes in the economy, the U & D could not last. By the 1930s and the beginning of the Great Depression, the U & D declined and then failed. Finally, in 1932, the U & D, once the pride possession of Thomas Cornell, was purchased by the New York Central Railway Company for $2.5 million.

In this regard, the inherent irony of this event is interesting to note. For although it was the success of this new means of transportation that initially brought continued wealth to Rondout and enabled this community to adapt temporarily to a changing commercial scene, it was the railroad that ultimately contributed to Rondout's inevitable decline: When the railroad began to ship more and more freight, it was only a matter of time before the D & H Canal closed. And the canal had *made* Rondout. It had always been the vein, so to speak, through which Rondout's lifeblood had flowed. Consequently, when the economy changed once again during the early twentieth century and American society decided that the railroad had become obsolete, Rondout found itself with nowhere to turn. But in 1890, at the time of the death of Thomas Cornell, things in Rondout looked very fine, indeed.

15 : Castles on the Point

 IT WAS NOT UNTIL 1895, when the vast estate of Thomas Cornell had been settled after lengthy litigation, that the man who was to continue Cornell's financial leadership of Rondout assumed the presidency of the U & D Railroad. From the death of Cornell until this time, Samuel Decker Coykendall, Cornell's son-in-law, had managed Cornell's narrow gauge railroads, as well as his lucrative towing business, called the Cornell Steamboat Company. By the time Coykendall took the reins of the U & D—upon the death of Edwin Young, Cornell's attorney, executor of his estate, and temporary president of the U & D—he had positioned himself well for the task ahead. With complete control of the railroad's stock in his hands at last, the new president promptly placed friends and relatives in key positions, thus assuring that the U & D would become a family enterprise. Samuel's oldest son, Thomas Cornell Coykendall, was elected vice president, son Harry treasurer, and son Frederick and Coykendall's brother, George, became directors. Edward, Coykendall's third son, was made U & D superintendent. According to railroad historian Gerald Best, unaided, the Coykendalls, with Samuel at the head, ran the U & D "for better or for worse" (101).

Once Samuel Coykendall had gained control of the U & D, he extended his paternalistic and personalized management style to all of the Cornell interests. With dispatch, Coykendall initiated a program of coordinated improvements to his steamboat, railroad, and hotel businesses. Among these changes were the replacement of wooden with iron railroad bridges, the building of a new repair shop in Rondout, with powerhouse and electric generator, and the conversion of all narrow gauge railroads to standard gauge by 1899 (103). Most notable to students of Rondout, however, was the project which he undertook between 1893 and 1897 out at the point, just north of where the Rondout Creek debouches into the Hudson River.

Fulfilling the original vision of Horace G. Young, U & D director and brother of Edwin Young, Coykendall purchased this conveniently situated riverside district of Rondout. Here, he built a steamboat landing that could accommodate the ships of the Hudson River Day Line. Prior to this time, these huge steamboats, filled with thousands of tourists, had docked at Rhinecliff across the river, necessitating passengers to take an additional ride on the ferryboat *Transport* (owned by Coykendall) to Rondout, where they would board the U & D for the final leg of their trip to the Catskills. Next, Coykendall extended the tracks of the U & D from central Rondout out to the new landing. Henceforth, tourists could disembark from dayliners, cross a platform, enter the vestibuled or open cars of the U & D, and in an hour or two find themselves breathing the salubrious air of the mountains.

Finally, to the west of the new landing, in what had been for the most part worthless swampland, Coykendall developed an amusement park. This eagerly sought destination, beloved by locals and tourists alike, became known as Kingston Point Park. Although seemingly insignificant in Coykendall's overall plan of improvements, Kingston Point Park was, in fact, an act of genius, for it linked directly the great steamboats of the Hudson River with the hotels in the Catskills in one master stroke. As a result of this inspired business strategy, not only would greater numbers of people travel on the U & D Railroad, but many of these tourists would also vacation at Coykendall's Pine Hill hostelry, the Grand Hotel. In short, by constructing Kingston Point Park, Coykendall placed himself in a very favorable position to take advantage of the contemporary rise in Catskill Mountain tourism.

Originally an uninhabited rocky bluff on the Hudson River backed by marsh and tidal flats, Kingston Point, or Columbus Point as it had been called in the early days of European settlement, was reached at first by boat or by crossing a "pole road laid across the swamp" (Schoonmaker, 470). It was a "tiresome jaunt" by stage, one writer remembers, "frequently very risky to life and limb, as the road in many places was in poor condition, full of holes and precipices" ("Kingston Point Park"). Undoubtedly, Henry Hudson and his crew had noticed this prominent landmark as they sailed up the river in 1609, and it might have been the initial site at which trading had occurred between the Dutch and the Indians in the seventeenth century. The Livingstons, a large, wealthy, and land-rich family who lived across the river almost within sight of the point, seem to have been its first recorded owners. By the eighteenth century, a small ferry plied its way back and forth across the Hudson to Rhinecliff from the point.

About this time, title to the land was transferred from the Livingstons to a most interesting and eccentric man. The grandson of a Frenchman who had immigrated from Bordeaux, Moses Cantine was to take the first steps of the long transformation of Columbus Point.

In 1796, when Moses Cantine learned that a toll road was to be built linking Columbus Point with the Delaware River, his excitement ran high. Certainly, few local entrepreneurs were more enthusiastic about the proposed road's prospects than he. Responding promptly to the good news, Cantine directed Christopher Tappan to survey, map, and lay out in lots and streets the environs of Columbus Point. Hoping to benefit by his strategic location on the new Ulster and Delaware Turnpike, as it was to be called, Moses' vision was to create what might be considered Ulster County's first housing subdivision. By 1802, when the state legislature finally incorporated the turnpike, Cantine had sold a number of lots and had built himself a large, two-story mansion of stone. A few of his purchasers also followed suit, constructing dwellings of a more modest nature at the point. To Cantine's great disappointment, however, the development was not a success, for although the turnpike was built to the point, it never prospered, and soon went bankrupt.

By 1820, writes one local historian, a visitor to the point would have observed only "some seven or eight stone houses, at least one half of them unoccupied and falling in ruins." (Schoonmaker, 470). "Although founded on rocks," writes the reporter, Cantine's "airy castles had crumbled. . .as if their foundation had been nothing but sand" (470). Yet, although Moses Cantine's idea had been a bit ahead of its time, his imagination and foresight *had* actually initiated the first extensive activity at the point, and so he must be given credit for this. Nonetheless, in 1857, the site of Cantine's abortive housing development was purchased by the D & H Canal Company. In subsequent years, a dock and office, which burned in 1886, as well as a small, private boatyard, were erected there. By the time Samuel Decker Coykendall purchased the land in 1893, much of the point had begun to return to its original state.

Considered by some to be the place where Captain Kidd had buried his treasure, the point during the nineteenth century never completely lost an aura of mystery. On January 14, 1853, for example, the Rondout *Courier* reported that a "brace of sturdy fellows" had been seen digging at the point. One of these strange men, it was said, had pulled a book from his pocket and had written something in an exotic mixture of Dutch and English. Although, by all accounts, Kidd's booty was never found at the point and the piratical legend associated with the place was eventually forgotten, Kingston Point Park nonetheless yielded another less romantic sort of treasure: For its owner, Samuel Decker Coykendall, it was for a time a not inconsiderable source of income.

The project at Columbus Point, however, did not advance as quickly as Coykendall had intended. Although by 1893 he held the deed to most of the land where British soldiers had come ashore in 1777 and where Moses Cantine had attempted his unsuccessful housing subdivision, Coykendall did not own all the land he needed. And even though much of the area was swampy, considered a "slough of mud and despond," its value skyrocketed when Coykendall's plan to extend the railroad out to the point became known (Schneider). As a result, Coykendall's efforts were stalled temporarily when landowners, whose acreage sat in the path of the proposed track, held out for higher prices. Ultimately, however, after lengthy negotiations and with the assistance of the Kingston Board of Trade, the matter was resolved to Coykendall's satisfaction. Thus, by the summer of 1896, Coykendall had converted the old D & H Canal Company wharf at the point into a suitable landing place for steamboats, and the new railroad track had been laid. Work then could begin on the park to the west.

Although nearly a century had passed since Moses Cantine had first envisaged constructing "castles" on the point, it would take Samuel Decker Coykendall only about a year to realize Moses' dream. Born in Wantage, New Jersey on May 28, 1837, Samuel Decker Coykendall's beginnings were surprisingly humble compared to the wealth, position and power he would command in his later years. Commencing his working life as a clerk in a general store in Port Jervis, New York, on the D & H Canal, Coykendall came to Rondout in 1859 after having proven himself in a dry goods emporium in Newburgh, and as a result having been promoted to the managership of a branch store in Rondout. In 1862, at the age of twenty-five, Coykendall enlisted in the 156th Infantry Regiment, which was organized in Kingston, leaving the area in December to fight in the Civil War. While with the 156th, Coykendall served as its quartermaster and later as a member of the staff of Gen. Nathaniel P. Banks during the Red River Campaign. Undoubtedly, the experience he gained during the war in obtaining and transporting large quantities of supplies aided Coykendall when he returned to Rondout in the spring of 1865, for he was quick to take advantage of his new knowledge and prestige as a war veteran. Within the year, Coykendall had married the daughter of Thomas Cornell, Mary Augusta, five years his junior, and had become a partner in the Cornell firm. From this day forth, Samuel Decker Coykendall's course was set and his future secure.

Bright, able, hardworking and ambitious, by the late 1860s Coykendall had perfected his business skills well. And Thomas Cornell, a good judge of men, had noticed this fact, and made Coykendall a director and vice president of his many enterprises. Placing increasing trust in Coykendall and bestowing greater and greater responsibility on him, during his second term in Congress (beginning in 1881), Cornell made Coykendall his primary deputy in Rondout and kept in constant contact with him. Temporarily assuming the presidency of all Cornell's railroads and his steamboat company, Coykendall ran these operations successfully. Thus, when Thomas Cornell died in the winter of 1890, Coykendall, the heir apparent, had already sat in Cornell's throne.

By 1895, Coykendall had taken firm control of what had been Cornell's interests. In later years, Coykendall would add to these extensive holdings. Among his many and diverse acquisitions would be the Rosendale Cement Company, the Colonial Trolley line, the Kingston *Daily Freeman* (which he acquired and ran during the 1880s), heavy interests in the local ice and bluestone industries, and even the D & H Canal, to list only a few. In addition, Coykendall would obtain large tracts of wild and picturesque land deep in the Catskills, creating a private preserve for himself and his family at Alder Lake in the town of Hardenburgh in the far western corner of Ulster County.

In his three decades of management of the Cornell-Coykendall family enterprises and in his deep involvement in the political and economic life of Ulster County, Samuel Decker Coykendall was without rival or peer. Although he seems to have avoided publicity and was reticent about revealing the facts of his personal life, refusing to appear in the biographical sections of the standard histories of Ulster County (Sylvester, 1880; Clearwater, 1907), as well as its *Commemorative Biographical Record* (1896) and directory of *Representative Business Men* (1892), there were few people in the area who had not heard of Coykendall or whose lives had not in some way been touched by him. Slight of frame but erect in carriage, with penetrating eyes and the suppressed intensity and concentration of a sparrowhawk, Ulster County's "leading citizen" was a man whom some hated and others feared (*The Hundred Year Book*, 169). According to one source, Coykendall "had the power to kill anyone financially," and at times, he did just this (Dwyer).

In addition to his vast transportation, mining and lodging interests, Coykendall was also involved in local finance, maintaining a prominent presence in both Rondout banks. A personal friend of Governor Charles Evans Hughes, Coykendall was courted three times by the Republican Party to run for state and national public office—for governor and for U. S. senator. In each case, he refused. Tough-minded, determined and ruthless in competition, Coykendall found the *laissez-faire* conditions and relaxed business ethics of the time perfectly suited to his temperament.

Swift to pursue his own needs and to defend his interests, Coykendall often took decisive action. When he discovered that a stop on the U & D Railroad at the Fair Street Extension in uptown Kingston was not making money, he petitioned the city to eliminate this station. The city rejected Coykendall's appeal, however, and his attorney, A. T. Clearwater, counseled against taking any action. Nonetheless, in typical Coykendall fashion, the president of the U & D took the matter into his own hands: On a quiet Sunday morning, while Kingston slept or attended church, Coykendall directed his train crew to hook a locomotive to the little frame building that served as uptown's station. In a matter of minutes, this uneconomical stop disappeared from the U & D's run. Comparing Coykendall to the industrialist Henry Ford in the defense of his property, a younger contemporary wrote, "I never knew two men more alike." (De Witt, 71).

Coykendall could also be outspoken in his opposition to projects that he believed threatened not only his own but also the public's interest. For years he prevented the City of Kingston from altering the railroad tracks where they crossed Union Avenue (De Witt, 69-70). He strongly opposed the construction of the Ashokan Reservoir, speaking at the public hearing held in Kingston in 1906 (Steuding, 32). And he even prevented the development of an open-air sanatorium for tubercular patients in Phoenicia, declaring that such a facility would decrease the number of tickets sold on the U & D and also lower property values (Evers, *Catskills*, 674-75; 710). Coykendall's close-fisted competitiveness is probably best exhibited in a statement he is reported to have made in regard to the competition between Rondout and Kingston. Expressing himself with unusual candor and feeling, Coykendall declared, "We'll have grass growing on Wall Street" (Shultz).

Although Coykendall could be a man of daunting will and self-interest, he was not without his public-spirited and philanthropic side. For many years, Coykendall served as a trustee of Vassar College, an institution which, at the time, enrolled only women. He also was known to donate generously to a number of civic projects, including the exhumation and reburial of the remains of George Clinton in Kingston and the erection of a monument to Thomas Chambers in Montrepose Cemetery. In September 1911, he even put a special train "at the service" of the members of the New York Historical Association who were meeting in Kingston. The train took these dignitaries up to the site of the Ashokan Reservoir, which was under construction at the time (*Brink*, 7: 308).

Coykendall was also known to pay his debts punctually and without hesitation. The same man who compared Coykendall to Henry Ford was bound to acknowledge that Coykendall "paid on the dot and liberally" (De Witt, 71). Coykendall, remembers this individual, was also a genuinely reasonable man and the "easiest millionaire" for one to gain an interview with. An appointment was not necessary; after a short wait outside his private office at 22 Ferry Street in Rondout, Coykendall would see anyone. "He was always there, too," adds this source (71). A family man and typical late-Victorian, Coykendall and his wife Mary produced seven children: Thomas, Harry, Edward, Frank, Robert, Frederick, and Katherine, who, according to one contemporary source, were "all fine people, well-educated and considerate" (Spangenberger).

When Samuel Decker Coykendall died unexpectedly on January 14, 1913, at his home at 90 West Chestnut Street, the Cornell-Coykendall empire was at its highest point: Passenger travel on the U & D would reach its zenith during this year, with a new line of track north of the Ashokan Reservoir being turned over to the railroad in June; the Cornell Steamboat Company would hold a virtual monopoly on the transportation of freight up and down the Hudson River, with hundreds of barges being towed every day; and, with a few exceptions, Coykendall's other investments would do well, too.

Sadly, however, the Cornell-Coykendall dynasty would end with Samuel's death. For his sons, although able in many ways, lacked their elders' shrewdness and aptitude for business, and thus were unable to deal successfully with drastically changing political and economic conditions. Within a few years after Coykendall's death, the predominance in Rondout and the county that he and Thomas Cornell had established and maintained for over half a century began to decline. By the time of the "crash" and the advent of the 1930s, the house of Cornell-Coykendall no longer held sway.

Back in early 1897, however, nearly two decades before his death, Samuel Decker Coykendall's plans for Kingston Point Park were nearly complete. The land, which had been deserted for some time and become overgrown, wild with brush and weeds, was cleared and landscaped. Downing Vaux, the noted landscape artist who had created Downing Park in Newburgh and Riverside Drive in New York City, was hired by Coykendall to design his new park. Vaux, the son of Calvert Vaux (together with Frederick Law Olmstead and others, Vaux designed New York City's Central Park), developed a plan in which brick paths wove throughout the park, and gardens, containing interesting plants, delighted visitors and refreshed them. Each path was assigned a bucolic name, such as Ulster Ledge Path, Over-knoll Walk, Briarwood Path, Mulberry Path, Piney Ridge Path and Shadow Walk to Shadow Bay (Ringwald, *Hudson River Day Line*, 90). Coykendall spared no expense in making Kingston Point Park a beautiful and pleasant place to spend a day. A sandy bathing beach was prepared where visitors could wade or swim; there were shady places to picnic, and lagoons were created where one could rent a boat. In one of these placid bodies of water a bandstand had been erected on a man-made island, called Harmony Island. The site of afternoon and evening concerts, this gazebo looked like a Chinese pagoda, or like a structure one might see floating in a pond in the Forbidden City in Peking. There was a merry-go-round on the hill, with horses named for heroes of the Spanish-American War after 1898. Coykendall even provided for his guests an example of the newly invented Ferris wheel, which had just been introduced to thrill-seeking Americans at Chicago's Columbian Exposition. Near the river could be found a large, open-air casino, where patrons could dance or enjoy the penny arcade and shooting gallery.

A two-story pavilion stood proudly at the landing. The first sight of the park one noticed when approaching from the river, this long, graceful structure was crowned by matching peaked observation towers. Between these points, in tall capital letters, stretched the words "Kingston Point Park." Downstairs, light refreshments were sold, and on the second floor a large space was set aside for eating. Conveniently located for day line passengers, the U & D Railroad station perched adjacent to this pavilion.

Probably the most memorable building at the park for locals, however, was the plaza, or trolley station. Here, eager citizens from Rondout and Kingston disembarked from packed streetcars on hot summer evenings. In 1897, a trip from Washington Avenue in Kingston to the park cost only five cents. At night, the park was brightly lit with electric lights—the electricity provided by the park's own generators. In this regard, one observer remembers: "Words would fail to portray the wonderous beauty. . . . The electric and incandescent lights made a solid mass of fire in all imaginable colors. . . . There is nothing that can 'hold a candle to it' " ("Kingston Point Park").

To the north of the park and outside its confines could be found the clubhouse and dock of the Rondout Yacht Club. In later years, humorously called the I.J.B. Club, or an organization to which Irish, Jewish, and "Binnewaters," or everyone else, no matter how rich or poor, could belong, the club's headquarters were situated near a large wooden icehouse and the Oriental Hotel, which echoed the Chinese motif of the park bandstand and surmounted the bluff. Once safely outside Coykendall's park, one might purchase an alcoholic drink at this famous hotel owned by a local brewery (Steuding, Robert; Woods, 29).

It is a shame that Kingston Point Park had not yet been constructed when photographer and author of *Picturesque Ulster*, Richard Lionel De Lisser, visited Ulster County in 1896. For although many interesting photographs and postcards exist today that amply document the life of this fragile and short-lived park, it would have been interesting to have seen this locale through the eyes of such a talented artist. On his "ramble through the county," as he called his photographic excursion, De Lisser offers us a seat beside him in his buggy and comments on the passing scene (5). As evidenced by the extensive portfolio of perceptive photographs De Lisser took of Rondout itself prior to the establishment of the park, it is not unrealistic to suggest that he might have produced a unique and distinctive view of the park, one that could be of considerable interest to us today.

Although Coxey's ragtag "army" had marched on Washington, D.C., in 1894, and four years later a four-month Spanish-American "war" had been fought, the period in which the Kingston Point Park was developed was, for the most part, a more genteel time than our own. It was an era before radio, television and cinema changed the manner in which Americans spent their leisure hours, a time when candidates like the profoundly proper William McKinley would be elected president, defeating the dynamic, populist orator from Nebraska, William Jennings Bryan. In short, it was a moment in history when people flocked to "pleasure-grounds" such as Kingston Point Park. On Sundays and holidays during the first two decades of the twentieth century, this popular park nearly burst at the seams. Many families came for the day from cities up and down the river and returned home in the late afternoon on specially scheduled day liners. As river historian Donald Ringwald wrote, "If all the members of the Sunday Schools and graduating classes from the Albany area who made the pilgrimage to Kingston Point. . .were gathered in one spot, they would form an army of formidable proportions" (*Hudson River Day Line*, 90). Coykendall charged no admission fee to Kingston's only public park at the time, and many people took advantage of his generosity; in 1903, for example, more than one million railroad passengers arrived at the park. And although the average daily attendance at the park was about 3,000, on the July 4, 1903, more than nine times that number visited the park (Woods, 29).

Kingston Point Park also became the scene of two important public celebrations. On May 29, 1908, the remains of hero and statesman George Clinton were brought ashore at Kingston Point, a flotilla of U.S. Navy ships attending. And the following year ceremonies were conducted at the point in commemoration of the maritime contributions of Henry Hudson and Robert Fulton. At this time, the river was "full of ships including replicas of the *Half Moon* and the *Clermont*" (Woods, 33).

Many visitors to the park remember it with affection. Philip H. Du Bois, in his memoir *A Catskills Boyhood*, recalls fondly that "youngsters" from Catskill often celebrated their birthdays by being "taken on an excursion to Kingston Point" (73). Donald Ringwald describes the park as "attractive" and "splendid." Even today, he wrote in 1965, mention in Albany of the word Kingston "inevitably kindles happy recollections of Kingston Point" (*Hudson River Day Line*, 90). Ralph Caterino of Kingston, who grew up in Ponckhockie near Kingston Point, recollects watching children dive for coins thrown by steamboat passengers at the day line dock (Caterino). And Kingston resident and notable collector of local memorabilia, John Matthews, also remembers the park, as he did in a 1985 interview in the Kingston *Daily Freeman*: "We used to go to the trolley stand and carry bags for extra money," he states. "It was exciting as a child to see the day liners."

In his interesting and informative books about the day line and the history of steamboating on the Hudson River, Donald Ringwald has painted a clear and vibrant picture of the bright maritime heritage, not only of the river but also of Rondout and Kingston Point. A most gracious and elegant mode of travel, the steamboat of the late nineteenth and early twentieth centuries effectively symbolized the acme of Rondout's fame, affluence and power, dramatically representing the era when Rondout was considered one of the most important ports of call on the Hudson River. Although Thomas Cornell had believed that the halcyon days of the steamboat had passed with the coming of the railroad after the Civil War, these great, "floating palaces" continued to be constructed and sailed, to the delight of their many passengers, well into the twentieth century.

Among the many ships operated by the Hudson River Day Line in its 122 years of service—the *Daniel Drew*, the *Armenia*, the *Chauncey Vibbard*, the *Albany*, the *New York*, the *Hendrick Hudson*, the *Robert Fulton*, the *De Witt Clinton*, the *Alexander Hamilton*, the *Chauncey M. Depew*, the *Peter Stuyvesant*, and the *Mary Powell*—the *Washington Irving* was the largest and one of the most luxurious. Built in 1912 to a length of about 400 feet, this ship, sporting three smokestacks and four decks above water, could carry as many as six thousand passengers. One of these lucky individuals remembers this steamboat as being a veritable "giant." It had "every imaginable extra, lounge chairs indoors and deck chairs outside, space for picnics, a. . .dining room with huge windows, an orchestra, and a continuous panoply of views on either side of the river" (Du Bois, 73).

Most everyone's favorite steamboat, however, seems to have been the *Mary Powell*, the "Queen of the Hudson," as she was respectfully called. Constructed in Jersey City in 1861 for Captain Absalom Anderson, she was lengthened an additional twenty-one feet in the following year. Operated by a subsidiary of the Hudson River Day Line from 1903 to 1917, during her mature and more dignified years this "family boat" traveled daily except Sunday between Rondout and New York, and later Albany. Although considerably smaller than the *Washington Irving*, this sidewheel craft was for a time one of the fastest boats on the river. Making the round trip in approximately fourteen hours, passengers could leave Rondout at 6 A.M. and reach New York by 11. Leaving New York at 3:30 P.M., these same travelers could step ashore in Rondout by about 8 P.M. Ridden by such notables as President Ulysses S. Grant, J. P. Morgan, the Grand Duke Alexis of Russia, Oscar Wilde, and Walt Whitman, the *Mary Powell* was known not only for her speed, reliability and record of safety, but also for her trim, graceful lines. During the early twentieth century, she was completely overhauled, and in her last two of fifty-nine seasons, the *Mary Powell* inaugurated "Saturday Specials" between New York and Albany. On these trips, her first stop after Yonkers was Kingston Point Park. Observing the *Mary Powell* pass his Esopus estate, Riverby, on its way northward, the naturalist John Burroughs is said to have remarked, alluding to the ship's long white wake, "There goes Mary rustling her skirts" (Benson, "Watching the Steamboats Go By," 12). When the *Mary Powell* made her final run with passengers on September 5, 1917, and was later sold for scrap, many people were heartbroken. Capt. William O. Benson recalls the sadness his father, who had served as a carpenter on the *Mary Powell*, felt at this time. Benson writes, "to him, like many others, the *Mary Powell* was more than a steamboat. He thought of her almost as a person" ("The Last of the Mary Powell at Port Ewen," 2).

A single journey on a steamboat, or the sight or sound of one, could become a memorable event, never to be forgotten during an entire lifetime. In his entry for July 1, 1847, Nathaniel Booth, who was returning by steamboat to Rondout from New York, described his trip rhapsodically in his diary:

> Every mile now brings us nearer home and opens to the sight some familiar objects—the Palisades are passed and now the Highlands loom into view—I am truly on the beautiful Hudson again though I can scarce believe it. . . . Our boat glides like an arrow through the quiet stream.

Thirteen years later, an equally enthusiastic steamboat traveler would exclaim in the Rondout *Courier* on August 17, 1860, "give me a Steamer before a railway car." anytime. Remarking on the cleanliness and perfect order of the steamboat *North America*, commanded by Capt. Jacob Tremper, this "veteran-traveler" stated with the assurance of long experience, "the steamers between Rondout and New York are better calculated for the real comfort and enjoyment of travelers, than any on the Hudson." Another man remembered how, as a young boy living along the banks of the Hudson in Cornwall, he had paddled his canoe out toward the great leviathans so that he might ride the wash created by their huge, churning paddlewheels (Martin). Yet another man recalled how, as a child, he had heard the music from riverboat orchestras float across the water as he lay in bed on hot summer nights (Smith, Alonzo). One local author recalled an overnight trip on the *James W. Baldwin*: "Oh what fun," he wrote, sitting down to a "special dinner," as the boat left Rondout harbor (De Witt, 67). Susan P. Hasbrouck, reminiscing about her Ponckhockie childhood, recalled the great "searching" light of the *Mary Powell*, as it reached the mouth of the Rondout Creek. In winter, she related, she and her friends would skate out to the *Mary Powell* on the flats and warm themselves at the woodstove of its friendly caretaker (1; 5-8). Children occasionally even stowed away on riverboats. Clearly, the romance of the steamboat is profound, and the response of many individuals to its spell is incalculable.

Carrying on the great tradition of Rondout steamboating and steamboat families were Thomas Cornell, Absalom L. Anderson, William F. Romer, and Jacob H. Tremper. Thomas Cornell we have met; Capt. Absalom Anderson became famous as the builder, occasional owner, and captain of the *Mary Powell*.

Born in Croton during the War of 1812, Anderson married Catherine Eltinge, the daughter of a physician who practiced in Rondout, and settled with her near Port Ewen in a home called Fair View, which commanded a sweeping view of the Hudson River and can be seen in Beers' 1875 *County Atlas of Ulster New York* (49). In 1882, after many seasons on the Hudson, Capt. Anderson sold his interest in the *Mary Powell*, retired from steamboating, and moved to California. His two sons, Capt. Jansen H. and Capt. A. Eltinge Anderson, however, continued the family connection with steamboating. Stepping into his father's shoes, A. Eltinge Anderson captained the *Mary Powell* for twenty-eight of its remaining seasons. In 1895, the father of this line of distinguished Rondout steamboat captains died in Santa Barbara, as a result of being thrown from a cart drawn by a horse. Anderson was nearly 83 years of age at the time.

A bit younger than Cornell, Anderson, and Tremper, who were about the same age, William F. Romer, who was born in 1822, was a bank cashier in Kingston when he resigned and became a partner in the steamboat line of Anderson, Romer and Company in 1848. A man of impressive financial talents, William Romer remained ashore and ably managed this steamboat company. In the next decade, Romer joined forces with the man whose practical nautical skills and maritime acumen, combined with Romer's own fiscal ability, would create a Rondout steamboat company of significance. The co-owner of this enterprise, known as Romer & Tremper, was Jacob H. Tremper.

Tremper, born in Kingston in the same year as Absalom Anderson, was one of the great steamboat captains of Rondout. Commanding for a time in the 1830s the *Congress*, the first passenger steamboat in Rondout, Tremper soon made his presence felt in the developing world of river transportation. By 1847, Tremper was in business for himself, having taken charge of the steam barge *Ulster County*, which ran from Rondout to New York. In the 1850s, he joined with William Romer and began his long and successful career as entrepreneur and captain of his own Hudson River steamers. The major rival of Thomas Cornell's line of freight and passenger steamboats at the time, Romer & Tremper had built and then sailed a number of popular night boats during the second part of the nineteenth century. Among these craft were the *James W. Baldwin*, commissioned in 1861, and the *North America*, which it replaced. Both these ships were commanded personally by Tremper for many years. The first of the classic Rondout steamboat captains to pass away, Jacob Tremper died far from his beloved Hudson River in 1888, during the winter of the "great blizzard."

Since August 17, 1807, and the trip of Robert Fulton up the Hudson in his *North River Steam Boat*, or the *Clermont* as it was later called, and since the dramatic entrance into Rondout Harbor in 1826 of the first steamboat, the *New London*, followed in 1829 by the arrival of the *Congress*, steamboats have played a significant role in the history of the port. The music of their whistles, the black smoke puffing from their big stacks, their brightly-painted hulls have become synonymous with Rondout. Rondouters have set their clocks by the arrivals and departures of the great steamboats. They watched the Cornell steamers *Pittston* and *Norwich* pull long tows of canal boats up the creek to the tidewater lock at Eddyville. Many locals spent their lives working on the boat or earned their livelihoods in related industries. James F. Dwyer, for example, whose parents had come from Ireland, bought his first canal boat in 1876 at the age of sixteen, and eventually accumulated a large fleet. In later years, he would open a ship's chandlery in Rondout, as well as enter other businesses such as brick-making, ice-cutting, and boatbuilding. In addition to Dwyer, Rondout names such as Allen, Everson, Williams, King, Gokey, Christie, Mc Causland, Hiltebrant, and Feeney, as well as "Island Dock," are all associated with the ancient and noble art of building, fitting out, and repairing water craft.

In Rondout, sloops and schooners were built during the first years. Canal boats, barges, small steamboats, lighters and scows followed. And finally, ocean-going rescue tugs, minesweepers, submarine chasers, and landing craft were constructed during the Korean and the two world wars. In World War I, one of the largest wooden steam freighters ever produced was launched in South Rondout. Possessing a 3,500-ton capacity, the *Esopus* was designed and built of wood in order to conserve steel. Even some of the boilers of the grandest Hudson River day liners were made in Rondout. In 1866, for example, John Dillon, husband of painter Julia Dillon, installed new boilers in the *Mary Powell*. Once again, in 1880, his company, now called the Rondout Iron Works, owned by McEntee & Dillon, replaced the aging iron boilers of the "Queen of the Hudson" with ones made of steel; in 1890, the job was done in Rondout another time by the same company, now called the McEntee and Rodie Boiler Works. James Rodie, the new partner, was the inventor of the Rodie steam heater. This company also fabricated many of Kingston and Rondout's cast-iron storefronts.

Truly, from the opening of the D & H Canal, and even earlier, the sights, smells, and sounds of shipbuilding have been extant in Rondout. According to local historian and steamboat authority Roger Mabie,

> For a full century, a prodigious number of vessels first became waterbourne on the Rondout. The ring of the caulker's mallet, the whine of the band saw, the thud of the bull gang's mauls against wedges on launching day, the smell of freshly cut yellow pine, the odor of oakum and hot pitch, and the humid aroma of steam escaping from the large steam boxes used to make timbers pliable. . .were once as common along Rondout Creek as the rise and fall of the tide ("The Hudson River Port of Rondout," 14).

16 : Dear Old Rondout

 LIKE THE HUDSON'S TIDE flowing in and then out, Rondout's "salad days" were not to last. For from its beginnings, Rondout's dynamism and its ability to adapt to changing conditions had been fundamental to its very existence. When these qualities ebbed in the late nineteenth century, Rondout's position in the commercial Northeast began to decline. Long before the difficult days of the Depression, things in Rondout had taken a turn for the worse. Some might trace this turning point to that fateful day in 1872 when Kingston and Rondout merged and the momentum of Rondout's municipal thrust was checked. Others point to the closing of the D & H Canal.

Although no surprise to anyone, the closing of the D & H Canal in 1898, during the second season of Kingston Point Park, marked the end of Rondout's greatest years. Without fanfare or ceremony, as had been the case in 1828, the ditch that seventy years earlier had created lucrative markets, drawn a large and willing labor supply to Rondout and inspired considerable entrepreneurial talent, was terminated with regret, but with little protest. As early as 1881, the canal company had publicly announced that the abandonment of the canal was imminent. And Thomas Cornell, who sat on its board, petitioned the state legislature to allow canal companies to construct and to operate railroads along or in the right of way of canals. By 1891, the D & H Canal had become so unprofitable, being superseded by railroads that could carry freight more quickly, cheaply, and in all seasons, that boatmen formed a committee and asked the company for assistance. In 1853, New York State canals moved over a billion tons of freight, and in 1863, a billion and one-half. Yet, within twenty years, railroads were doing double this amount of business. And by the mid-1890s, canals were carrying less freight than they were back in 1853, and railroads were moving thirteen times as much (Hacker, 44). In 1894, the company laid off 150 boats. Finally, on November 5, 1898, the last shipment of coal left Honesdale in Boat No. 1107 for Rondout.

The following year, Samuel Decker Coykendall purchased the entire canal at auction. The canal, which had built Rondout and brought untold millions to its inhabitants, sold for the unbelievable sum of $10,000. Even more surprising is the fact that Coykendall was the only individual to tender a bid. Subsequently, the D & H Canal was operated in part for a few more seasons in order to accommodate Coykendall's cement mines in Rosendale (Wakefield, *Coal Boats to Tidewater*, 200). But finally, Coykendall sold sections of the canal to the New York Ontario & Western Railroad in 1901, and in 1904 abandoned the canal and shipped his cement by rail (Best, 113). In 1899, the D & H Canal Company reorganized and quietly changed its name to the D & H Company. This new corporation promptly purchased the Albany & Susquehanna Railroad and ironically, without pause or reservation, entered the railroad business itself.

The "most important factor" in the prosperity of Kingston and Rondout, writes A. T. Clearwater, had been the construction of the D & H Canal (*History of Ulster County*, 221). As a result of its creation, trade increased and the growth of commerce was "greatly enhanced" (221). Rondout "owed its development almost entirely" to the opening of the canal (221). And when the canal outlived its usefulness and was abandoned, it was "a sad blow" for the area, he writes (222). Unwilling to end this discussion on a pessimistic note, however, Clearwater adds that although Rondout was no longer "wholly dependent" on the canal, the harbor remained active (222).

Nonetheless, although Rondout did remain "active" to a certain extent, by the time these words were written in 1907 even the most myopic booster of Rondout could see the handwriting on the wall. Without a doubt, life in Rondout was different. For one thing, the many vital, local industries which had supported Rondout for so long were failing, and they would vanish, leaving faint trace in the coming years. Bluestone was no longer used for sidewalks and ornamental work, and Rosendale cement, mined along a ridge from north of Rondout to Rosendale in the south, was gradually being replaced by Portland cement. Although Rosendale cement was cheaper and set well under water, Portland was stronger and dried more quickly. Samuel Decker Coykendall, who owned much of the local cement works by the turn of the century, experimented at great cost to make Portland, a mix of rocks, clays and shales, at Rosendale. This last-ditch attempt to save the local cement business was unsuccessful, however, and in due time, the loss of yet another source of income in Rondout ensued (Evers, *The Catskills*, 574).

Within a few years, ice-cutting and brick-making also declined and then disappeared along the Hudson with the depletion of the clay banks, the change in building materials and techniques, and the introduction into American households of electricity and refrigeration. Even the major modes of transportation—the railroad and the steamboat—were threatened. In 1917, the most famous Hudson River passenger steamboat, the *Mary Powell*, was decommissioned, sold for scrap in 1919, and later broken up. To the surprise and horror of Rondouters, the demise of this once beautiful steamboat was observed every day as she was rudely dismantled across the creek. Although the day line would enjoy its most successful year in 1925, with two million passengers riding its steamboats, its days of greatness were past. For changes in lifestyle and the manner in which Americans recreated and spent their vacations, as well as the development of the automobile, soon made the steamboat seem antiquated. To many, it began to appear like some quaint and genteel throwback to a bygone time.

An even more significant sign of Rondout's decline was the fate of the U & D Railroad. During the first years of the 1930s, as mentioned previously, this carrier, which had helped to make the canal obsolete, itself went bankrupt and was sold. In 1932, the New York Central Railroad, which purchased the U & D, closed its shops in Rondout. To add insult to injury, a noted local political figure, Judge Alton B. Parker, was defeated in the presidential election of 1904, taking only 29 percent of the electoral vote and losing New York State. The winner and incumbent, Theodore Roosevelt, concerned with international affairs, looked elsewhere than Rondout and the Hudson River Valley for his field of action. The defeat of Judge Parker, who maintained a residence in West Park a few miles south of Rondout, suggests this shift of interest in the country at the time. It seemed to many, and with good reason, that the Hudson Valley and Rondout, which had enjoyed such prominence in the nineteenth century, were being left behind.

Even Kingston Point Park's days were numbered. The final flowering of optimism concerning Rondout's future, and one of its last, major expressions of entrepreneurial imagination and vision, Kingston Point Park's popularity began to recede in the 1920s. In 1922, the Oriental Hotel burned to the ground, as if to herald the beginning of the end. The previous year, Rondout's beloved chain ferry, the *Skillypot*, had been retired when a suspension bridge was completed over the creek from the foot of Wurts Street. Then, Downing Vaux, who had designed Kingston Point Park, jumped to his death from an upstairs window of the Y.M.C.A. Clearly, change was in the wind.

In 1931, the amusement center at Kingston Point closed. In due time, the railroad ceased its service to the point. In 1936, the D & H Company office in Rondout was dismantled. And on September 13, 1948, the day liner *Robert Fulton* made the last regular steamboat landing at Kingston Point.

Then, as the second half of the century dawned, the event which everyone had thought impossible occurred. After over 100 years of activity, a Rondout institution came to an end: In 1958, the oldest continually existing business in Rondout, the Cornell Steamboat Company, was purchased by New York Trap Rock and its assets sold. By 1965, when Cornell Steamboat was discontinued by its succeeding owners, Lone Star Industries and Martin-Marietta, its revered name, synonymous with that of Rondout since 1847, had begun to fade from the minds of most local women and men. Only a small public park, donated by the grandchildren of Thomas Cornell and situated adjacent to the site of the family mansion on Wurts Street, along with a street in central Kingston, remain to perpetuate the Cornell name. Today, when one hears the word Cornell in Ulster County, most likely one thinks of the university and not the man or the company by which Rondout was made. In the upper level of Cornell Park, a monument has been erected to veterans of the World War II. At its top, almost unnoticed, an eagle proudly sits. Removed from a Cornell tugboat, this memento of past vigor and enterprise reminds those who remember old Rondout of the brilliance of its early "glory days" (Mabie, 14).

During the 1950s, Rondout continued its long decline. Another bridge was built, this time across the Hudson to the north, and the ferry from Rondout to Rhinecliff was decommissioned, further isolating Rondout and removing it from the mainstream. Fires swept through sections of Rondout, and once-impressive buildings became vacant and fell into disrepair. Although the Kingston *Daily Freeman* continued to be published in Rondout, and two banks, a branch post office, as well as a few commercial establishments, such as Yallum's clothing store, Weber's Pharmacy, and Forst's Packing Company continued to survive, many businesses began to leave Rondout for more desirable locations in midtown. Stock and Cordts, a renowned quality furniture store, had already vacated its historic building in 1942, moving to central Broadway. Some religious congregations sold their places of worship and left, also. In 1946, the large, late Victorian structure on Wurts and Abeel Streets owned by the Rondout Presbyterian Congregation was disposed of and later demolished. Little by little, fleeing the decay and despair, the population of Rondout was moving out.

As early as 1929, the writer H. P. Lovecraft had described Rondout as a "somewhat picturesque slum" (338). By the 1960s, there was no longer the possibility of doubt. In addition to the presence of many empty and boarded up buildings, derelict ships rotted in the creek and junkyards lined the Strand. Rondout even became the place where Kingston's sewage was sent. Out at Kingston Point, oil tanks perched on the bluff where the Oriental Hotel had stood. And although a new lighthouse had been built at the mouth of the Rondout Creek in 1913, it was vacant, too. Like an old person living alone in shabby circumstances, Rondout was quickly being forgotten.

Remembering life in Rondout during better times, Susan Hasbrouck wrote in 1964 that old Rondout was "a far cry from the Rondout of today. The gracious homes and gardens have largely disappeared, passenger boats have gone from the Hudson, [and] Kingston Point has become an overgrown wilderness."(8). Extolling the delights of early Rondout, songwriter and Rondout native J. W. Barton wrote in "Dear Old Rondout," "There's a place of fond remembrance 'tis the spot where I was born/ When the flow'rs of May were blooming did the forest path adorn./ It is some miles from old New York/ A place you all do know/ And they call it dear old Rondout where the Hudson River flows."

Thus, Rondout was ripe for what, in the 1960s, became known as urban renewal. As early as 1955, however, when the Orpheum Theatre finally closed its doors, urban development of some sort had been considered for Rondout. By 1959, in response to this pressing civic concern, the City of Kingston had engaged the services of Raymond & May Associates, a professional planning firm; by 1961, Raymond & May had completed a "Comprehensive Development Plan" for Kingston and a "Marketability and Land Utilization Study" for the "Rondout General Neighborhood Area." In this study, Raymond & May described in graphic terms the "setbacks" from which, they believed, Rondout had "never recovered."(6). The area, they reported, "presently houses a substantial portion of low income groups." In addition, "retail trade is at a minimum; most wholesaling functions have disappeared; and the greatest percentage of the building inventory is either physically or environmentally substandard" (6). A considerable number of Rondouters were found to live in "tenements," which one researcher remarked were in "deplorable condition" (Shuster). In a total, habitable land area of some 171 acres, these planners estimated that approximately 14 percent of all residential acreage was vacant. And of a population in 1960 of 4,294—less than half the number at the time of the Rondout-Kingston merger—the average per capita income was about $1,250. (The average income in the rest of Kingston ten years earlier was twice that sum. As a result of these and other findings, the study recommended that in a substantial portion of Rondout, "demolition" was "necessary" (6).

A term that strikes fear in the hearts of contemporary historians, architectural buffs, and preservationists, urban renewal first surfaced on the national scene in 1949, and by the 1960s had become a national priority. In the bright sunshine of our present enlightened hindsight, this fundamentally well-intentioned and hopeful government program, ironically has come to suggest the arbitrary and irresponsible destruction of landmarks and historic buildings, as well as the dispossession of ethnic minorities and the poor. Today, a similar prescription for the problems of urban areas such as Rondout would most likely be found unacceptable. And the "elimination of slums and blight," as the process of urban renewal was defined in government and private publications at the time, seems short-sighted and simplistic to us now (*Planning the Community*, 17). As the twentieth century comes to an end, we can perceive more clearly how "renewal" of the sort that occurred in the 1960s and '70s could have been conducted in a very different way. But back in the turbulent '60s, to many the idea, without qualification, looked pretty good.

Not surprisingly, therefore, only faint negative public opinion surfaced when news of the proposed project was heard. Of course, angry community meetings were held in Rondout, chaired by president of the Ulster County Board of Elections and Rondout cigar store owner Joe Epstein, the unofficial "mayor" of Rondout, and a few individuals did express their concern at the urban renewal office and at public hearings, but little came of this. Some people in Rondout even welcomed urban renewal, hoping to sell their properties at a profit and get out. The rest of Kingston, more interested in Viet Nam and the space program at the time, for the most part were either apathetic or mildly favored the "renewal" of Rondout. Most inhabitants of Rondout, therefore, many of them uneducated, elderly and poor, felt powerless before the juggernaut of this federal program. As a result of this perception, they accepted its inevitable fulfillment with resignation and, ultimately, moved out.

And so, without significant opposition, the project moved ahead. By 1965, plans had reached the model stage and properties were being acquired by the Kingston Urban Renewal Agency, which had been established the previous year. However, on June 1, local alderman Leonard Van Dyke was to report to the Kingston *Daily Freeman* that there was "increased dissatisfaction" among the people of Rondout concerning the prices they were being paid for their land. The compensation was "unjust and inadequate," he stated. And although property owners had the right to submit their own appraisals, few had done so. In addition, he pointed out, the relocation effort on these Rondouter's behalf had been extremely poor. "Where are all these people going to go?" he asked.

In the future, two housing developments would be built to house these Rondout-ers, but a significant number would search, frustrated and bewildered, for their own lodgings. Some would find no new homes in the area, for the number of new housing units constructed in Rondout never equaled the number lost. In addition, many people believed, as they had been told by the Urban Renewal Agency, that one day they would be able to repurchase their old home sites and rebuild with low-interest loans. This, however, did not happen, or as one urban planner has stated recently, it proved "a bit more optimistic" than possible (Shuster). For the process of urban renewal was so complicated bureaucratically, and took so long, that by the time this step could be considered things had changed—the plan had become obsolete—and such a prospect was no longer feasible.

As properties were purchased and people gradually displaced, Rondout began to look more and more like a ghost town. Each night, as the last remaining inhabitants returned to Rondout after work, they found their neighborhoods silent and dark. By 1966, of eighteen addresses on Broadway between the Freeman Building and the Rondout Savings Bank on the corner of Mill Street, many were partially empty and ten were totally vacant. Only a few residences and commercial addresses, such as Knust & Sons men's clothing, Stone's liquor store, and Manos' Market, were tenanted. On Ferry Street, the enduring Rondout tavern, Ray's Riverside Rest, remained.

Near the end of 1967, the demolition began. When this work was completed, all structures would be leveled and a giant swath cleared through the core of Rondout from the east side of Broadway to Hasbrouck Avenue, and from Newkirk Avenue to the Strand; among the many historic buildings that would be taken was the elegant Rondout National Bank. Gone, too, would be Thomas Chambers' ancient pear tree, the Stock & Cordts Building (possibly the tallest in Kingston), Samuel Decker Coykendall's offices, and the buildings and wharves where the great steamboats had docked at the Strand. By 1971, streets would be relocated, housing developments built, and nearly $7 million of state and federal money spent.

About this time, the state would also relocate Route 9W, constructing an arterial highway over the Rondout Creek and the Strand. In addition, a new fire station and city hall would be erected in Rondout, situated roughly in the upper portion of the recently cleared land. Though not a part of the original urban renewal plan, the idea of Kingston Mayor Raymond Garraghan to move the seat of government to Rondout seems both prudent and just. For not only did this decision prevent future city administrators from ignoring Rondout, making it evident that the job of renewal was unfinished there, but it also restored to Rondout, if only symbolically, a measure of civic pride and identity it had lost in 1872, when Rondout and Kingston had been made one.

Nonetheless, by the mid 1970s it had become apparent that something had been lost in Rondout. The place definitely was not the same. The land east of Broadway, so crowded and vibrant with life in earlier times, as depicted in the photographs of Richard De Lisser and in this book, looked like a deserted wasteland—except for the new housing developments. What the city had hoped would happen in Rondout after the demolition had not occurred. Private enterprise had not stepped in as had been expected. In its study, undertaken more than a decade earlier, Raymond & May had estimated greater market demand for this area than had developed. Few, if any, retail, wholesale, or industrial buyers could be found for this devastated land. And the potential development which the firm had predicted for Rondout was occurring elsewhere to the west and in the suburbs. Well into the next decade, Rondout continued to be neglected, with many buildings empty and little traffic moving on lower Broadway.

Considering the widespread apathy regarding historic preservation and the general state of dilapidation of much of Rondout at this time, in addition to the availability of federal funding and the pervasive feeling of antipathy toward Rondout in Kingston, it is not surprising that, during the 1960s, this area was razed rather than renovated and restored. Samuel Decker Coykendall had predicted that he would see grass growing on uptown Kingston, but he was wrong.

If Coykendall had lived another ten years, it is tempting to speculate whether the fate of Rondout might have been different. Could Coykendall's leadership have enabled Rondout to meet the challenge of change and rescue itself from its sad demise? Probably not. As early as 1860, J. B. Hageman, the editor of the Rondout *Courier*, had pointed out that Rondout lacked "manufacturing enterprise." On July 6, 1860, he had written, "We are rapidly progressing now, but our advancement would be much greater if we were a fabricating as well as a trading people." Certainly, Rondout had not taken Hageman's prophetic words concerning economic diversity to heart. Indeed, according to the Kingston Board of Trade, in 1902 nearly five thousand Kingston and Rondout residents were employed on a regular basis. Within three decades, however, fewer than three thousand would be so employed. In this regard, acknowledging the existence of *some* jobs in Rondout, a Kingston *Daily Freeman* article of November 3, 1958, nonetheless suggests that the problem of declining employment is caused by the "lack of long-range planning." With clarity and emphasis, the article states, "While large business enterprises were built [in the past] by progressive men, those who followed failed to look. . .beyond the changes that were gradually taking place."

So, uptown Kingston had gotten the last word, after all. Natchez, as Rondout had been called by Congressman Root in the early nineteenth century, no longer festered "under the hill." Its infancy spent in the roaring 1820s and '30s, its adolescence in the 1850s and '60s, its adulthood during the years between the end of the Civil War and the closing of the D & H Canal, Rondout had spent a long, ailing old age and had finally been put out of its misery. Or so it seemed.

Certainly, much of old Rondout had been irretrievably lost. Yet, contrary to the predictions of urban renewal's most bitter critics, Rondout had not died. A small part of its central core had not been taken, some suggested, because a substantial portion of its population was Black. In the late 1960s, cautious governments took great care to avoid the mistakes of Newark and Detroit, and there was significant fear of the possibility of a race riot. Whether this supposition is well founded or not cannot be proven. Possibly, the fact that all of Rondout was not demolished is due to other unrelated factors, such as the precipitous nature of the terrain to the west of Broadway, the amount of government money that was available, or simply the factor of time. Be that as it may, the Freeman Building, originally the Sampson Opera House and presently Mary P's Restaurant, George Von Beck's Mansion House, the West Strand, as well as the entire west side of Broadway and the rest of Rondout to Wilbur, where the first canal workers had lived, mercifully remained untouched and intact. Although not in the best condition, this area and these structures formed the living nucleus from which a new Rondout could grow.

Although the supporters of urban renewal had misunderstood, and therefore devalued the interesting subculture which flourished in Rondout—made up of Blacks, Jews, economically disadvanaged Whites and other ethnic groups—they had provided, if unwittingly, for the rebirth of Rondout by preserving the area that is left. A controversial subject to this day in Rondout and Kingston, urban renewal and its effects can now be seen by some of its detractors as not without some benefit. What might have happened to Rondout, or "downtown" as it was disparagingly called, if there had been no urban renewal? Might any historic buildings exist today in a condition worthy of being saved? Or might Rondout have gone the way of many other Hudson River towns? It is difficult, of course, to say.

At first, after the bulldozers had left, it looked like Rondout was not going to make it, as mentioned earlier. But within a decade or so, like the phoenix rising from the ashes, Rondout began to come to life again. Never without its supporters, in 1970 a community development organization called S.C.O.R.E. was formed to rehabilitate the Strand. Nine years later, Rondout and the West Strand were added to the National Register of Historic Places. In March 1983, work began on the restoration and conversion of the Mansion House into luxury apartments. Soon thereafter, the widespread renovation and preservation of many other Rondout buildings followed. The gentrification of Rondout had begun.

Museums and an Urban Cultural Center have developed in Rondout, too. In 1980, the Hudson River Maritime Center was founded, inhabiting a converted building formerly owned by the Cornell Steamboat Company. The Trolley Museum of New York also settled nearby on the Strand. The waterfront has been cleaned up, with the development of West Strand Park, a marina, a boat landing, and river rides on the cruise boats *Rip Van Winkle* and the *Rondout Belle*. Lectures have been given on Rondout architecture and photographic exhibitions presented of its contemporary scene. Even Kingston Point Park, long disappeared and thought lost for good, is being rescued by the Kingston Rotary Club and others, wrested from the grip of brush and swamp.

Today, Rondout is considered an interesting place to live and to visit. On weekends and holidays, tourists flood the streets of Rondout's historic district so thickly that it is often difficult to find a place to park. With expensive boutiques, art galleries, antique shops, exotic restaurants, summer concerts and theater, and recently the completion by Rondout developer John Mc Clelland of an upscale commercial-residential complex on the east side of Broadway, Rondout seems to have eschewed its working-class origins and become strangely stylish and chic. Certainly, if the ghosts of Thomas Cornell, George Von Beck, and Samuel Decker Coykendall were to return to Rondout and walk its once familiar streets, they might not even recognize the place, so different in flavor and spirit has this section of Rondout become. Ironically, the people who worked for Cornell and his associates, as well as most of those who were recently dislocated by urban renewal, could probably not afford to live on the Strand today. As one long-time observer of Rondout remarked recently, "Rondout has taken on a new life of its own" (Shuster).

Yet, if Rondout no longer throbs with the rich, full beat of industry and commerce, as it once did many years ago; if the *Mary Powell* and the *Jacob H. Tremper* no longer steam into the creek; if cement is no longer mined under Hasbrouck Park, and bluestone is not finished at Fitch's stoneyard in Wilbur near the railroad bridge; if ice is left in the river uncut, and bricks no longer bake at North Street out near the point; if Julia Dillon and Catherine Murdock no longer follow their daily round, and the memory of Rondout's patriotic schoolteacher, Joseph Corbin, who died during the first day of battle at Gettysburg, is forgotten; if the Dutch and Indians who traded in Rondout have long ago returned to the soil, and the red hair of Rondout's founder, Thomas Chambers, is turned to dust; if all this is gone—the human hopes, the fervent dreams, the artful deals—somehow, Rondout, although altered, has not been lost. If not renewed, as many had hoped, or even reborn as a copy of its former self, Rondout has nonetheless survived. For once again, miraculously, Rondout has been transformed.

Works Cited

Abbey, Henry. *The Poems of Henry Abbey*. 3rd ed. Cambridge, Massachusetts: Riverside, 1895.

Adams, Henry. *The Education of Henry Adams: An Autobiography*. Boston: Houghton Mifflin, 1918.

Aldrich, T. B. "Among the Studios." *Our Young Folks* 2 (October 1866): 622-25.

Avery, Kevin, et al. *American Paradise, the World of the Hudson River School*. New York: Abrams, 1987.

Bacon, George F. *Kingston & Rondout: Its Representative Business Men & Its Points of Interest*. Newark, New Jersey: Merchantile Publishing, 1892.

Barrus, Clara. *John Burroughs----Boy and Man*. Garden City, New York: Doubleday, Page, 1920.

Beers, F.W. *Country Atlas of Ulster New York*. New York: Walker & Jewett, 1875.

Benson, William O. "The Last of the 'Mary Powell' at Port Ewen." *Sunday Freeman* 27 May 1973.

_____. "Watching the Steamboats Go By." *Sunday Freeman* 7 October 1973.

Best, Gerald M. *The Ulster and Delaware Railroad*. San Marino, California: Golden West, 1972.

Blum, John et al. *The National Experience*. 2nd ed. New York: Harcourt, 1968.

Blumin, Stuart M. *The Urban Threshold*. Chicago: U. of Chicago, 1976.

Booth, Nathaniel. Manuscript diary. 2 vols. Senate House Museum, Kingston, New York.

Boyds's Kingston & Rondout Directory 1857-8. New York: William H. Boyd, 1857.

Brink, Benjamin, ed. *Olde Ulster*. 10 vols. Kingston, 1905-1914.

Brown, Harriet Connor. *Grandmother Brown's Hundred Years 1827-1927*. Boston: Little, Brown, 1929.

Bunton, William M. "Ulster Academy & School #2." In *Picturesque Ulster*, 69-70. Cornwallville, New York: Hope Farm, 1968.

Burroughs, John. *The Life and Letters of John Burroughs*. Vol. I. Ed. Clara Barrus. New York: Russell & Russell, 1968.

_____. *Locusts and Wild Honey*. Boston: Houghton Mifflin, 1879.

_____. *My Boyhood*. New York: Doubleday, 1922.

Calhoun, Betsy. "Julia Mc Entee Dillon." In *Julia Mc Entee Dillon Commemorative Art Exhibit*. 1987.

Caterino, Ralph. Interview by author. 29 September 1994.

Chamberlain, John. *The Enterprising Americans: A Business History of the United States.* New York: Harper, 1963.

Clearwater, Alphonso T. *The History of Ulster County New York.* Kingston, New York: W. J. Van Deusen, 1907.

_____. *Kingston: A Tribute.* Kingston: Freeman Publishing, 1929.

Cochran, Thomas, and William Miller. *A Social History of Industrial America.* Rev. ed. New York: Harper, 1961.

Commemorative Biographical Record of Ulster County, New York. Chicago: J. H. Beers, 1896.

Cooper, James Fenimore. *The Pioneers.* In *The Tavern Lamps Are Burning.* Ed. Carl Carmer. New York: David McKay, 1964.

Crevecour, St. John. *Letters From an American Farmer.* First American edition, 1782.

Currey, Cecil. "The Dutch Colonial Failure in New York." *Mankind* 2: 14-29.

Dankers, Joseph. Diary entries in *Chronicles of the Hudson.* Ed. Roland Van Zandt. New Brunswick, New Jersey: Rutgers, 1971.

De Lisser, Richard Lionel. *Picturesque Ulster.* Kingston: Styles and Bruyn Publishing, 1896-1905. Reprint Cornwallville, New York: Hope Farm, 1968.

De Witt, William C. *People's History of Kingston, Rondout & Vicinity.* New Haven, Connecticut: Tuttle, Morrehouse and Taylor, 1943.

Dickens, Charles. *American Notes for General Circulation.* New York: D. Appleton, 1872.

Dillon, Julia Mc Entee. *Old Gardens of Kingston.* Kingston: Ulster Garden Club, 1915. Reprint 1987.

Drago, Harry Sinclair. *Canal Days in America.* New York: Clarkson N. Potter, 1972.

Du Bois, Philip H. *A Catskills Boyhood: My Life Along the Hudson.* Hensonville, New York: Black Dome, 1992.

Dumond, Dorothy. "John Vanderlyn: Noted American Artist." In *Historic Kingston.* Kingston: Anniversary Booklet Committee, 1952.

Dunshee, Kenneth Holcomb. *As You Pass By.* New York: Hastings House, 1952.

Dupuy, Ernest and Trevor Dupuy. *The Compact History of the Civil War.* New York: Warner, 1960.

Dwyer, Peter. Telephone interview by author. 22 October 1988.

Evers, Alf. *The Catskills: From Wilderness to Woodstock.* New York: Doubleday, 1972.

_____. Public lecture. High Falls, New York. 2 May 1993.

_____. "The Rise and Fall of the U & D." In *In Catskill Country: Collected Essays on Mountain History, Life and Lore*, 131-37. Woodstock, New York: Overlook, 1995.

Forry, Samuel. "Account of a Malignant Fever Which Prevailed at Rondout." *The New York Journal of Medicine, and Collateral Sciences 1* (November 1843): 293-347.

The Freeman's Sixth Annual Directory of the City of Kingston. Kingston: Freeman Job Printing House, 1900.

Fried, Marc B. *The Early History of Kingston and Ulster County, N.Y.* Kingston, New York: Ulster County Historical Association, 1975.

Gates, Theodore B. *The Civil War Diaries of Col. Theodore B. Gates 20th New York State Militia*. Ed. Seward R. Osborne. Hightstown, New Jersey: Longstreet House, 1991.

_____. *The Ulster Guard and the War of Rebellion*. New York: B.H. Tyrrel, 1879.

Gazetteer & Business Directory of Ulster County, N.Y. For 1871-2. Ed. Hamilton Child. Syracuse, New York: Hamilton Child, 1871.

Hacker, Louis, et al. *The United States: A Graphic History*. New York: Random House, 1937.

Handlin, Oscar. *The History of the United States*. 2 vols. New York: Holt, Rinehart & Winston, 1967.

Hasbrouck, Susan P. "At the Turn of the Century." *Ulster County Gazette 2* (December 1964): 1, 5-8.

Hickey, Andrew S. *The Story of Kingston*. New York: Stratford House, 1952.

Hone, Philip. *The Diary of Philip Hone*. Ed. Allan Nevins. New York: Dodd, Mead, 1936.

The Hundred Year Book. Ed. Philip Schuyler. New York: A. S. Barnes, 1942.

Johnson, Clifton. *The Picturesque Hudson*. New York: Macmillan, 1909.

Kingston Comprehensive Development Plan. Kingston: Raymond & May Associates. 1961.

Kingston, Ellenville & Saugerties Directory for 1873-1874. Kingston, New York: J. H. Lant, 1873.

"Kingston Point Park." Kingston *Weekly Leader* 18 August 1900.

Krom, John B. Letters to John Wurts. 14 February 1863-10 March 1864. McHugh Collection.

Lindsley, James G. "A Description of the Geological Formations of Ulster County." In *Picturesque Ulster*, 25-31 Cornwallville, New York: Hope Farm, 1968.

_____. "The Story of Rondout." In *Picturesque Ulster*, 37-42. Cornwallville, New York: Hope Farm, 1968.

Lovecraft, H. P. *Selected Letters*. 3 vols. Sank City: Arkham House, 1971.

Mac Creery, Amos. Interview by author. 6 November 1986.

Mc Entee, Jervis. "The Jervis Mc Entee Diary." In *Journal of the Archives of American Art 8* (July-October 1968): 1-29.

_____. Manuscript diary. New-York Historical Society. In *Charmed Places*, 71; 81; 112-113. New York: Harry N. Abrams, 1988.

Mabie, Roger W. "The Hudson River Port of Rondout." *Sea History* (Autumn 1985): 12-15.

Marketability & Land Utilization Study Rondout General Neighborhood Renewal Plan Area. Kingston: Raymond & May Associates, 1961.

Martin, Michael Andrew. Interview by author. 26 March 1989.

Miller, Douglas T. *Jacksonian Aristocracy: Class and Democracy in New York 1830-1860.* New York: Oxford, 1967.

Miller, William. *A New History of the United States.* New York: Dell, 1962.

Nevins, Allan and Henry Steele Commager. *A Pocket History of the United States.* New York: Pocket Books, 1967.

O'Connor, Julie. "Ulster County's Brickmaking Heritage." *Ulster* 4 (Summer 1989).

Phisterer, Frederick. *New York in the War of the Rebellion 1861-1865.* 3rd ed. 5 vols. Albany, New York: J. B. Lyon, 1912.

Planning in the Community. Publication No. 299. Washington, D.C.: League of Women Voters, March 1964.

Pratt, George. *An Account of the British Expedition Above the Highlands of the Hudson River and of the Events Connected With the Burning of Kingston in 1777.* Collections of the Ulster County Historical Society 1 (1860). Reprint, 1977.

Rayback, Robert J. "New York State in the Civil War." *New York History* 42 (January 1961): 56-70.

Ringwald, Donald C. *Hudson River Day Line.* Berkeley, California: Howell-North, 1965.

Rosenberg, Charles E. *The Cholera Years: The United States in 1832, 1849, and 1866.* Chicago: U. of Chicago, 1987.

Schneider, Gail. "Cornell Steamboat Company: An Annotated Chronology." In *Rondout and the Cornell Steamboat Company 1847-1964.* Catalog of an exhibition at the Hudson River Maritime Center, Kingston, New York, 1983.

Schoonmaker, Marius. *The History of Kingston, New York.* New York: Burr Printing House, 1888.

Sciaky, Leon. "The Rondout and Its Canal." *Proceedings of the New York State Historical Association* 39 (July 1941): 272-89.

Sheldon, G. W. *American Painters.* New York: Appleton, 1879.

Shultz, Herbert L. Letter to author. 16 September 1994.

Shuster, Dan. Interview by author. 20 July 1995.

Smith, Alonzo. Interview by author. 18 February 1989.

Smith-Rosenberg, Carroll. "Beauty, the Beast and the Militant Woman: A Case Study in Sex Roles and Social Stress in Jacksonian America." *American Quarterly* 23 (1971): 562-84.

Spangenberger, C. W. Interview. 23 August 1995.

Sterne, Simon. *The Railway in Its Relation to Public and Private Interests: Address of Simon Sterne before the Merchants and Business Men of New-York at Steinway Hall, April 19, 1878.* New York: Press of the Chamber of Commerce, 1878.

Steuding, Bob. *The Last of the Handmade Dams: The Story of the Ashokan Reservoir.* Rev. ed. Fleischmanns, New York: Purple Mountain, 1989.

Steuding, Robert [Sr.]. Interview by author. 16 September 1988.

Sutherland, Daniel E. *The Expansion of Everyday Life 1860-1876.* New York: Harper & Row, 1989.

Sylvester, Nathaniel Bartlett. *History of Ulster County, New York.* Philadelphia: Everts & Peck, 1880.

Thompson, E. P. "Time, Work-Discipline, and Industrial Capitalism." *Past and Present* (December 1967): 56-97.

Tocqueville, Alexis. *Democracy in America.* First American edition, 1838.

Van Buren, Augustus H. *A History of Ulster County Under the Dominion of the Dutch.* Kingston, New York, 1923. Reprint Astoria, New York: J. C.& A. L. Fawcett, 1989.

Van Der Donck, Adriaen. *A Description of the New Netherlands.* Ed. Thomas F. O'Donnell. Syracuse: Syracuse U., 1968.

Van Santvoord, Cornelius. *The One Hundred and Twentieth Regiment New York State Volunteers.* Kingston: Rondout Press, 1894. Reprint Cornwallville, New York: Hope Farm, 1983.

Van Zandt, Roland. *Chronicles of the Hudson.* New Brunswick, New Jersey: Rutgers, 1971.

Vogel, Morris J. and Charles E. Rosenberg, eds. *The Therapeutic Revolution: Essays in the Social History of American Medicine.* Philadelphia: U. of Pennsylvania, 1979.

Wakefield, Manville B. *Coal Boats to Tidewater.* South Fallsburg, New York, 1965.

Welter, Barbara. "The Cult of True Womanhood: 1820-1860." In *The American Family in Social-Historical Perspective.* Ed. Michael Gordon, 224-250. New York: St. Martin's, 1973.

Whittredge, Worthington. *Autobiography.* New York: Arno, 1969.

Wiebe, Robert H. *The Search for Order.* New York: Hill and Wang, 1967.

Wilstach, Paul. *Hudson River Landings.* Reprint Port Washington, New York: Ira J. Friedman, 1969.

Woods, Ron. *Kingston's Magnificent City Parks.* Kingston, New York, 1992.

Additional Sources

Abbey, Henry. *May Dreams*. New York: Abbey & Abbot, 1862.

_____. Scrapbook. February 1894-27 September 1898. Local history collection, Kingston Area Library, Kingston, New York.

The Act of Incorporation of the Village of Rondout, Passed April 4, 1849. Rondout, New York: J. P. Hageman, 1853.

Adams, Arthur G. *The Hudson River in Literature, An Anthology and History*. Albany: State University of New York, 1981.

Adams, Arthur G. *The Hudson Through the Years*. Westwood, New Jersey: Lind, 1983.

Adams, Samuel Hopkins. *Canal Town*. Chicago: Consolidated, 1944.

"American Painter—Jervis Mc Entee, N.A." In *Art Journal* 2 (1876): 178-79.

Anjou, Gustave. *Ulster County, N.Y. Probate Records*. 2 vols. 1906.

Annual Reports of the Delaware & Hudson Canal Company, 1823-1897. High Falls, New York: D & H Canal Museum, n.d.

The Antifederalists. Ed. Cecelia A. Kenyon. Indianapolis: Bobbs-Merrill, 1966.

Austin, Erik W. *Political Facts of the United States Since 1789*. New York: Columbia U., 1986.

Averill, Louise Hunt. *John Vanderlyn, American Painter, 1775-1852*. PhD dissertation, Yale University, 1949.

Bacon, Edgar M. *The Hudson River from Ocean to Source*. New York: Putnam's, 1907.

Barber, John W. and Henry Howe. *Historical Collections of the State of New York*. Reprint Port Washington, New York: Kennikat, 1970.

Blumin, Stuart M. "Rip Van Winkle's Grandchildren: Family and Household in the Hudson Valley, 1800-1860." *Journal of Urban History* 1 (1975): 293-315.

Boyle, Robert H. *The Hudson River, A Natural & Unnatural History*. New York: Norton, 1979.

Breslin, Howard. *Shad Run*. New York: Crowell, 1955.

Brodhead, John R. *History of the State of New York*. 2 vols. New York: Harper, 1853 and 1871.

Brown, Dee. *The Year of the Century: 1876*. New York: Scribner's, 1966.

Bruce, Wallace. *The Hudson*. New York: Bryant Literary Union, 1894.

_____. *The Hudson by Daylight*. New York: Bryant Literary Union, 1907. Reprint New York: Walking News, 1982.

Buckman, David Lear. *Old Steamboat Days on the Hudson River*. New York: Grafton, 1907.

Burroughs, John. *A River View and Other Hudson Valley Essays by John Burroughs*. Ed. Edward Renahan. Croton-on-Hudson, New York: North River, 1981.

Butler, B.C. *The Summer Tourist Descriptive of the Delaware and Hudson Canal Company's Railroads, and Their Summer Resorts*. Boston: Franklin, 1879.

Carmer, Carl. *The Hudson*. New York: Farrar & Rinehart, 1939.

Catton, Bruce. *The Civil War*. New York: Fairfax Press, 1960.

A Century of Progress: History of the Delaware and Hudson Company, 1823-1923. Albany: J. B. Lyon, 1925.

Charmed Places. Ed. Sandra Phillips and Linda Weintraub. New York: Harry N. Abrams, 1988.

Charter of the City of Kingston, Passed May 29, 1872, and as Amended in 1875 and 1877. Kingston: H. G. Crouch, 1877.

Coffin, Tristram. *The Last Gold Mine of the Hudson by a Summer Visitor*. New York: Knickerbocker, 1923.

Compendium of the Tenth Census of the United States, 1880. Washington, D.C.: Government Printing Office, 1883.

Corwin, Edward T., ed. *Ecclesiastical Records State of New York*. 7 vols. Albany: University of State of New York, 1901-16.

Craig, Gordon. *The Germans*. New York: Putnam's, 1982.

Curtis, George William. *Lotus-Eating, A Summer Book*. New York: Harper, 1852.

Dangerfield, George. *Chancellor Robert R. Livingston of New York 1746-1813*. New York: Harcourt, 1960.

Dayton, Fred Erving. *Steamboat Days*. New York: Frederick A. Stokes, 1925.

De Noyelles, Daniel. *Within These Gates*. Thiells, New York, 1989.

"The Departure of the One Hundred Twentieth." *Olde Ulster* 7 (July 1911): 193-206.

"The Departure of the Twentieth Regiment." *Olde Ulster* 7 (June 1911): 161-172.

Documents Relative to the Colonial History of the State of New York. Vol. 13. Albany: Secretary of State of New York, 1877-87.

Dornbusch, C.E. *The Communities of New York and the Civil War*. New York: The New York Public Library, 1962.

Eighmey, Henry. "The Iron Horse Arrives." In *Kingston's 350th Anniversary 1609-1959*, 32-37. Hudson-Champlain Souvenir booklet. Kingston, 1959.

Elting, Irving. "Dutch Village Communities on the Hudson River." In *Municipal Government and Long Tenure*, 5-68. Baltimore: Johns Hopkins U., 1886. Reprint New York: Johnson Reprint Corporation, 1973.

Evans, Sara M. *Born for Liberty: A History of Women in America*. New York: Free Press, 1989.

Evers, Alf. "Bluestone Lore and Bluestone Men." In *I Walked the Road Again: Great Stories from the Catskill Mountains*. Ed. Janis Benincasa. Fleischmanns, New York: Purple Mountain, 1994.

Ewen, William. "Steamboats on the Hudson." In *Days of the Steamboats*, 28-40. New York: Parents' Magazine, 1967.

Fiske, John. *The Dutch & Quaker Colonies in America*. 2 vols. Boston: Houghton Mifflin, 1900.

Fister, Ruth. "The British Destroy a Capitol." In *Historic Kingston*, 19-22. Kingston: Anniversary Booklet Committee, 1952.

Forsyth, Mary Isabella. *The Beginnings of New York, Kingston the First State Capitol*. N.P., 1909. Also published as *Kingston, The First State Capitol*. Boston: Richard G. Badger, 1909.

Fowler, Everett. *The Founding and Early Development of Kingston, New York*. N.P., 1924.

Fox, William. *New York at Gettysburg*. 3 vols. Albany: J. B. Lyon, 1900.

_____. *Regimental Losses in the American Civil War 1861- 1865*. Albany: Albany Publishing, 1893.

Gekle, William F. *A Hudson Riverbook*. Poughkeepsie: Wyvern House, 1978.

"General Sharpe and Lee's Surrender." *Olde Ulster* 8 (September 1912): 257-79.

"General Sharpe at the Unveiling." *Olde Ulster* 8 (November 1912): 321-31.

German American Genealogy. Ed. Elizabeth Ann Sharp. North Hollywood, California: Immigrant Genealogical Society, 1987.

Gerow, Joshua R. *Alder Lake*. Privately published, 1953.

Gilchrist, Ann. *Canalling Along the Delaware and Hudson*. D & H Historical Society, 1982.

_____. *Footsteps Across Cement, A History of the Township of Rosendale, New York*. Privately published, 1976.

Ginger, Ray. *Age of Excess*. New York: Macmillan, 1965.

Glaab, Charles and A. Theodore Brown. *A History of Urban America*. London: Collier-Macmillan, 1967.

Glanz, Rudolf. *The Jew in Old American Folklore*. New York: Walden, 1961.

Griffen, Clyde. "The Study of Occupational Mobility in Nineteenth-Century America: Problems and Possibilities." *Journal of Social History* 5 (1972): 310-30.

Handlin, Oscar. *Immigration As A Factor in American History*. Englewood Cliffs, New Jersey: Prentice-Hall, 1959.

Haring, H.A. *Our Catskill Mountains*. New York: Putnam's, 1931.

Hasbrouck, G.D.B. *Thomas Chambers, Founder of Kingston*. Paper read at the spring meeting of The Ulster County Historical Society, Kingston, New York, June 6, 1931.

Hendricks, Howard. *The City of Kingston, Birthplace of New York State*. Kingston: The Kingston Board of Trade, 1902.

Higginson, Francis J. "A Short Account of the Early History of Kingston, Ulster Co., New York." *Pocumtuck Valley Memorial Association Proceedings* 6 (1914): 122-47.

Hill, Dewey D. and Elliot R. Hughes. *Ice Harvesting in Early America*. New Hartford, New York: New Hartford Historical Society, 1977.

Hilton, George W. *The Night Boat*. Berkeley, California: Howell-North, 1968.

Hine, Charles Gilbert. *The West Bank of the Hudson River, Albany to Tappan: Notes on its History and Legends, its Ghost Stories and Romances*. Newark, New Jersey: Hines Annual, 1906.

Hingham, John. *Strangers in the Land, Patterns of American Nativism 1860-1925*. New York: Atheneum, 1965.

The History of Ulster County With Emphasis Upon the Last 100 Years 1883-1983. Ed. Kenneth E. Hasbrouck. Ulster County Historians, 1984.

Hoffman, A.W. "The Harbor of Rondout." In *Picturesque Ulster*, 73-77. Cornwallville, New York: Hope Farm, 1968.

_____. "Ulster County Bluestone." In *Picturesque Ulster*, 119-122; 126-129. Cornwallville, New York: Hope Farm, 1968.

Horton, John. "Rondout in the Fifties." Kingston *Daily Express* 25 November 1895.

Howatt, John K. *The Hudson River and its Painters*. New York: American Legacy Press, 1972.

The Hudson By Daylight. Map with descriptive pages. New York: William F. Link, 1878.

Illustrated & Descriptive Kingston, N.Y. Kingston, 1906.

Ingersoll, Ernest. *Illustrated Guide to the Hudson River & the Catskill Mountains*. Chicago: Rand Mc Nally & Co., 1908.

Isaacs, Lei. "Getting to the Point." *Ulster* (Summer 1993): 50-57.

Jarrold, Ernest. "Peg-Leg, the Musician." *Harper's Weekly* 29 September 1894.

Jervis, John B. *The Reminiscences of John B. Jervis, Engineer of the Old Croton*. Ed. Neal Fitzsimons. Syracuse: Syracuse U., 1971.

Jervis Mc Entee, N.A. Catalog of oil paintings by Jervis Mc Entee, N.A. New York: Ortgies & Co., 1888.

Johnson, Clifton. "Farming Beside the Hudson." In *John Burroughs Talks: His Reminiscences and Comments*, 126-52. Boston: Houghton Mifflin, 1922.

Jones, Chester Lloyd. *The Economic History of the Anthracite-Tidewater Canals*. Philadelphia: U. of Pennsylvania, 1908.

Jones, Nathan W. "Esopus Indians and Their Language." *Olde Ulster 1 (1905): 70-75*.

Josephson, Matthew. *The Robber Barons*. New York: Harcourt, 1934.

Kass, Alvin. *Politics in New York State, 1800-1830*. Syracuse: Syracuse U., 1965.

Keller, Allan. *Life Along the Hudson*. Tarrytown: Sleepy Hollow, 1976.

Kenney, Alice P. *Stubborn For Liberty: The Dutch in New York*. Syracuse: Syracuse U., 1975.

Kimball, Francis P. *New York: The Canal State*. Albany: Argus, 1958.

Kingman, William C. *A History of the Rondout Presbyterian Church, 1829-1933*. Kingston: C. M. Thomas, 1936.

Kingston Point Park. A pamphlet published for the Consolidated Railroad Company. Kingston: The Freeman Press, 1903.

Kurtznacker, Arthur G. "Thomas Chambers, Lord of the Manor." In *Historic Kingston*, 7-10. Kingston: Anniversary Booklet Committee, 1952.

Lamont, Thomas W. *My Boyhood in a Parsonage*. New York: Harper, 1946.

Langdon, William Chauncy. *Everyday Things in American Life, 1776-1876*. New York: Scribners, 1945.

Larkin, Jack. *The Reshaping of Everyday Life, 1790-1840*. New York: Harper & Row, 1988.

Leach, Douglas Edward. *The Northern Colonial Frontier, 1607-1763*. New York: Holt, Rinehart and Winston, 1966.

Leander, Bishop J. *A History of American Manufacturers from 1608 to 1860*. 3rd ed. 3 vols. Philadelphia: Edward Young, 1868.

Lee, John Wiltsee. *Stories of the Hudson*. New York: Putnam's, 1871.

Le Roy, Edwin. *The Delaware & Hudson Canal: A History*. Honesdale, Pennsylvania: Wayne County Historical Society, 1950.

Letters About the Hudson River And Its Vicinity. New York: Freeman Hunt, 1837.

Lewis, Jack. Watercolors and text, 1964.

The Literature of the Mid-Hudson Valley. Ed. Alfred Marks. New Paltz: Center for Continuing Education, State University of New York, 1973.

Litt, Robert Stephen. "Urbanization and Social Control: An Analysis of Kingston, New York, 1820-1872." Senior honors thesis at Howard University, 1971.

Lossing, Benson J. *The Hudson, From the Wilderness to the Sea*. London: Virtue, 1868.

Mc Caffrey, Lawrence J. *The Irish Diaspora in America*. Bloomington, Indiana: Indiana U., 1976.

Mc Clelland, Elisabeth. *History of American Costume, 1607-1870*. New York: Tudor, 1937.

Mc Kinley, Albert E. "The English and Dutch Towns of New Netherland." *American Historical Review* 6 (1900): 5.

Maass, John. *The Gingerbread Age: A View of Victorian America*. New York: Rinehart, 1957.

Magee, Irving. *Semi-Centennial Celebration of the Rondout Presbyterian Church, Kingston, N.Y.* Albany: Weed, Parsons, 1884.

Manners, Ande. *Poor Cousins.* New York: Coward, McCann & Geoghegan, 1972.

Merritt, Edward L. "Kingston Academy," *Proceedings of the Ulster County Historical Society* (1937-38), 22-53.

Merten, Alfred A. "The Ulster & Delaware Railroad: A Brief History." Unpublished manuscript, Senate House Museum, Kingston, New York, 1969.

Meyer, Balthasar Henry. *The History of Transportation in the United States Before 1860.* Washington, D.C.: Carnegie Institute of Washington, 1917.

Miller, Douglas T. "Immigration and Social Stratification in Pre-Civil War New York." *New York History* 49 (1968): 157-88.

Miller, Geoffrey. "'Are You All Unhappy At a Twenty Dollar Bill?': Text, Tune and Context At Antique Auctions." *Ethnomusicology* 28 (May 1984): 187-208.

_____. "The Diary of Nathaniel Booth: A Contemporary Account of the Antebellum Culture of the Hudson Valley." Unpublished manuscript, 1989.

Morgan, Hal. *Symbols of America.* New York: Viking, 1986.

Morris, Edmund. *The Rise of Theodore Roosevelt.* New York: Ballantine, 1979.

Morris, Robert John. *Cholera, 1832: The Social Response to an Epidemic.* New York: Holmes & Meier, 1976.

Mumford, Lewis. *The City in History.* New York: Harcourt, 1961.

Myers, Kenneth. *The Catskills, Painters, Writers, and Tourists in the Mountains 1820-1895.* Yonkers: The Hudson River Museum of Westchester, 1987.

Mylod, John. *Biography of A River: The People and Legends of the Hudson Valley.* New York: Crown, 1969.

Neighborhood Conservation and Property Rehabilitation. Washington, D.C.: U.S. Department of Housing & Urban Development, 1969.

Nelson, Frank L. "Economic Geology of Ulster County." In *Thirteenth Annual Report of the State Geologist (NY) For the Year 1893.* Ed. James Hall. Albany: James B. Lyon, 1894.

Newland, D.H. *The Mining and Quarry Industry of New York State.* Albany: New York Museum Bulletin 174, 1914.

Nye, Russel B. *The Cultural Life of the New Nation: 1776-1830.* New York: Harper and Row, 1960.

_____. "John Humphrey Noyes." *A Baker's Dozen.* East Lansing: Michigan State U., 1956.

_____. "The Slave Power Conspiracy, 1830-1860." *Science and Society* 10 (Summer 1946): 262-74.

_____. *The Unembarrassed Muse: The Popular Arts in America.* New York: Dial, 1970.

Osborne, Seward R. *Holding the Left at Gettysburg, The 20th New York State Militia on July 1, 1863.* Hightstown, New Jersey: Longstreet House, 1990.

Ostrander, Jonathan D. Manuscript diary. Senate House Museum, Kingston, New York.

Partridge, Bellamy, and Otto Bettmann. *As We Were, Family Life in America, 1850-1900, in Picture and Text.* New York: Whittlesey House, 1946.

Payne, Robert. *The Canal Builders.* New York: Macmillan, 1959.

Peluso, A. J. *J. & J. Bard, Picture Painters.* New York: Hudson River Press, 1977.

Phillips, B.T. *Thanksgiving Discourse Delivered in the Presbyterian Church, Rondout, N.Y., November 30, 1854.* Rondout, New York: J. P. Hageman, 1854.

Pierson, George. *Tocqueville in America.* Abridged by Dudley C. Lunt. Garden City, New York: Doubleday, 1959.

Plank, Will. *Banners and Bugles.* Marlborough, New York: Centennial Press, 1963.

Plass, John Brice. *The History of Tuberculosis in Ulster County.* Ulster County, New York, 1970.

Poor, Henry Varnum. *History of the Railroads and Canals of the United States.* New York: J.H. Schultz, 1860.

Programs for People. New York State Division of Housing and Community Renewal. April 1967/March 31, 1968.

Reflections: A Jewish Bicentennial Edition. Kingston: Temple Emanuel, 1976.

Rigby, Harry. "A Brief History of the City of Kingston." In *The History of Ulster County With Emphasis Upon the Last 100 Years 1883-1983.* Ed. Kenneth Hasbrouck, 122-137. Ulster County Historians, 1984.

Ringwald, Donald C. *The Mary Powell.* Berkeley, California: Howell-North, 1972.

_____. *Steamboats for Rondout.* Providence: Steamship Historical Society of America, 1981.

_____. "When Steamboats Reigned." In *Kingston's 350th Anniversary 1609-1959.* Kingston, 1959.

Rockwell, Charles. *The Catskill Mountains and the Regions Around.* New York: Taintor Brothers, 1867. Reprint Cornwallville, New York: Hope Farm, 1973.

Rosten, Leo. *Religions in America.* New York: Simon & Schuster, 1963.

Rush, Benjamin. *Selected Writings.* Ed. Dagobert D. Runes. New York: Philosophical Library, 1947.

Ruttenber, Edward Manning. *Indian Tribes of Hudson's River: Their Origin, Manners and Customs, Tribal and Sub-Tribal Organizations, Wars, Treaties.* Port Washington, New York: Kennikat, 1917.

Salomon, Julian Harris. *Indians of the Lower Hudson Region, The Munsee.* New City: Historical Society of Rockland County, 1982.

Sanderson, Dorothy Hurlbut. *The Delaware and Hudson Canalway: Carrying Coals to Rondout.* 2nd ed. Ellenville, New York: Rondout Valley Publishing, 1974.

Schoonmaker, Marius. Manuscript fragment of "History of Kingston," Vol. 2. Senate House Museum, Kingston, New York.

_____. Unpublished biography of the "Life and Works of John Vanderlyn." Senate House Museum, Kingston, New York.

Sears, Mary Hun. *Hudson Crossroads.* New York: Exposition Press, 1954.

Shannon, William V. *The American Irish: A Political and Social Portrait.* New York: Macmillan, 1964.

Shaughnessy, Jim. *Deleware & Hudson.* Berkeley, California: Howell-North, 1967.

Sherwood, Warren G. *Revolutionary War Times in the Highland Area and Ulster County.* Bicentennial celebration pamphlet, 1976.

Shultz, Herbert Lloyd. "Kingston's Last 100 Years." In *Historic Kingston*, 33-51. Kingston: Anniversary Booklet Committee, 1952.

Sinclair, Peter. "A Short History of Hurley, New York." Unpublished manuscript, 1989.

Sketch of the Life and Career of James F. Dwyer. Kingston: Freeman Publishing, 1940.

Smith, Agnes Scott. "Dutch Days." In *Historic Kingston*, 11-14. Kingston: Anniversary Booklet Committee, 1952.

_____. "The Dutch Had a Word For It." *New York Folklore Quarterly* 4: 182-94.

Smith, Richard. *A Tour of the Hudson, The Mohawk, the Susquehanna, And the Delaware In 1769.* Fleischmanns, New York: Purple Mountain, 1989.

Stampp, Kenneth. *America in 1857, A Nation on the Brink.* New York: Oxford, 1990.

_____. *The Era of Reconstruction 1865-1877.* New York: Random House, 1965.

"The Story of the One Hundred and Fifty-Sixth." *Olde Ulster* 7 (November 1911): 321-28.

Tanner, H.S. *A Description of the Canals & Railroads of the United States.* New York: T.R. Tanner & J. Disturnell, 1840.

Taylor, George Rogers. "American Urban Growth Preceeding the Railway Age." *Journal of Economic History* 27 (1967): 309-39.

This is Kingston. Rev. ed. Kingston: League of Women Voters, 1972.

Town of Esopus Story. Ed. Mary Polhemus. Hannacroix, New York: Town of Esopus Bicentennial Committee, 1979.

Tyrell, William J. "Kingston's 300 Years." *American Heritage* 4 (Fall 1952): 12-15.

Ulster County in the Revolution. Ed. Ruth P. Heidgerd. New Paltz: The Huguenot Historical Society, 1977.

Van der Zee, Henri, Barbara Van der Zee. *A Sweet and Alien Land, the Story of Dutch New York.* New York: Viking, 1978.

Van Wagenen, Jared. *The Golden Age of Homespun.* Ithaca: Cornell U., 1953.

Vaux, Calvert. *Villas & Cottages.* New York: Harper, 1857.

Verplanck, William E. and Moses W. Collyer. *The Sloops of the Hudson.* Putnam's, 1908. Reprint Fleischmanns, New York: Purple Mountain, 1985.

Wakefield, Manville B. *To the Mountains By Rail*. Grahamsville, New York: Wakefair, 1970.

Walam Olum or Red Score: The Migration Legend of the Lenni Lenape or Delaware Indians. Indianapolis: Indiana Historical Society, 1954.

Whitford, Noble E. *History of the Canal System of the State of New York*. 2 vols. Albany: Brandow Printing, 1906; 1914.

Whitson, Skip. *The Hudson River One Hundred Years Ago*. Albuquerque: Sun Books, 1975.

Williamson, Jeffrey G. "Antebellum Urbanization in the American Northeast." *Journal of Economic History* 25 (1965): 592-608.

Wilson, Edmund. *Patriotic Gore*. New York: Oxford, 1962.

Wise, Daniel. *Summer Days on the Hudson*. New York: Hunt & Eaton, 1889.

Zimm, Louise Hasbrouck. "Beginnings in Ulster County, New York." *Americana* 37 (October 1943): 535-62.

Zimm, Louise Hasbrouck, et al. *Southeastern New York*. 3 vols. New York: Lewis Historical, 1946.

Acknowledgements

Writing the story of a place like Rondout is a formidable task, one not to be undertaken lightly or without friends. Fortunately, I have been blessed in this respect, for countless individuals and institutions have helped me immensurably in my work. From the many informants who lived the adventure of Rondout and freely shared their memories with me, to the intrepid historians whose pioneering work in regional history inspired me and set a standard which was often difficult to maintain, to the private collectors who generously opened their treasure troves of historic photographs and memorabilia and whose fascination with and dedication to the past preserves for posterity what would otherwise be lost, to the museums, historical societies and historic sites whose exhibitions and presentations furthered my research, and finally, to the competent, courteous, and exceedingly patient staffs of archives and libraries who aided me unstintingly, responding with good humor to my every request, I wish to proffer my most sincere and wholehearted gratitude. If I have gotten the story right, it is assuredly to their credit; if I have not, the responsibility is not theirs.

With pleasure, I list the following names in recognition of the assistance these people and their organizations have rendered to me: Denise Abbey; Arthur Adams; Max Aduchefsky; Shirley Anson; Donn and Mary Ann Avallone; Ray Berardi; Jack Bierhorst; Herman Boyle; Mim Brown; Jim Burggraf; Lynn Burstein; Fred Carpenter; Ralph and Lois Caterino; Harry Collins; Tram Combs; Rodman Conklin; Richard and Linda Cooper; Ernie Costello; Herbert Cutler; Gene Dauner; Bill and Tildy Davenport; Diane De Chillo; Bill Dederick; Bert Delamater; George Donskoj; John Dwyer; Peter Dwyer; Dorothy Dumund; Martha Belle Elias; Henry Ellenbogen; Alf Evers; Mark and Kayla Feldman; Jan Kellermann Fletcher; Edwin Ford; Dan Freer; Richard Frisbie; Eloise Gardner; Abel Garraghan; Ray Garraghan; Bill Golden; Sibyl Golden; Ethel Gray; Bob Haines; Herb Haufrecht; Kathryn Heavey; Justine and Hillard Hommel; Bob Johnson; Colton Johnson; Rich Katims; Joe Keefe; Hugh Kelly; Les Kiersted; Arthur Kurtznacker; Sherwood Landers; Walter Lang; John and Janice Lanzarotta; Pat Law; Amos Mac Creery; Tom Mc Grath; Marilyn Mc Hugh; Roger Mabie; Polly Maouris; Al Marquart; Michael Martin; Jack Matthews; Jim Matthews; Haig Meshejian; Geoff Miller; Kathy Neopolitan; Tom and Lynda and Lauren Ocker; Seward Osborne; John Overbagh; Mary Polhemus; Frank Rafferty; Jay Rifenbary; Barry Samuels; Thelma Schwab; Joe Schwarz; Dorothy Shapiro; Dick Shults; Herb and Bolly Shultz; Dan Shuster; Peter Sinclair; Robert Slater; Agnes Scott Smith; Alonzo Smith; Alton Smith; Jackie Soltis; Bill Spangenberger; Harry Spiegel; Joe and Hilarie Staton; Dorothy and Fred and Katherine and Kevin and Miles and Robert and William Steuding; Mike Thaler; Lowell Thing; Gene Turgeon; Fernando Valdivia; Julian Weiner; Dianne Whitmore; and Bob and Scrappy Yallum.

Also, Rosalie Burgher and Ruth Ann Muller and the staff of the Olive Free Library; Mrs. Ryan, curator of the local history collection at the Elting Memorial Library; the staff of the State University of New York Library at New Paltz; George Allen, Jean Smith, Dorothea Tracey-Warren and the staff of the Kingston Area Library; Patricia Carroll-Mathes, curator of the local history collection, Lawrence Berk, Richard Arnold, Marie Mastronardo and the staff of the MacDonald Dewitt Library at Ulster County Community College; the staffs at the State Library in Albany, the New York Public Library (the Berg Collection), the Adriance Public Library, The Bard and Vassar College libraries, the Catskill, Hurley, Phoenicia, Rosendale, Saugerties, Stone Ridge, West Hurley, and Woodstock libraries, and the staffs at the Franklin D. Roosevelt Library and the Hamilton Fish Library.

In addition, the D & H Canal Historical Society; the Klyne Esopus Historical Society; the New-York Historical Society; the New York State Historical Association at Cooperstown; the Ulster County Genealogical Society; and the Ulster County Historical Society.

Also, Susan Lewis, Tina Green, and Linda Loomis of the D & H Canal Museum; Kathleen Mc Fadden, Dick Albert, and Richard Goring of the Senate House State Historic Site; Melinda Terpening, Jenny Sponberg, and Cynthia Bushnell of the Hudson River Maritime Center & Museum; Christine Howard, Deborah Mc Clain and Debra Albright of the Kingston Urban Cultural Park; and the staffs at the Snyder Estate/Century House, the Empire State Railway Museum, and the Trolley Museum of New York.

I would also like to thank my superlative publishers Wray and Loni Rominger— our good relationship stretches back over a decade; my colleagues at Ulster County Community College, with whom it has been a joy to work; President Robert T. Brown of Ulster County Community College, who has been a stalwart supporter of my writing all these years; Bob Amundson and the U.C.C.C. Faculty Development Committee, who provided me with a faculty development grant to aid in the researching of this project; and my talented wife and life-partner Martha, who listened to my ceaseless Rondout nattering and read the manuscript of this book, making invaluable suggestions.

Finally, and most importantly, I am indebted to Monica Kiersted Freer, my research assistant and friend. Her intelligence and ingenuity, her generosity and dedication to the task, her warmth and humanity have made the writing of this book a delightful experience. Once again, I am grateful to Monica. The next book is hers.

Photo Credits

I wish to thank the following collectors, local historians, publishers, and institutions who graciously allowed me to view, and in some cases granted me permission to reproduce, photographs from their collections, publications, and archives: Herman Boyle; Bill Dederick; the D & H Canal Museum; John Dwyer; Jan Kellermann Fletcher; Monica Freer; Richard Frisbie of Hope Farm Press; Bob Haines; the Hudson River Maritime Center; a special thanks to Jack Matthews; Tom Ocker; Seward Osborne; Wray and Loni Rominger of Purple Mountain Press; the Senate House Museum Library; Dan Shuster; Robert Slater; Martha Steuding, who took the author's photo; the Ulster County Community College Local History Archive and all the local history collections housed in area libraries; and the Arthur A. Warrington Collection.

Also I would like to recognize and to express my unbounded admiration for, and my gratitude to, the following photographers, who captured Rondout through the years—although they have passed from the local scene, they will live forever in their work: Richard Lionel De Lisser; Louis Hoysradt; Cornelius Hume; Will Longyear; Henry B. Snyder; and the many other professional and amateur photographers whose images are extant but, sadly, unsigned.

Index

Rondout before urban renewal.

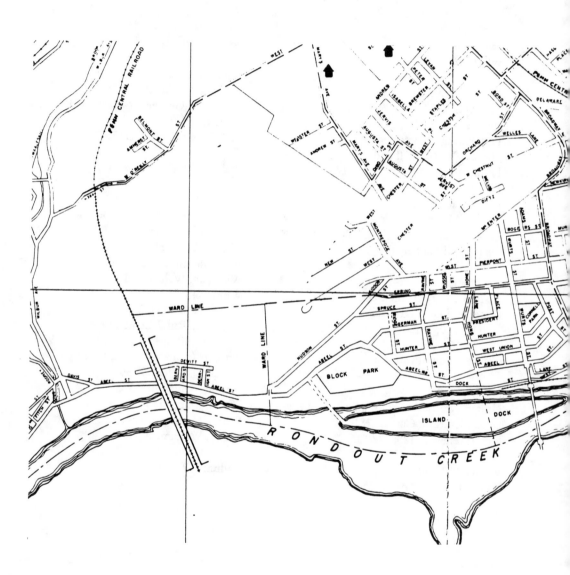

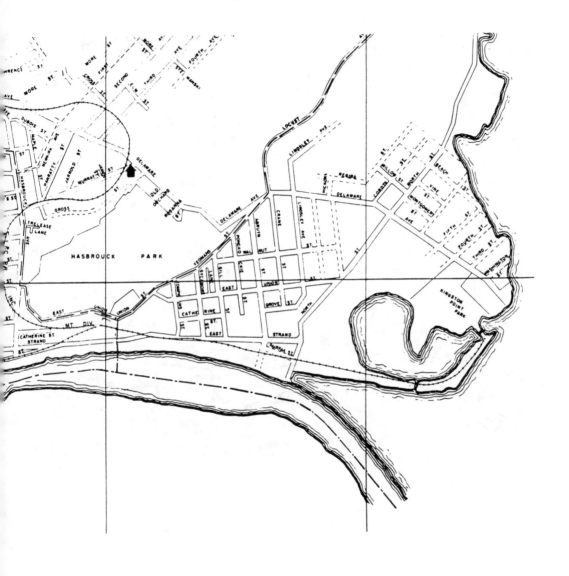

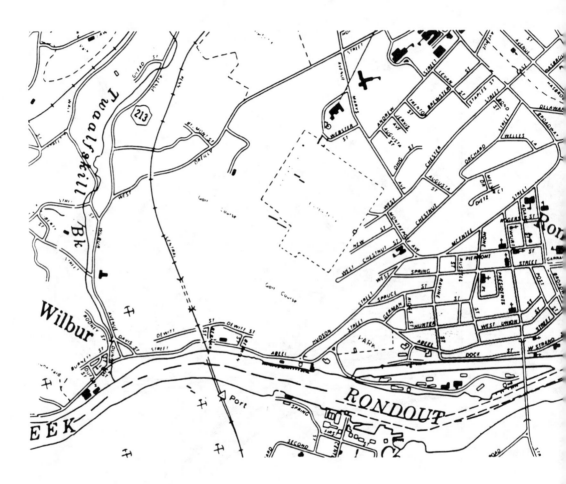

Rondout after urban renewal.

Courtesy of Kingston Urban Cultural Park

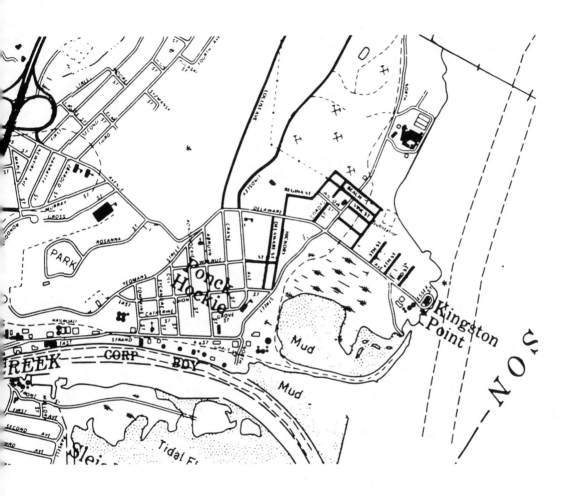